LISTENING TO CHILDREN ABOUT KINSHIP CARE, CHILD WELFARE, AND PERMANENCE

A Child-Centred Approach to Navigating Relational Spaces

Paul Daniel Shuttleworth

P

First published in Great Britain in 2025 by

Policy Press, an imprint of
Bristol University Press
University of Bristol
1–9 Old Park Hill
Bristol
BS2 8BB
UK
t: +44 (0)117 374 6645
e: bup-info@bristol.ac.uk

Details of international sales and distribution partners are available at policy.bristoluniversitypress.co.uk

© Paul Daniel Shuttleworth 2025

The digital PDF and ePub versions of this title are available open access and distributed under the terms of the Creative Commons Attribution-NonCommercial-NoDerivatives 4.0 International licence (https://creativecommons.org/licenses/by-nc-nd/4.0/) which permits reproduction and distribution for non-commercial use without further permission provided the original work is attributed.

DOI: https://doi.org/10.51952/9781447374909

British Library Cataloguing in Publication Data
A catalogue record for this book is available from the British Library

ISBN 978-1-4473-7488-6 paperback
ISBN 978-1-4473-7489-3 ePub
ISBN 978-1-4473-7490-9 OA PDF

The right of Paul Daniel Shuttleworth to be identified as author of this work has been asserted by him in accordance with the Copyright, Designs and Patents Act 1988.

All rights reserved: no part of this publication may be reproduced, stored in a retrieval system, or transmitted in any form or by any means, electronic, mechanical, photocopying, recording, or otherwise without the prior permission of Bristol University Press.

Every reasonable effort has been made to obtain permission to reproduce copyrighted material. If, however, anyone knows of an oversight, please contact the publisher.

The statements and opinions contained within this publication are solely those of the author and not of the University of Bristol or Bristol University Press. The University of Bristol and Bristol University Press disclaim responsibility for any injury to persons or property resulting from any material published in this publication.

Bristol University Press and Policy Press work to counter discrimination on grounds of gender, race, disability, age and sexuality.

Cover design: Andrew Corbett
Front cover image: Shutterstock/Maxim Ibragimov

Dedicated to my father, Malcolm Shuttleworth,
writer, poet, playwright, and inspiration.

Contents

List of figures and tables — vi
Acknowledgements — vii

1 Valuing different perspectives — 1
2 Valuing kinship care support — 15
3 Valuing permanence for kinship care — 37
4 Valuing child participation — 58
5 Valuing a 'what matters' approach — 81
6 Valuing ethics and 'what matters' participation approaches — 104
7 Valuing connection/separation — 124
8 Valuing care and protection/independence and risk — 149
9 Valuing recognition/(mis)recognition — 173
10 Navigating relational spaces — 197

References — 212
Index — 251

List of figures and tables

Figures

2.1	The impact of welfare state typologies on valuing kinship care support	18
2.2	The circular debates on kinship care	34
5.1	Tree diagram of three ontological levels: empirical, actual, real	87
5.2	Values that mattered to the children who participated in the 'What matters to children living in kinship care' study	100
5.3	Three central mechanisms that emerged from how the children in the study managed family life and permanence	102
6.1	Kitbag contents	116
6.2	Images used to elicit words and pictures narratives with the children	122
7.1	Connection/separation – one of the three central mechanisms that emerged from how the children in the study managed family life and permanence	125
8.1	Care and protection/independence and risk – one of the three central mechanisms that emerged from how the children in the study managed family life and permanence	150
8.2	Maslow's hierarchy of needs pyramid	151
9.1	Recognition/(mis)recognition – one of the three central mechanisms that emerged from how the children in the study managed family life and permanence	174

Tables

4.1	Lundy's model of participation	77

Acknowledgements

This book is not only about the meaning of family – it has flourished from the love and support of family. Like the children I spoke to, I recognise that my family constantly evolves and extends beyond genetic ties. Thank you to my mother, Marcia Randell; my sister, Jo Shuttleworth; Jack; James; my nieces, Lila and Isis; my cats, Leo and Jack; and all my relatives. You have all provided me with the space, sometimes literally, to reflect on the essential values of responsibility, dedication, and compassion, and have created moments of joy.

I must also thank my friends, who I also consider part of my family, especially Kirsty, Gemma, Manuel, Emily, Fee, Fi, Susie, Mikey, Mo, Ken, Wendy, Paul, Antonio, Tomasz, Sarah Flagg, Hayley, Beverley, Jennifer, Raj, Rebekah, Michelle, Rainbow Chorus, and even Jack (the nice one). Thank you to my enduring friends and colleagues from Liverpool Hope, Edinburgh University, the University of Sussex, and Kingston University. Special mentions go to Louise, Rosa, May, Rea, Barry, Janet, Lisa, Gemma C., Rick, and Josie. You are inspirational and have helped me navigate my 'wobbles' with appropriate but kind challenge when necessary (both/and).

To all those no longer physically present, I miss you, but you remain connected within me: my father, Malcolm Shuttleworth, and those who have recently passed – Willis, Indra, Paul Jewson, and Joe McCann, to name a few.

Thank you to International Futures Forum and their Kitbag, and Walsh and Evans (2014) for the use of their diagrams. Thank you to SENSS (ESRC funding), Policy Press, and the University of Sussex for supporting the book. In particular, their courage, hard work, and generosity in making this work open access and freely available online means that everyone can hear about and be inspired by how children living in kinship care navigate their lives.

Thank you to the practitioners, colleagues, and families who have inspired and guided me throughout my career. And how could I possibly forget my husband, Gareth Pugh? Through the veneer of indifference, you show your support and care for others, sighing your way through it all while sparking joy and laughter. You're welcome.

Finally, I want to thank the children and families who dedicated their time, thoughts, and energy to the initial research, ongoing conversations, and this book. I could only complete this work because each of you has contributed so much. You have enhanced the understanding of family life in kinship care. You provided me with profound reflection and inspiration, which I feel privileged to share. You have proved that your views really do matter.

1

Valuing different perspectives

> Kids should always stay safe in their family.
> Jordan, child research participant

Inspired by children's insights, this book offers a fresh perspective on listening to children, understanding kinship care, promoting child permanence, and valuing family life. It invites readers to reflect on navigating relational spaces, a theme that unfolds throughout the book.

The book draws on PhD research titled 'What matters to children living in kinship care' (Shuttleworth, 2021). It also shares valuable insights from subsequent publications, journal articles, presentations, life story work training with kinship carers, practice experience, and ongoing discussions with child welfare practitioners, policy makers, researchers, academics, carers, and, most importantly, children themselves. The original research embraced creative approaches to listen to and understand children's views. This book builds on the original PhD findings by further employing critical realism and dialogical participation, as explained later. It emphasises the importance of incorporating children's perspectives into child welfare policies, practices, and everyday family life. By genuinely listening to children, we can better protect, support, and nurture their flourishing and sense of permanence. The book illustrates how children can help us ensure, as requested by Jordan, that they 'always stay safe in their family'.

This opening chapter introduces the 'what matters' child-led approach to understanding the dynamics of family life for children in kinship care. It begins by defining kinship care and emphasising the key challenges regarding permanence and safety for these children. I then share my experiences in practice, explaining how ongoing debates about kinship care prompted me to explore a different perspective, centred on children's views. Next, the chapter examines various categories of kinship care through historical, anthropological, and legal lenses. It also considers how general insights from international research can enhance our understanding of kinship care. After a cautionary note on representation, generalisation, correlation, causation, and neologisms, the chapter concludes with an overview of the book's structure.

Introducing kinship care and permanence

Under English law, which applied to the children in the PhD research this book builds on, kinship care refers to the full-time care provided to children by relatives when the children cannot remain with their birth parents. Kinship carers may be biologically related, legally connected, or have established significant prior relationships with the child (Children Act 1989). Globally, kinship care is the fastest-growing solution for children who cannot stay with their birth parents (Hallett et al, 2021). In the UK, the 2021 Census reveals that around 121,000 children are in kinship care arrangements.

In high-income nations, kinship care is often regarded by child welfare policy and practice as an alternative to intrusive statutory care (Delap and Mann, 2019). The United Nations Convention on the Rights of the Child emphasises the importance of the child's best interests and their right to family life (United Nations General Assembly, 1989). This principle informs policies such as England's Children Act 1989, which prioritises maintaining the child's family connections over more costly state care options like fostering and adoption. In low- and middle-income countries, kinship care is not typically seen as either a child welfare intervention or an alternative to fostering and adoption. Instead, it more accurately reflects their cultural norms of shared collective responsibilities (Delap and Mann, 2019).

Beyond preventing costly and intrusive state interventions and reflecting cultural norms, kinship care is thought to provide another significant benefit. It is commonly regarded as a more favourable option for children than fostering, adoption, or residential care as it can help maintain and strengthen a child's sense of permanence (Winokur et al, 2018). Permanence is a crucial aspect for child welfare services, particularly when children cannot remain in the care of their birth parents. According to English legislation, achieving a sense of permanence involves ensuring that all children experience 'a sense of security, continuity, commitment, identity, and belonging' with their family, not just during childhood but also into adulthood (Department for Education, 2010, pp 22–3). While the concept of permanence has sparked much discussion in social work, its ultimate aim is to cultivate a safe, supportive, and lasting family environment (Boddy, 2017).

Although numerous studies suggest that kinship care is likely to foster child permanence more successfully than statutory care (Winokur et al, 2018), some research, like the literature review by Hassall et al (2021), presents findings that could question this notion. The review revealed that kinship care alone, as a practice, did not always genuinely strengthen the relationships between children, their caregivers, biological parents, and their culture and community. Therefore, without authentic positive connections to those around them and their environment, questions can arise about whether a child's true sense of permanence, belonging, and identity can always be achieved just through kinship care.

This type of challenge illustrates that merely scratching the surface of kinship care and permanence reveals complexity and potential confusion. Such uncertainty arises because kinship care fundamentally challenges traditional notions of permanence and placement, which are primarily rooted in foster care and adoption practices (Kirton, 2020). These placement models often overlook the kinship care experience, where children are not simply moved from one family to another but remain in their existing family networks, presenting additional challenges and risks. Kinship care and the relationships within it are complicated and in flux. This raises critical questions about what it means for children to, as Jordan expressed, 'always stay safe in their family', and whether kinship care should be viewed in the same light as adoption and fostering, or even as a definitive means to preserve safe family relationships. Such ambiguities can confuse how child welfare professionals, policy makers, and caregivers define, understand, and support this distinct family arrangement (Ponnert, 2017).

More concerning is the relative absence of the child's voice in policies and practices related to kinship care and permanence (Clements and Birch, 2023). The lack of their perspectives leads to assumptions about preferred outcomes, often without a genuine understanding of what truly matters to the children themselves. When social workers, policy makers, and other researchers do seek a child's perspective, they frequently use significantly different ways of considering, accessing, and interpreting the child's voice and experiences. Without a consensus on how to obtain and realise children's views, a dominant, adult-centric understanding often emerges regarding family life in kinship care arrangements. This allows policy and practice to take conventional notions of child participation, permanence, family, and care for granted, often without critical challenge.

Chapters 1 to 6 of this book summarise these traditional perspectives derived from prior research and literature, which primarily focus on what adults feel matters. This is crucial as it provides context and highlights the various issues and circular arguments that, despite best efforts, remain unresolved. Chapter 7 to 10 illuminate how children's views can offer new explanations and support for kinship care that more closely align with their lived experiences.

My social work practice background and a vision for more child-centric, valued-led research

Before becoming a social work researcher, lecturer, and amateur podcaster, I had the privilege of spending over ten years in social work practice, working alongside children and families. After working in in child protection for eight years, I joined a team focused on assessing and supporting kinship care arrangements within the Fostering, Placements, and Permanence Service. The challenges of placing kinship care within a service aligned with fostering, adoption, and placements are discussed throughout the book.

My work with the team integrated my aspiration to keep families together with the fundamental mandate that social workers must ensure children's wellbeing and protection from harm. It allowed me to balance process-driven procedural tasks, such as court work and legal permanence planning, with opportunities to support families in a less authoritative manner. I soon became aware this presented a tension in practice with families in kinship care arrangements. I had to consider an optimistic perspective of families and their inherent desire to care for and protect their children, but also be realistic about possible risks that family members may pose to a child's safety and wellbeing (Kettle and Jackson, 2017).

This tension was also apparent when observing a wide range of diverse and ambivalent views on kinship care from others, alongside the ongoing debates about whether it can be considered a legitimate permanence option or even defined as a placement. The ambivalence was evident in the differing opinions of child welfare practitioners, legislation, court rulings, and local authority panels. It seemed that the more people explored kinship care, the more they questioned its nature, meaning, and validity.

Amid this complex web of questions and challenges, it also became evident throughout my practice experience that children's perspectives were often regarded as mere additions to assessments and decision-making or, unfortunately, overlooked entirely. This disregard for children's voices seemed particularly perplexing considering that a child's desire to remain in their home with their carers is one of the key factors determining how long they will stay there (Boddy, 2017).

One day, I was sat at the lunch table with an array of my social work colleagues, each with different roles and responsibilities within the Children and Families Service. We discussed the benefits and challenges of kinship care. Afterwards, I wondered what the conversation might be like if the children living in kinship care arrangements were seated at that table instead of adult professionals. Imagine if the children came together to talk about their lives. How would they define their family lives and kinship care circumstances? Would they speak about educational achievement, legal orders, safety, permanence, resources, and their physical, mental, and emotional wellbeing – things that are typically discussed by child welfare professionals? My previous experience indicated that the children were unlikely to characterise their lives in such a service-driven manner. I was curious to know whether they could cut through all the debates, definitions, and adult-centric dilemmas. Would the children contribute anything valuable to our understanding of kinship care? Ultimately, could children guide child welfare professionals and families toward better ways of supporting them?

Since then, I have been intrigued by how debates about the meaning, value, and definition of kinship care can spark such heated discussions, professional disagreements, and personal inner conflicts. In my view, these debates arise not only from differing perspectives on how kinship care should be conceptualised and supported but also from the emotive issues concerning family, state responsibility, and child abuse. We possess strong feelings about love, risk, and harm, especially regarding children and our families. This can lead to passionate, emotive clashes both with others and within ourselves. Holding conflicting views and needing to prioritise seemingly opposing values creates a split mindset. Kinship care challenges both professional and personal values, which can lead to both external and internal conflict (O'Brien, 2012).

This book emphasises the significance of professional and personal values, along with our choices to prioritise those that resonate most with us. We are all guided by values in our approaches to child welfare research, policy making, and practice, as well as in our everyday lives. When we think about it, values motivate us and help determine what truly matters most. For example, in my professional life, social work is guided by essential values like integrity and promoting dignity, as emphasised by organisations such as the International Federation of Social Workers and the British Association of Social Workers. In my personal life, I also value integrity and my family, which, for me, is not reliant on genetic ties. Acknowledging the impact of these values highlights why anyone interested in child welfare must engage in reflection and reflexivity. Values significantly influence our actions, and we must strive to do what is helpful rather than harmful. Such reflection and reflexivity become even more essential regarding issues like kinship care, which often elicits ambivalence, split mindsets, and visceral emotional responses.

Concepts of kinship care

The origins of kinship care

One of the first steps in exploring a subject is to consider its history and context. The concept of kinship care is not new. Numerous instances exist of children being raised by their family network when they cannot be cared for by their birth parents (Hegar, 1999). Kinship care can be traced historically through anthropological studies worldwide, as it is one of the oldest traditions in child-rearing. One of the most well-known expressions related to kinship care originates from the African maxim that it takes a whole village to raise a child (Swadener et al, 2000) – a phrase popularised by Hillary Clinton (2007).

The Bible contains numerous references to children being raised by relatives. In ancient Greece and Rome, adoption and fostering within families were regarded as practical means of safeguarding successors (Enke, 2019). Additionally, Chinese culture has a rich tradition of emphasising the importance of family members supporting one another. Multiple generations often lived together under one roof with one head of the family (Cong and Silverstein, 2012).

The term 'kinship care' itself allegedly originated from the documentation of enslaved Black individuals in the US (Geen, 2004). Approximately one-fifth of the children of enslaved people, having been separated from their biological parents during transportation, were cared for by other enslaved individuals. It was a cultural pact with an understanding that the caring arrangement would be reciprocated if the carers' own biological children were separated from them.

Legal definitions of kinship care

Shifting away from anthropological explanations, in high-income countries, kinship care is generally categorised into two types: formal and informal (Delap and Mann, 2019). Formal kinship care involves intervention from social services, with children typically placed in statutory foster arrangements within their birth families. For example, in England, a child in formal kinship care is placed under a legal order such as a care order or an interim care order (Children Act 1989, s 31), thereby becoming 'looked after' while remaining with their family members, who are enrolled as foster carers. In the UK, for formal kinship care, the local authority shares joint parental rights and responsibilities alongside the birth parents (Wijedasa, 2015). Kinship carers do not possess legal parental rights or responsibilities.

Informal kinship care involves situations where no public legal order secures the arrangement. As a result, a family member or family friend takes on the responsibility for a child without any state involvement. Research indicates that approximately 95 per cent of kinship care arrangements in the UK are informal (Selwyn and Nandy, 2014).

Much speculation exists regarding why this percentage is so high. MacDonald et al (2018) conducted an international literature review on informal kinship care. They discovered that the negative portrayal of some social workers as overly intrusive and ineffective fostered distrust and caution among family networks. Numerous informal carers expressed concerns about invasive bureaucratic processes, hesitated to involve social work, and refrained from seeking support.

In England and Wales, the classifications of formal and informal care can become muddled. For example, a child under a special guardianship order or a child arrangement order (explained in Chapter 3) may not formally be part of the 'care system'. However, under these supposedly informal arrangements, some families may still receive formal social work intervention as part of a court-ordered care plan. This can result in such arrangements being described in regulations as formal (MacDonald et al, 2018). The complexities surrounding legal definitions and their implications for support is explored in greater depth in Chapter 2.

The confusing terminology surrounding kinship care and kinship carers has led to calls for clearer definitions in legislation and policy. The England and Wales Independent Review of Children's Social Care by MacAlister (2022) urged the government to 'develop a new legal definition of kinship care, taking a wide range of circumstances into account' (MacAlister, 2022, p 108). In April 2022, the Family Rights Group launched the #TimeToDefine campaign, advocating for a clear definition of kinship care to be included in primary legislation. Although it is evident that definitions are scattered and somewhat obscured within English and Welsh laws and guidelines, attempting to simplify kinship care into a single definition could produce unintended consequences. While distinguishing between formal and informal kinship care can be challenging, this does not necessarily mean that the government should categorise the 'wide range of circumstances' of kinship care arrangements too broadly or into overly specific groups. These approaches may lead to menus of care and tiers of financial and practical support that are not tailored to actual needs, but instead depend on definitions and legal classifications.

Characteristics of kinship care

Another way to understand kinship care is through analysis of the demographics of caregivers and children, along with the support systems available and the challenges they face. What follows is a summary of international research on kinship care, using data from the UK's 2021 Census, Hunt's (2020) *Two Decades of UK Research on Kinship Care*, and global studies (for example, Delap and Mann, 2019).

Demographics of kinship carers

- Gender: Most kinship carers are female. In the UK, about 70 per cent of kinship carers are women. Similar trends are observed internationally, as women frequently assume the primary caregiving role.
- Age: Kinship caregivers are often older adults, typically in the 45–64 age range. This trend is seen in several countries, including Australia, Canada, and the US.
- Employment: A significant number of kinship carers are either unemployed or retired. Approximately 40 per cent of kinship carers in the UK are

not in the workforce. This pattern is also evident in other countries, as kinship carers may leave their jobs to provide full-time care.
- Education: Many kinship carers worldwide have a high school education or lower. This trend is seen globally, as numerous carers encounter restricted opportunities for higher education.

Demographics of children in kinship care

- Ethnicity: The ethnic composition of children in kinship care varies by country. In the UK, children from minority ethnic backgrounds are over-represented in kinship care. Similar patterns are seen in the US and Australia, where Indigenous and minoritised children are more likely to enter kinship care.
- Age: Kinship care children are of all ages from infants to teenagers, with many at the younger end of this range. This is consistent globally.
- Disability: Many children in kinship care experience disabilities, creating extra challenges for caregivers. This is a widespread issue globally, necessitating additional support and resources.

Support and challenges

- Financial assistance: Kinship carers often receive less financial support than foster carers, creating economic pressure, especially for those already living below the poverty line. This is a widespread concern, and many countries acknowledge the need for enhanced financial assistance for kinship carers.
- Social support: Many kinship carers lack access to formal support services and rely on informal networks. This challenge is widespread worldwide, and numerous carers require more organised support systems.
- Legal support: Kinship carers frequently encounter unclear legal standing since many lack formal guardianship or custody. This complicates their access to services and support. This issue is apparent in various countries, highlighting the necessity for more straightforward legal frameworks.

The challenges of kinship care research

While these insights provide valuable information, the research to date has several limitations. First, there are significantly fewer studies on kinship care compared research on other living arrangements for children unable to remain with their biological parents (Kallinen, 2021). More research and information aligned specifically with kinship care are needed.

Second, accurately tracking the number of kinship care arrangements presents challenges. For example, in the UK, at the time of writing, descriptive data is drawn from the 2021 Census, which does not ask about kinship care specifically; the data is compiled from questions on relevant aspects, such as household relationships.

Third, the current data tends to generalise kinship care by merging findings from international research or framing it solely as a social work service intervention. It is often overlooked that kinship care also represents a family lifestyle. Research frequently evaluates kinship care 'more as a technology and less as a family' (Skoglund and Thørnblad, 2017, p 438). However, Skoglund and Thørnblad (2017; 2022) emphasise that anthropologists and historians have long studied kinship, childhood, parenthood, and the role of relatives in raising children. These disciplines offered rich insights into familial care long before kinship care became a significant part of child protective services in the 1990s. Even so, the complex theories put forward on kinship diversity and functioning have received little attention in much kinship care research, literature, and policy. Additionally, perspectives on kinship care from low- and middle-income countries are often neglected. One notable exception is the extensive work by Delap et al (2024), which examines lessons learned from around the world. To address the limitations of existing literature, this book incorporates international literature beyond child welfare, including a broad range of sociological literature.

Lastly, children's viewpoints and experiences are often overshadowed by what are considered more reliable adult perspectives, such as adult notions of permanence, and the concerns of adults, which can be seen as being more important. When children's views are included in UK research (for example, Broad, 2004; Aldgate and McIntosh, 2006; Farmer and Moyers, 2008; Farmer et al, 2013), few studies focus exclusively on children's perspectives without incorporating adult views.

In summary, there is still insufficient understanding of kinship care, and research often explains children's experiences of kinship care and their sense of permanence through the lens of what adults consider significant. This emphasis on adult concerns can also lead to an over-reliance on particular methodologies, such as the 'what works' approach.

What works and what matters?

The 'what works' approach, which originated in the late 1990s, emphasises the importance of robust evidence that meets rigorous criteria to inform decisions in public services such as criminal justice, health, and social care (Davies et al, 2000). It aims to identify the most effective interventions and practices to ensure efficient use of resources and improved outcomes. Often, it does this through randomised controlled trials. It is suggested that a 'what works' approach can enhance accountability and transparency by providing a clear rationale for decision-making. Implementing proven interventions can also promote efficiency in addressing health disparities and social inequalities, ensuring that the most suitable communities are targeted to benefit from public health strategies. It is proposed that the approach facilitates continuous improvement as new evidence becomes available, ensuring that public service practices and strategies remain relevant and effective (Davies et al, 2019).

The 'what works' approach has faced various critiques over time (for example, Pampaka et al, 2016; Tomkins and Bristow, 2021). For example, it tends to over-emphasise quantitative data and statistical techniques, which can simplify complex human behaviours and interactions into simple measurable variables. This may overshadow the qualitative insights essential for understanding individuals' nuanced experiences. The approach can also easily sideline professional judgments. 'What works' research might fail to capture the unique contexts in which care is provided. Due to cultural, social, or economic differences, what works in one environment may not produce the same results in another. The approach can also minimise broader systemic political challenges that influence lived experiences (Pawson, 2006).

There are concerns for child welfare practice regarding 'what works' research focusing on efficiency and cost-effectiveness at the expense of the wellbeing and preferences of individuals receiving care. This focus can contribute to the de-professionalisation of child welfare and social care, diminishing autonomy and professional curiosity by confining roles to set interventions. Even when evidence-based practices are recognised as beneficial, applying them effectively in real-world situations can be difficult due to limitations in resources, staff training, and rigid organisational cultures (Pawson and Tilley, 1997).

One of the most significant ethical issues with the 'what works' approach is to do with its handling of representation and generalisation. The approach can reduce groups and classifications to simple variables, and can confuse correlation with causation. Misinterpreting correlations may lead to misleading conclusions and inappropriate policy decisions. For example, the MacAlister (2022) review attributed poor child welfare outcomes primarily to inadequate and inefficient social work practice. It paid minimal attention to underlying structural issues such as poverty, and it did not mention political choices like austerity even once. Austerity was the economic policy implemented by the UK government to reduce public spending and debt, often involving spending cuts to public services and welfare benefits as well as tax increases. This was implemented widely under the Conservative government from 2010 to 2019 in response to the financial crisis in 2008, and it impacted child welfare services and families across the UK.

The 'what works' approach can also fetishise groups, labels, and typologies. Fetishising characteristics can create a misleading sense of diversity and lead to essentialist labelling, thereby oversimplifying complex social realities. People may be grouped by traits, such as age and gender, and other identities, and this helps researchers organise the data into tables of analysis. This can foster a deceptive logic suggesting that the diversity within populations has been replicated in studies, allowing definitive correlations to be drawn. Personally, as a Jewish Queer individual, I do not wish to be reduced solely to my sexuality and ethno-religion. Much less do I wish to be regarded as the representative of the exceptionally diverse groups to which I belong.

You may notice in this book that I refuse to place ages, placement types, or ethnicities beside the children's quotes – this is the approach I take in my research generally. The aim is to avoid, as much as possible, naming, defining, classifying, stereotyping, or comparing characteristics. While characteristics are dispersed throughout the work, they are not readily apparent; they hold significance, but they are not the focal point. Instead, through critical realism, dialogical participation, and a 'what matters' approach, the deeper structural mechanisms of power relationships, including child–society, child–carer, and participant–researcher relationships, are explored more authentically (Sayer, 1992). For example, it was essential to have some children participating who were racially minoritised in their local environment, rather than having one child who was Black, one who was White, one who was Jewish, and so on. This allowed for power relationships to be discussed in more depth. We discussed what it felt like to be marginalised for being seemingly different rather than just discussing what it felt like to be of, for example, Traveller heritage.

Design of the original study and neologisms

Language can consciously and unconsciously create obstacles to understanding. For example, both the original study and this book highlight the need to implement a different methodology – a 'what matters' approach. This was necessary so that the children's perspectives had reliability and validity, and we approached generalisability through the emergence of new theoretical paradigms not often associated with kinship care. For the first time, critical realism was employed in conjunction with dialogical participation to illuminate, through reflexivity, the children's underlying values, their inner conversations, and the generative mechanisms that motivate their family lives. This approach relied on the stratification of reality, providing empirical validation alongside a nuanced interpretive awareness of diverse contexts. The insights of the children were collated through a series of person-centred, creative, participatory, and task-oriented interviews. Notably, a diverse range of literature has been incorporated and referenced throughout this book, frequently diverging from traditional discussions surrounding kinship care, participation, permanence, social work, child welfare, and childhood studies.

The previous paragraph likely illustrates that employing various techniques, methodologies, theories, and concepts presents a significant drawback.

It requires the use and mixing of specific technical jargon from multiple disciplines, which can hinder readability and accessibility. This issue is particularly problematic because I value the importance of allowing children's insights to be heard by as many people as possible to ensure they have an impact. The blending of terms and inaccessibility is especially troubling when many of the disciplines, including child welfare and social work, are already saturated with jargon. Critical realism, central to this study, is also frequently criticised for creating new terms, known as neologisms, or even altering the meanings of everyday words. Examples include the terms emergence, mechanisms, and absence. Language and accessibility are made even more complex by the extensive personal jargon used by family members and the children themselves. For instance, before beginning the research, I was unaware of what a slime station was or how to distinguish between relations and family. I also did not realise the extent to which the word 'like' can be used – like a verbal tic rather than as a comparative term.

Language has been a central consideration in my research and practice. Our choice of words is linked to power dynamics. For example, in social work, the language we use shapes interactions and influences power relationships (Fook, 2016). Effective communication between child welfare professionals and families is essential. If we are not careful, our language can limit our openness to other viewpoints and may reinforce unnecessary hierarchies or authority. Research, particularly involving children and child welfare professionals, must always take this into account. I have been mindful when speaking with children and writing this book. While still tied to my own way of expressing myself, I have consistently tried to ensure that the words and ideas are accessible.

At times, there is a need for jargon and neologisms. I hope I have, therefore, leaned into them thoughtfully, with appropriate explanations. I also hope others will discover the beauty in some of the words, such as Sayer (2011) using the term flourishing instead of developing. Personally, discovering new words has introduced me to new ideas, methods, methodologies, and concepts. New words, especially those used by children, can facilitate an evolution of language and thought that better connects with the realities of children's lived experiences.

Structure of the book

This book invites readers to rethink and revalue kinship care, research methods, child permanence, and participation. By prioritising children's voices, it challenges dominant narratives and offers new insights for a more inclusive and thoughtful approach to family life and care. The book is structured into ten chapters. Chapters 1 to 3 summarise what is currently known, highlighting the challenges of kinship care support, permanence, and participation. Chapters 4 to 6 are more reflective, philosophical, and practical in nature. Chapters 7 to 10 showcase the power of children's insights and the implications of them. They demonstrate how incorporating the voices of children can help us theorise, understand, and support kinship care and better navigate relational spaces.

Following on from this chapter, which introduced kinship care and my perspective, Chapter 2 – Valuing kinship care support – offers further context on the uncertainties surrounding child welfare in relation to supporting children and families living in kinship care. This discussion is critical as kinship care is often poorly supported and frequently exploited worldwide. The chapter draws on international literature to summarise how cultural norms regarding family and state responsibilities influence the availability of support. It also explores current trends in kinship care support in England. The politically charged chapter advocates for acknowledging lived experiences and operating from the in-between as the basis for advancing kinship care policy and practices.

Chapter 3 – Valuing permanence for kinship care – attempts to set aside political debates and focuses on children's lived experiences of permanence. Providing brief histories of permanence illustrates how traditional child welfare and legislative concepts of permanence do not align with the realities of kinship care practice. Such concepts are rooted in the concerns and debates surrounding fostering and adoption. Instead, it is crucial to acknowledge a permanence paradox, where emotional and physical stability can be provided even though permanence is in constant flux, placing kinship care in the middle space between substitute psychological parenting and birth family preservation.

Chapter 4 – Valuing child participation – emphasises the importance of child participation and the voices of children in kinship care, welfare research, policy making, and practice. While participation is vital for upholding rights and ethics, it is necessary to exercise caution to prevent further marginalisation and exploitation of children. This concern is supported by the relatively few studies highlighting the voices of children living in kinship care. The chapter advocates for a more reflective approach to child participation, progressing from either/or frameworks to a dialogical approach that acknowledges the political and ethical dimensions and more effectively respects the realities of child agency.

Chapter 5 – Valuing a 'what matters' approach – highlights the importance of philosophy for ethical child participation and child welfare research and practice. It presents a new framework, based on Sayer's book *Why Things Matter to People*. This chapter demonstrates how critical realism connects two contrasting research paradigms: positivist and interpretivist. It acknowledges the limitations of both paradigms while also drawing on their strengths to establish a middle ground. Critical realism is presented as a helpful underlabourer for research and effective policy making, underscoring the need to acknowledge the importance of values. When combined with dialogical child participation, this value- and theory-driven 'what matters' approach encourages the inner conversations of children to emerge.

Chapter 6 – Valuing ethics and 'what matters' participation approaches – is both practical and reflective. It delves into the essentials of ethical practice, introduces helpful, creative methods, and emphasises reflexivity as essential for child welfare practice and research. The methods discussed include Kitbag, photo-elicitation, child-led walking tours, drama, visual methods, and an interviewing process with children that debates emerging theories. My positionality and identity, and their contradictions, are also further presented/exposed. The chapter concludes with a new critical realist-based conceptual model that promotes collaborative reflexivity.

Chapter 7 – Valuing connection/separation – allows children's views to take centre stage. The chapter explores how children navigate fuzzy family boundaries, ambivalent relationships, and absence/presence through the skilled and nuanced sharing of time, space, and family narratives. Conceptualising children's family lives in this manner ensures that practices such as life story work appropriately recognise a child's agency and abilities.

Chapter 8 – Valuing care and protection/independence and risk – delves deeper into family relationships by considering what care, safety, and permanence mean to children living in kinship care. Discussions with the children illuminate how navigating autonomous interdependence and the ethics of care and justice can equip practitioners with a framework to address the children's need for a sense of permanence while remaining mindful of risk.

Chapter 9 – Valuing recognition/(mis)recognition – ties all the children's insights together. It explores how using modified versions of recognition theories can ensure that policy, practice, and legislation are more attuned to the realities of children's experiences and support needs. It also shows that recognition should not just extend to children's challenges, deficits, and troubles. Recognition must also extend to how children make do and get by.

Chapter 10 – Navigating relational spaces – summarises the book. It reflects on and honours the children's insights into navigating relational spaces. It reiterates the benefits of finding innovative ways to gain children's perspectives and commit to their worth. The chapter also shows how child welfare practice and policy making can navigate the in-between by applying theoretical insights gleaned from children, even for contentious issues such as contact. Overall, the chapter and the book robustly demonstrate that understanding and supporting a child's family life always begins with including children in discussions. Children can help provide clearer understandings of what permanence, kinship care, and a good, safe family life truly mean.

2

Valuing kinship care support

> I think that the important thing to me is about, like, the whole kinship care thing – it is really undermined for the job that it is. Like it's not a job, but it's also like a way of life. But I don't … I really don't think that people understand it at all. Like, I did a speech to my English class about the difference in kinship care and foster care. And I feel like kinship care has a lot more of a hard job because they already have that emotional connection, but then just nobody really knows about them. My Nan and Grandad get little to no funding for anything that they do, and it's just, like, I don't think that's right.
>
> Danielle, child research participant

Danielle explains how a lack of understanding surrounding kinship care affects support. She also emphasises that it is unjust for families involved in kinship care to receive insufficient assistance. This concern is echoed in the findings of a 2024 survey of kinship carers in England and Wales conducted by the charity Kinship. The survey revealed that not only do carers lack vital support for themselves and their families, but they also feel misunderstood, undervalued, overburdened, and exploited by child welfare services and the government (Kinship, 2024). If the lack of understanding and support and the potential exploitation are concerns for families living in kinship care, they should also be concerns for policy makers, practitioners, researchers, and anyone interested in kinship care, child welfare, and, indeed, social justice.

Chapter 1 demonstrated that even scratching the surface of kinship care reveals its complexities and ambiguities. Kinship care is a multifaceted concept that fulfils various roles worldwide. This chapter expands the exploration of kinship care by highlighting the broader issues that affect it. Overall, the chapter examines the complex concept and practice of kinship care support, focusing on navigating between the two primary perspectives often associated with it: kinship care as a social work intervention and kinship care as a reflection of family life – or as Danielle describes it, a 'job' but also a 'way of life'.

The chapter begins by examining the foundations of a concept known as familialism and explores its influence on child welfare policies across various countries. Then the norms, ideologies, and cultural perceptions of family and gender roles that shape kinship care are addressed. The discussion explores the sociopolitical context, highlighting how neoliberalism, individualism, and managerialism impact kinship care. Additionally, it considers the perception of risk and the concept of 'risky families' for kinship care, along with the systemic challenges these families face, which include racism and poverty, and kinship care's use as a cost-effective child welfare solution for governments and local jurisdictions.

The chapter concludes by examining current English policies and legislative frameworks, emphasising the need for a balanced, long-term approach that better recognises the complexities of kinship care. It advocates for a nuanced understanding of family dynamics and sociopolitical influences. It calls for policies that provide adequate support and resources to families in kinship care, starting from the middle, from lived experiences. This can ensure that child welfare policies and practice better reflect the realities of these families' lives and what matters to those living them.

Kinship care as a reflection of familialism

Worldwide, kinship care as a concept and practice exists somewhere between two seemingly contrasting dominant narratives (Xu et al, 2020). One views kinship care primarily as a social work intervention, prioritising measurable child outcomes and formal monitoring, assessment, and support. The other perceives kinship care as a reflection of the diversity of family life, emphasising social relationships and cultural beliefs and relying more on informal family and community support than on state resources.

The stance taken by governments, policy makers, and individuals largely depends on the political belief of whether the primary responsibility for ensuring individual wellbeing lies with the state or the family. Regarding kinship care, most opinions about who should be responsible for child welfare fall somewhere in between the two. Hunt (2001) emphasised this middle ground, characterising kinship care as a unique bridge between care provided by birth parents and state care. Many researchers support this notion, recognising that kinship care navigates both private and public spheres (for example, Cossar, 2004; Munro and Gilligan, 2013; McCartan et al, 2018; Xu et al, 2020).

The theory of familialism can help provide a deeper exploration of this middle space. Familialism is a sociological concept proposing that families should take responsibility for their kin rather than relying on the government or other institutions (Leitner, 2003). Nations with strong familialism traditions, such as Poland, are less inclined to involve social workers in child welfare matters (Furstenberg, 2020). In contrast, countries that rely less on familialism, like Norway, advocate for greater state involvement to attempt to ensure equity. Countries like Norway consequently experience relatively higher instances of social service intervention (Skivenes and Thoburn, 2016).

Saraceno and Keck (2010) examined the sociopolitical context of familialism and its influence on child welfare policies. They identified three key types:

- familialism by default: no direct state support or alternatives to family care;
- supported familialism: assistance through tax relief and paid leave without direct state aid;
- de-familialisation: state support tailored to individual needs.

Hantrais (2004) examined familialism specifically for the UK, emphasising that child welfare is generally de-familialised. The state provides tailored support for families in need and facilitates the removal of children from harmful family environments when necessary. Nevertheless, kinship care stands out and disrupts the de-familialised ideal. Instead, kinship care in the UK promotes a shift from de-familialisation back to re-familialisation, where, in the first instance, extended family, friends, or non-governmental organisations (NGOs) are expected to provide care when a child cannot remain with their primary carers.

Other studies examining family support systems across Europe (Albertini et al, 2016) and the role of grandparents in welfare states (Herlofson and Hagestad, 2012) also illustrate the unique interplay between familialism and kinship care. For example, McCartan et al (2018) used Esping-Andersen's (1990) welfare state typologies to compare kinship care approaches in the UK. While Esping-Andersen's framework has received criticism for neglecting gender norms and offering a narrow perspective on family, it nevertheless provides an insightful anchor for analysing kinship care practices across various high-income and European nations. Figure 2.1 summarises these studies on familialism and kinship care.

Different countries' stances on welfare and support for kinship care are shaped by cultural notions and ideologies surrounding family and responsibilities, and perceptions of what is normal, risky, deserving, and undeserving. The following section delves deeper into some of the norms and ideologies that affect support for families living in kinship care arrangements.

Factors and norms influencing kinship care support

What is normal?

Before further exploring some key factors and norms that influence how kinship care can be supported, it is vital to reflect on what is considered 'normal'. When the term normal is mentioned, the immediate reaction, especially among child welfare practitioners, may be to dismiss it and its

Figure 2.1: The impact of welfare state typologies on valuing kinship care support

Nordic model	Liberalism	Conservative model	Mediterranean model	East European model
Norway, Sweden, Finland Denmark, Netherlands	UK, US, Canada	Austria, Belgium, France, Germany, Luxembourg	Italy, Spain, Greece, Portugal, Turkey	Poland, Slovakia, Romania, Czech Republic, Moldova, Estonia, Hungary
General social policy and programmes to all citizens through local authorities	Central regulation and guidance of services	Social support is given to those on the labour market	Minimal State intervention	Diverse welfare systems with social security separate from the state
Tax-funded universal benefits	Local authorities play a central role	Problems should be solved primarily without interference from the state or markets	Reliance of family, church, community intervention and voluntary organisations	Move towards privatisation, and promotion of market principles
Family orientated, child-focused, and preventative services	Ambivalent attitude to welfare	Family-orientated services	Rooted in family and traditional values, and Catholicism	Respects and aims to re-establish the autonomy of the family
Readiness to intervene, which can be repressive	Separation of preventative services and child protection services	The state delegates responsibility for welfare and insurance to religious and voluntary organisations	Measures towards child-welfare, preventative and family-orientated services	Kinship care has little interference from the state and is seen as a private family matter
Kinship care has equal status to foster care	Separation into formal and informal kinship care	Kinship care is seen as a private matter	Line between informal and formal care is blurred	Paucity of support, resources, or training
Kinship carers are defined as foster carers	Minimal aim of reunification	Aim for reunification	Paucity of support, resources or training for kinship carers	Reliance on NGOs and foreign capitals
	Little financial or support parity with other services, such as adoption or fostering	Lack of practice guidance, standardised approaches, and support		

implications. A core value in child welfare and social work is to respect diversity and difference, which might suggest that there is no such thing as normal. However, as highlighted in Figure 2.1 and other child welfare research, various cultural norms affect whether a family receives or seeks assistance from the state. The goal is not to overlook cultural norms, but to understand and reflect on them, challenge them if necessary, and then address them thoughtfully with critical reflection.

A central critical realist argument of this book is that normality exists and is not merely subjective. Normality has both an objective empirical status (for example, mean, mode, and average) and a moral one. Social sciences, society, and child welfare work rely on normativity (Sayer, 2017). How society, child welfare, and individuals interpret what is expected of families influences how we determine what will satisfy a child's need and right to safety and wellbeing. Law, policy, practitioners, and society can and should make judgments about such things. What constitutes a good parent? What defines a safe family setting? These core assessments, essential for child welfare and support, all rely on norms. While these norms can and should be critiqued, there must be an agreed standard for determining what is considered right or wrong, safe or harmful, supportive or disruptive.

While it is essential to acknowledge that norms and expectations exist and are real, it is also the case that they are subjective, adaptable, and influenced by cultural contexts and historical periods. The norms that individuals and society hold as true – particularly regarding kinship, family types, and functioning – depend on many factors, including, unfortunately, the harmful influences of heterosexism, nationalism, misogyny, and White supremacy. Some of these are explored further next.

Family norms and gendered roles

Hopefully, we are progressing towards a broader acceptance of many types of families in different cultures. What is considered normal is expanding. In many cultures, family life has become more diverse and flexible in the past few decades due to the increased number of same-sex couples having children, the acceptance of divorce, and the movement away from gender-traditional work and family roles (McKie and Callan, 2011).

Family norms are also shaped by increased geographic mobility and multiculturalism. Modern family dynamics and remote work opportunities often allow the primary source of family income to be more geographically flexible (Pratchett and Rees, 2017). Parents can frequently work away from home, sometimes in different countries. Climate emergencies, global disasters, conflict, war, and migration have also significantly affected norms regarding how families form and function transnationally (Griffiths et al, 2013). These circumstances can lead to displacement, loss of homes and livelihoods, and loss of life. As a result, families may be forced to separate or to establish new structures to survive, and this is likely to involve changes in caregiving roles and social support.

The significance of genetic relationships in family composition norms is also increasingly questioned, particularly as new family types, such as chosen families, gain acceptance. Chosen families are groups of individuals who are not connected by blood or legal ties but build intimate, supportive relationships that function like families (Weston, 1991). Recently, chosen families have become more accepted in many cultures, especially within LGBTQIA+ communities, where members often face rejection from their biological families. As the visibility and acceptance of chosen families rises, they actively challenge and transform conventional ideas about family and belonging (Jackson and Ho, 2020). This shift has implications for the growing acceptance of non-familial kinship care, where the caregivers are not related to the children, and for ensuring that their specific support needs are met (Kiraly, 2019).

Another influence on normative views of the family is gendered expectations, which primarily assign caregiving responsibilities to women. This issue is evident throughout child welfare practices and policies. In many child protection scenarios, if mothers are labelled as not 'good enough', social workers, most of whom are women, recommend placing children with other women who are assessed as being 'good enough' (Lambert, 2019). Women are seen as both threats and protectors for children, with caregiving and protection responsibilities heavily weighted toward them compared to men. This is evident even in the distribution of blame for instances of child abuse and neglect. For example, women often face blame for child abuse perpetrated by males (Crawford and Bradley, 2016) and are more frequently convicted for child deaths, even if indirectly involved (Singh, 2021).

Despite their perceived threat, women worldwide remain the primary caregivers for children (Seedat and Rondon, 2021), shouldering social reproduction responsibilities alongside both paid and unpaid care tasks under patriarchal capitalist principles and constructions of motherhood. This perpetuates the oppression of women, especially in the context of kinship care (McGhee et al, 2018). Since most kinship carers are women and most kinship care is predominantly informal, the unpaid labour of kinship care could be viewed as shifting from one female family member to another who is seen as less risky, and in this scenario the caregivers often do not receive expensive state support (Lara, 2011).

Neoliberalism, individualism, and managerialism

Neoliberalism, individualism, and managerialism, or modernisation, also shape perceptions of responsibility for kinship care support. Understanding the impact of neoliberalism on kinship care and the expectations placed on families and the state is essential, although this is often overlooked in kinship care literature. Child welfare work, policy, and practice must be viewed within their sociopolitical context, as kinship care can be politicised and exploited. Budgetary pressures, rising managerialism, and the move towards individualistic ideologies drive new policies, including the potential deregulation of kinship care, which shifts responsibilities from the state to families (Sen and Kerr, 2023).

A simplified explanation of neoliberalism is that it initially aimed to release private businesses from excessive government involvement and control. It was proposed that this would liberate market processes from governmental restrictions and increase their profitability. Social work academics such as Ferguson (2012), Garrett (2013; 2017), Houston (2016a), Jordan (2011), and Webb (2016) argue that neoliberal goals, rather than social transformation, increasingly shape social policy and child welfare practices. Others contend that neoliberalism no longer holds the same significance as the initial free market ideals promoted by its chief proponent, Friedrich Hayek. Therefore, it has become a contentious term across various disciplines. Indeed, some suggest that while it can still dominate debates, it has lost its persuasive power. It may be more beneficial to view neoliberalism as a continually evolving process and refer to it as something actively occurring, such as 'neoliberalisation' (Brenner and Theodore, 2002, p 6).

Neoliberalisation, capitalism, and the belief that success is primarily based on a person's drive, skills, and abilities can promote individualism. This individualism is increasingly evident in contemporary child welfare and social work within Western and European societies (Webb, 2016). Families and children can be viewed as individuals who are monitored, compared to others, and normalised. Otherwise, they could be deemed undeserving, troublesome, and excluded. Individuals are depicted as self-interested rational agents who possess the capacity to address their challenges (Houston, 2016a). Those who cannot achieve their apparent potential are pathologised and moralised as lacking the necessary capacity, drive, or willpower (Skeggs, 2004).

Neoliberalisation and the subsequent individualism, along with the 'politics of withdrawal' (Edwards et al, 2012, p 739), have also contributed to a new form of punitiveness affecting not only families but also social workers (Pratt et al, 2013; Edwards et al, 2012). This shift has unveiled new 'truths' regarding the 'failed social worker', 'developmental kid', 'failing and pricey corporate parent', 'undervalued birth parent', and 'rights-bearing child' (Winter and Cree, 2016, p 1183).

Bringing the political abstract back to the realities of everyday child welfare work and kinship care, we often see how easily professionals are blamed for the deaths of children at the hands of caregivers. We can see how blame for events can become individualised. Notably, in the UK, social workers have faced public scrutiny following scandals involving child murders, such as those of Baby P, Star Hobson, and Ellie Butler. Ellie's case is explicitly related to kinship care. Ellie stayed with her kinship carer grandparents until she was ordered to return to her birth father, who murdered her. Newspaper headlines declared that the local authority had 'blood on their hands' (Taylor, 2018, np).

Over time, individualised blame directed at social workers or family members has led to bureaucratic child protection systems. This shift has transformed social work into what Harris (2003) describes as the social work business, influenced by market disciplines. This trend, known as modernisation and managerialism, emphasises best value, consumerism, and performance (Diaz and Hill, 2019). Social work's time and service user progress are now measured to improve efficiency by pushing people through the system as swiftly as possible. Together, these ideologies endorse a contradictory neoliberal and individualistic belief that families should self-support without intrusive state intervention, payment, or kudos, while paradoxically implying that social workers should be aware of and intervene sooner with at-risk families. Child welfare, and, therefore, state support for kinship care, is reduced to a lose-lose scenario of intervening too much or too little.

Risk

Questions about who bears the main responsibility for a child highlight the impact of concepts of risk on kinship care. This requires further exploration within its sociopolitical and historical context. What constitutes acceptable levels of risk, and who can be labelled as potentially riskier?

Although risk and responsibility for child safety are vital considerations in kinship care assessments and court decisions, many researchers, academics, NGOs, and policy makers often overlook them. This omission is surprising, as intergenerational risk and abuse are common concerns surrounding kinship care (Hallett et al, 2021; Skoglund et al, 2022). The saying 'The apple doesn't fall far from the tree' reflects fears that children may be vulnerable to harm if left within their families, suggesting dysfunction may be passed down through generations. Jonsson (1975) researched this as negative social inheritance from a cross-disciplinary perspective. From the viewpoint of child welfare policy and practice, Casey (2012) examined the impact of intergenerational abuse on 'troubled families'. The study found that issues such as domestic violence, sexual abuse, drug and alcohol addiction, neglect, arson, and starting families at a young age were prevalent and faced by 'troubled families' throughout the generations.

Specifically for kinship care, Crumbley and Little (1997) were among the first to address the issue of intergenerational risk and abuse. They explicitly questioned whether behaviour patterns are passed down through generations. According to Crumbley and Little, professionals and policy makers may overlook the extent to which kinship carers, particularly grandparents, may have contributed to birth parents' abuse and neglect of their children. They also proposed that even if the kinship carer interrupts the abusive behaviour, practitioners should still acknowledge that other family members or household members may continue the abuse.

The reluctance of many researchers, NGOs, and policy makers to mention risk in kinship care is even more perplexing given modern culture's focus on it for most other issues. Beck (1998) and Giddens (1991) famously proposed that risk mitigation concepts and behaviours have become organising principles in modern cultures, resulting in what they called a risk society (Garrett, 2013). The global economic crisis of 2008 (Aebi et al, 2012), the coronavirus pandemic (Domingues, 2022), climate emergency management (Maechler and Graz, 2022), and even Trump's wall (Clapton, 2021) are examples of various governments' obsession with risk and their attempts to control it. Most child welfare practices, other than kinship care, have offered an almost natural site for promoting the risk narrative, shaping expectations for assessing and managing the threat of harm, particularly in child protection (Hardy, 2020). Practitioners must provide concrete evidence to reassure that sufficient efforts are being made to detect and address any risks to a child's wellbeing (Smith, 2010).

One explanation for risk rarely being addressed in kinship care literature and policy is the reluctance to enter the emotionally charged moral and ethical debates surrounding assigning risk to kinship care families. Many may avoid discussing risk, to avoid appearing flippant, unjust, or unfair. Emphasising risk could lead to poorly evidenced generalisations and perpetuate negative stereotypes, causing families living in kinship care to be labelled 'risky' (Brown et al, 2002, p 72).

As noted in the previous chapter, broad generalisations and labelling can overlook underlying issues. Correlation is not the same as causation. For instance, it is now well recognised that poverty is associated with child maltreatment (Bywaters et al, 2016). Therefore, claiming that grandparents who have previously struggled with money and parenting cannot now be kinship carers is misleading and ethically dubious. When confronted with the uncomfortable reality that kinship carers may have been unsatisfactory and 'risky' parents to their own children, we must also recognise that situations can change and acknowledge that context is important. Grandparents will likely be in significantly different positions now than they were a generation ago.

Another political and ethical challenge with broad generalisations is that labelling victims of social and economic injustice as 'risky' and blaming them may serve as an excuse to avoid addressing the true causes of institutionalised poverty, racism, sexism, and unequal opportunity. With parallels to neoliberalisation and individualisation, it can individualise troubles without recognising the causes and impacts of social injustices. These 'risky' families can be dismissed as undeserving 'anti-social families' destined for the 'sin-bin', so there is less governmental motivation to provide them with individual investment or societal improvement (Garrett, 2017). Paradoxically, if social workers and the state do not invest in these families or in institutional change, it is likely that fewer opportunities will be available to help the families and this will increase the likelihood of them becoming 'risky'.

This notion that families labelled as 'risky' are not worthy of investment can also be seen in policy discussions about the previously mentioned 'troubled' families. Despite the growing recognition of diverse family arrangements, many policies for children and families, particularly those involving care away from birth parents, continue valuing the ideal family or 'family-like' norms as being more able to attend to a child's needs (Boddy, 2019). Many policies, particularly in high-income countries, still adhere to the ideal two-parent, White, heteronormative, Eurocentric, middle-class mother-and-father dyad caring for children (Kirton, 2020). Numerous laws routinely distinguish and categorise 'regular' families from 'troubled', 'troubling', or 'troublesome' households (Smith, 2015). These ideals mirror historical ones in the UK, such as David Cameron's 'Troubled Families' programme, the 'underclass' in the 1980s, 'problem families' in the 1950s, and the 'undeserving' in the 1880s (Lambert, 2019). Consequently, families in kinship care arrangements are often perceived in high-income countries' policies and practices as deviations from the norm. They can be marginalised as troublesome families living in an abnormal family set-up (Pratchett and Rees, 2017).

Systemic racism

The central dispute with labelling others is that due to marginalisation and discrimination, certain groups are more likely to be unjustly labelled as troublesome, risky, not good enough, or undeserving of support. Systemic and institutional racism is one of the most challenging, and increasingly acknowledged, factors negatively affecting how family and kinship care are attended to.

International research has noted that there are disproportionate numbers of children from ethnic minoritised groups in kinship care and a larger number of children from these groups in informal kinship care than in formal kinship care (Nandy et al, 2011). Studies on kinship care arrangements in England have supported these findings. For example, nearly one in three children in kinship care is from an ethnically minoritised group, and informal kinship care is twice as prevalent among Black children compared to the national average. There are known correlations between ethnicity and poverty in the UK (Webb et al, 2020), and compared to children growing up with at least one parent, children in kinship care are disproportionately likely to live in deprived areas and are significantly more likely to experience health problems and disabilities (Wijedasa, 2015). This disparity in provision is further amplified by the social gradient, which correlates family socioeconomic circumstances to children's chances of receiving child protection intervention and support (Goldacre and Hood, 2022). This shows a disproportionate number of Black families in the UK in informal kinship care compared to their non-Black counterparts, and these Black families are more likely to be poorly supported, in financial hardship, and have health issues.

Tackling disparities for ethnic and racially minoritised children is now a greater focus in child welfare. In recent years, there has been a concerted effort to instil anti-racist practice (James-Brown, 2022). In the UK, there are new initiatives and research into disparities of support for Black and ethnic minoritised families living in kinship care, such as the work of Sharon McPherson and Families for Harmony. However, acknowledgement of racial inequality is still in its infancy in kinship care literature, research, policy making, and practice.

Cost-effectiveness

One often underplayed yet significant reason kinship care is regarded as a valued alternative to state care is its cost-effectiveness for governments and local jurisdictions (McCartan et al, 2018). Considerable savings could be achieved if the number of children placed in foster care or adoption were to decrease through opting for or maintaining children in informal kinship care, where practical and financial support should not be, but usually is, discretionary. Even when local authorities fund kinship arrangements, the costs are lower due to reduced start-up expenses, no recruitment costs, and minimal training requirements. Kinship care is 'financially attractive for cash-strapped local authorities' (McGhee et al, 2018, p 1192). The economic benefits are particularly compelling given the financial pressures stemming from the 2008 crisis, the COVID-19 pandemic, and ongoing global conflicts impacting living and energy costs.

The underfunding of local authorities, along with governments frequently attempting to cut costs to public services, results in a strikingly unjustifiable lack of practical and financial support for children and their families living in kinship care. Worldwide, most families, advocates, lobbyists, charities, researchers, and child welfare professionals agree that children in kinship care and their families require better financial and practical assistance (Brown et al, 2019). Although many national governments recognise the importance of kinship care in their policies, this recognition is often not reflected in the levels of state support provided to carers, children, and families. For example, in Armenia, social workers are required to conduct only two official visits to formal kinship care arrangements each year, and visits are often less frequent in practice. In China, NGOs and the government offer little to no assistance. In India, kinship care is often informal. In Ghana, neither the law nor national policy addresses kinship care. In Ethiopia, 70 per cent of kinship carers reported no NGO or government assistance. In many high-income nations, support for kinship care is contingent on its classification as either formal or informal. Even with such distinctions, assistance for these categories varies based on local policy and practitioner attitudes (Delap and Mann, 2019).

Support for formal kinship care and informal kinship care

This section revisits the specific legislative and policy processes regarding support for the children in the original study. It returns to the distinctions between formal and informal kinship care in England and how these impacted the support for the children who participated in the PhD research. Additionally, this section critiques the tendency to tie in kinship care with fostering and adoption processes, whether directly or as an adjacent approach, particularly as some cash-strapped local authorities employ diversionary tactics to evade their responsibilities and support.

Assessment and support for formal kinship care

In high-income countries such as Australia, New Zealand, the UK, and the US, policy makers and statutory services often view kinship care as a solution to child protection issues and as the ideal means of keeping families together whenever possible. This perspective is grounded in human rights discourses, particularly the United Nations Convention on the Rights of the Child. Article 19 of the Convention mandates that children must be protected from abuse, violence, and neglect, and that governments should ensure parents do everything possible to achieve this. Article 9 states that a child should not be removed from their family's care unless remaining there poses significant harm. The Convention emphasises the right of children to remain in a family environment and to be safe. At times, there may be tension between keeping a child with their family and ensuring their safety. This is why some legislation, such as the Children Act 1989, attempts to address this for particularly precarious situations by formally asserting full or partial parental rights and responsibilities for the child.

In England, formal kinship care arrangements authorised by the local authority are governed by looked-after child fostering processes (Children's Act 1989, s 22) and child-in-care budgets. Potential kinship foster carers are assessed to meet fostering standards and regulations. Attempting to shoehorn kinship care into existing legislation and processes presents many challenges. Fundamentally, kinship care exists within a system initially designed for relatively short-term placements with strangers. However, kinship care in England is typically regarded as a permanent solution with known adults, usually with little chance of reunification (McCartan et al, 2018).

Research has also shown that many kinship carers find the formal fostering assessment processes intrusive and demeaning, especially when they believe they have previously raised their own children relatively well (Farmer and Moyers, 2008). In the UK, non-kinship foster carers typically choose foster care as a vocation, inviting scrutiny and intrusion. Non-kinship care foster carers also have long periods of training before approval and receive financial compensation for their caregiving responsibilities. In contrast, kinship carers are more likely to become carers due to emergency crises, and they have less time for preparation to ensure that their homes, lifestyles, other caring obligations, and work align with their new responsibilities (Taylor et al, 2020). They must also contend with legal guardianship issues (Nandy and Selwyn, 2013).

The starkest difference between kinship care foster carers and non-kinship care foster carers lies in the need to manage the ongoing relationships within the family that have led to the crisis. Non-kinship foster carers are not central to navigating the family tensions that may have caused children to be unable to stay in their birth parents' care. Kinship carers also often need to ensure the children's safety while at the same time attending to the distress and needs of the birth parents. Additionally, kinship carers frequently feel guilt, believing that their family, and possibly themselves, have played a role in the abuse and neglect (Hingley-Jones et al, 2020). Kinship carers' personal circumstances are also more likely to differ from those of non-kinship carers. As illustrated in the previous chapter, kinship carers tend to be older, face financial hardship, lack space, experience isolation, and deal with physical and mental health issues (Nandy and Selwyn, 2013). This means their housing and lives may not meet fostering standards and regulations.

The updated *Kinship Care: Statutory Guidance for Local Authorities* (DfE, 2024) provides advice on these matters. It states that although housing may not meet standards, and although the mental and physical health of the carers may be of concern, these are to be noted in the totality of the assessment for suitability. Concerns that are not typically attributed to foster carers must be balanced against other factors and documented for future support once the carers have been approved. The guidance also allows some leeway for potential kinship carers with criminal convictions. The concern here is that thresholds for appropriate care may be lowered, yet children still require and deserve safe family lives that focus on their needs.

Support for informal kinship care

Another option available for families in the UK is informal kinship care. This can be arranged without local authority intervention and is usually addressed in England with support from the child in need processes (Children's Act 1989, s 17). For informal kinship care, section 17 child in need support is intended to be a one-off support package that can be, and usually is, made multiple times. This means that, typically, the welfare of children in kinship care in England is treated in legislation as a private family affair with as little as possible state support provided (MacDonald et al, 2018). This is especially concerning given the high caseloads and competing priorities. Kinship carers who require more formal support and monitoring often do not pass kinship care fostering assessments. They are, therefore, encouraged to pursue a private law application, where the family is less likely to receive support compared to those requiring statutory care. As a result, families with the least support and monitoring are often the ones who need it the most (McCartan et al, 2018). The lack of adequate support is even more concerning given that many kinship carers faced with challenges later are reluctant to seek social work support or assessment (McGrath, 2021).

Fitting a square peg into a round hole

Particularly in the UK, both formal and informal kinship care, assessment, monitoring, and support are often wedged into the more established fostering, adoption, or early intervention policies, legislation, and funding, or at the very least viewed as an alternative to them. Commentators have described this bridging of kinship care into the child welfare system as piecemeal and reactive with limited research evidence (O'Brien, 2012). Merging kinship care with fostering and adoption can oversimplify the concept and practice by assuming that there are few differences between fostering, adoption, and the various types of kinship care arrangements. However, kinship care is a broad phenomenon with numerous intricacies. It is misleading to imply that all families who foster and adopt are the same, let alone categorise kinship care with them.

Even the differentiation between formal and informal kinship care is not enough. There are now numerous hybrid kinship arrangements where, for example, social work may have intervened or may intervene later in so-called informal placements (Berrick and Hernandez, 2016). Therefore, it is imperative not to essentialise kinship care and assume that all family arrangements are the same or similar. As discussed earlier, along with levels of local authority support, kinship care is influenced by perceptions of what constitutes a safe and normal family environment, societal attitudes toward gender roles, ideal family structures, ethnicity, identity politics, political economic choices, and prevailing political beliefs. The families, the carers, and the children, along with their contexts, are neither uniform nor singular in their characteristics, roles, or statuses (MacDonald et al, 2018). Kinship care has its own complex experience for children and should be treated as such (Harwin, Alrouh et al, 2019). This is why integrating kinship care into existing fostering and adoption ideals, or even those adjacent to them, is often described as trying to fit a square peg into a round hole (Dill, 2010).

Diversionary tactics

On one hand, English legislation and policy mandate the support of formal arrangements for children in kinship care. On the other hand, they provide pathways for deregulation and numerous potential diversionary routes from the system and social work, offering only discretionary practical and financial support. There are many ways that the state and local authorities can shirk responsibilities. Many local authorities attempt to dissuade kinship carers from pursuing the formal foster care route and do not make it clear that carers are likely to receive less support if they choose private arrangements (Farmer and Moyers, 2008; Hunt and Waterhouse, 2013; Selwyn et al, 2013; McCartan et al, 2018).

One study estimated that only 3.5 per cent of the approximately 180,000 children in kinship care in England at the time were legally entitled to financial and professional support (Davey, 2016). Another states:

> There is a long legacy of reluctance to help family members to do what many think should be done out of a sense of kinship affection and obligation (O'Brien 2000) and we found that only one-quarter (23%) received the help they had requested. Carers were often told that they were expected to manage without state assistance. The attitudes the carers encountered are likely to be underpinned by attempts to contain costs. (Farmer et al, 2013, p 32)

This is especially pertinent given that poverty continues to be the most significant driver impacting a child's health and wellbeing. Nevertheless, child welfare and UK government policy and practice have still not effectively addressed the issue of poverty (Davidson et al, 2017).

Current attempts to straddle the gap between private family life and state concern

This section explores and critiques some of the current English policy and legislative directions that have attempted to balance state responsibility with less intrusion into private family life.

Clear Blue Water

In 2018, England and Wales announced a family court crisis, responding to the highest number of children in care in three decades. It was found that too many children and families were subjected to care proceedings, resulting in separation from their families of origin, despite the Children Act 1989 prioritising children remaining with their families. The report *Care Crisis Review: Options for Change* (Care Crisis Review, 2018) identified multiple factors contributing to the rise in the number of children in state care. Although it did not explicitly reference kinship care, it acknowledged an untapped resource for some children on the verge of care: their extended family and community. The report argued that family was an underutilised and underfunded resource for child welfare initiatives.

The same year, Isabelle Trowler, the Chief Social Worker for Children and Families at the Department for Education in England, proposed a solution to the family court crisis in *Case Proceedings in England: The Case for Clear Blue Water* (Trowler, 2018). The report suggested that the legal principles of no order and least intervention should be applied more readily, meaning that making a care order for children or family life should be considered a last resort. It argued that section 20 of the Children Act 1989 should be reclaimed 'as a legitimate and respected support service to families for the long-term care of children' (Trowler, 2018, p 19).

Section 20 arrangements involve carers voluntarily agreeing, sometimes under significant pressure and threats of court action, that the local authority provide state care for children at home or in other settings. Parents maintain parental responsibility and rights, and often there is no need for the local authority to apply to the court for a care order. Trowler's report advised that increased use of section 20 would facilitate more family work before legal proceedings and be 'resurrected as the key point of hope' (2018, p 9) to avoid court whenever possible.

Advocates of *The Case for Clear Blue Water* believed that voluntary family solutions would be more ethical, improve outcomes, shorten time frames, and be more cost-effective. They would also increase broader family care, including kinship care. The report suggested that increased use of Section 20 would encourage more successful collaboration between families and child welfare services. Better engagement would counteract the negative influence of the 'culture of blame, shame, and fear' (Care Crisis Review, 2018, p 18) that has developed in recent years within social work. Trowler (2018) asserts that making the child welfare system more cooperative and less threatening would decrease animosity between statutory services and families, as well as within families themselves.

The adversarial nature of court proceedings among family members is a significant concern, particularly for kinship care (Harwin, Alrouh et al, 2019).

Relatives often find themselves engaged in contentious legal battles with one another over child custody. Afterwards, the family must work to rebuild relationships after court. Restoring family connections after separation is difficult enough without the added strain of previous legal disputes and serious allegations between relatives.

MacAlister's Independent Review of Children's Social Care

Isabelle Trowler is not alone in trying to resolve the issues of too many children in care, along with the challenges posed by antagonistic systems and fractious relationships. In recent years, England has continued its efforts to adjust the current system toward less intrusive family solutions. In 2021, the Independent Review of Children's Social Care was launched. Much of the final policy report by Josh MacAlister reiterated the importance of partnership working with families to '[u]nlocking the potential of family networks' (2022, p 93). According to the review, this would help keep families together by offering a more cost-effective and ethical alternative for children needing care away from their original parents. The review heavily promoted growing kinship care, suggesting, again, that it could reduce the number of children in state care by accessing the untapped resource of potential family carers. The MacAlister review also assumed this would lead to better outcomes for children.

The MacAlister review resulted in England's first National Kinship Care Strategy in 2023 (DfE, 2023), which also aimed to grow kinship care, provide a more explicit definition in legislation, and offer more recognition and improved support to kinship carers. Backed by £20 million, the strategy included financial allowances for kinship carers, matching those received by foster carers. It also expanded the role of virtual school heads, previously set up for children in statutory care, to prioritise the education of children living in kinship care.

Challenges to kinship care as a child welfare or child welfare-adjacent service

At first glance, the policy and legislative directions promoting kinship care may appear reasonable, well founded, and morally aligned. The idea of more children remaining with their families instead of placing them with strangers through intrusive and adversarial statutory social work intervention is highly appealing. However, there has been substantial resistance to these policies from various quarters. This includes concerns about nepotism (Rogowski, 2020; Hanley, 2021), the creeping privatisation and marketisation of children's services (Jones, 2018; McGrath-Brookes et al, 2021), the commodification of social work knowledge and research

(Tunstill, 2018), and the over-reliance on increasingly impoverished communities and peer support (BASW England, 2021). There are also fears that the ultimate goal is to deregulate and de-institutionalise child welfare, with kinship care serving as the ideal vehicle to facilitate this (Sen and Kerr, 2023).

Setting aside these contentious yet necessary political considerations, from a research and evidence perspective, caution is warranted regarding claims that increasing voluntary agreements and family-centred solutions effectively expand kinship care, reduce costs, and lessen animosity. Integrating kinship care into struggling systems and legislation without comprehensive data and research evidence is precarious (Shutleworth, 2023a). For instance, Trowler's optimism about enhancing the use of section 20s in family arrangements is speculative, with no definitive proof of its challenges or benefits. No study has been conducted on the impact of more frequent use of section 20s on kinship care.

Another issue is the assumption that increasing kinship care as an alternative placement will reduce the number of looked-after children due to an 'untapped resource' of prospective kinship carers. This is partly true. Factors such as deprivation, thresholds, and potential kinship carers' access to information and legal aid significantly affect the prevalence of kinship care (McCartan et al, 2018). However, it is misleading to definitively claim that increasing support for kinship carers, particularly without substantial economic assistance, will substantially boost the number of kinship care arrangements and lower the number of children in non-kinship 'out-of-home' statutory placements (Shuttleworth, 2023a).

Additionally, the number of kinship care placements has risen yearly in England, as has the number of children in non-kinship looked-after state care (Kinship, 2024). This does not align with the assumption that increasing the use of kinship care would reduce the number of children in non-kinship state care. Instead, it suggests that the complete data is not yet available and that the solution is more complex than merely increasing support and kinship care placements through existing systems or adding amendments.

What is certain is that, even with section 20 in place, the state must take steps to safeguard children's safety and wellbeing in kinship care settings. Children still have rights, and governments must ensure that these rights are upheld even if children are not in formal state care. When necessary for children's safety and wellbeing, the state is still expected to provide support (United Nations Convention on the Rights of the Child 1989), allowing sufficient time to assess what safe, valuable support means. The adversarial element of the judicial process might be diminished if section 20s were used more frequently. However, the process may still take a long time, and any prolonged family tension impacts adversarial family relationships even without statutory intervention.

Lastly, the political and economic contexts and choices are often not fully acknowledged. For example, the MacAlister review underscored a shift in child welfare tasks and resources without the corresponding and necessary increases in funding. While this may be due to the priorities of the sitting government rather than the review itself, its intermediate and final reports often overlooked sociological and political issues, issuing generalised calls for increased funding, with, as previously mentioned, terms like austerity conspicuously absent. Additionally, although the resulting 2023 Kinship Care Strategy (DfE, 2023) marks a positive step forward, initially, only up to eight local authorities were provided additional financial allowances under the scheme. This means that despite the advocacy for more kinship care arrangements, most kinship carers and children will not receive financial support for some time. In contemporary Global North politics, kinship care could arguably be viewed as a convenient tool to reduce costs, evade state intervention responsibilities, or delay them, which might enable further deregulation that could undermine children's rights (Willow, 2023).

Navigating the in-between spaces of kinship care

Many debates surrounding kinship care return to whether the responsibility for child welfare lies primarily with the state and society or with individuals and families. Stepping back to take an even broader view reveals that these discussions are often circular and seemingly unresolvable. Attempts to shoehorn kinship care into current policies and practices, or even to tinker with and modify kinship care definitions, result in circular discussions. So do attempts to inappropriately address or ignore the impact of sociological understandings, cultural family values, political contexts, and the influence of costs. As shown in Figure 2.2, the debates tend to loop around themes of support, responsibility, risk, regulation, resources, cultural and political values, norms, and, probably most importantly for governments and child welfare services, investments of time and money.

On the one hand, there are arguments for kinship care to be more of a private family matter, which is potentially more ethical and culturally aware than costly, intrusive, and judgemental state interference. On the other hand, over-reliance on family and community capital can allow risk, valuation of norms, and neoliberal capitalism to be ignored. Both provide many diversionary opportunities for the children living in the arrangements not to receive support from the state. Therefore, the argument returns to mandating support and monitoring it in ways like fostering and adoption.

Noting this cyclical debate does not suggest that any of the arguments put forward are not compelling or even necessary. However, while each discussion goes around in circles, one thing remains: children and families in kinship care are not getting the support they need (Kinship Care Parliamentary

Figure 2.2: The circular debates on kinship care

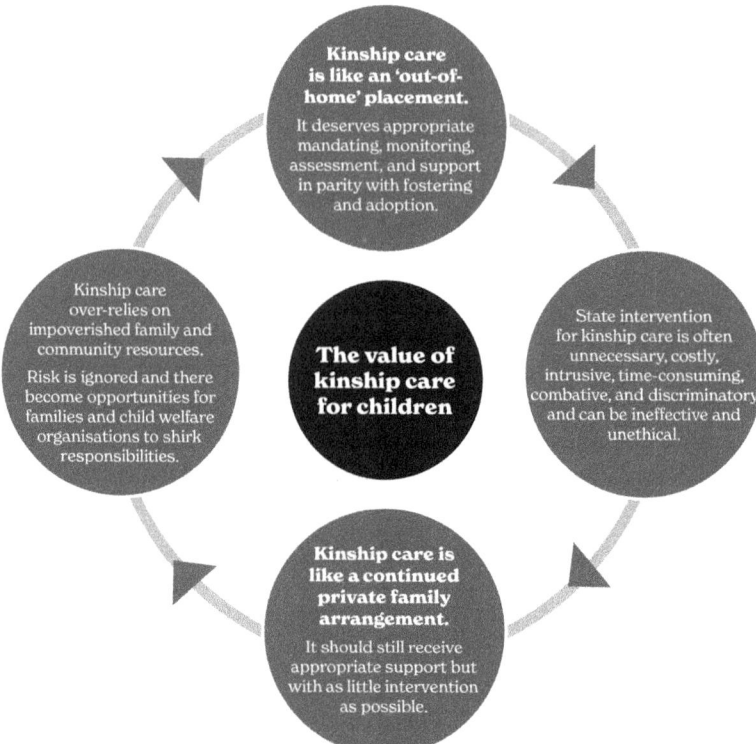

Taskforce, 2020). It is essential to start looking at their tensions, recognise and reflect on when we are persuaded by particular arguments, and start working in the middle space. It is time to acknowledge that kinship care lies in the push and pulls of an ambivalent, messy space, and work within it rather than against competing demands.

One approach is to apply theory to practice and recognise multiple meanings of family, the acceptance and challenging of norms and their implications, and the greater awareness around the gendered nature of family and care. Many academics (for example, Biehal, 2014; Boddy, 2023) now argue for a more sociological understanding of family life, focusing on relationality rather than just genetic relations (Smart, 2011). Other academics have suggested the inclusion of socio-genealogical connectedness (Owusu-Bempah, 2010) and meaning rooted in shared memories, togetherness, belonging, and personhood (McCarthy, 2013).

There also needs to be more critical social work that tackles kinship care and child welfare. These contrasting and seemingly contentious counter-narratives must be addressed during policy making. This includes critical social work critiques of neoliberalism (Marthinsen et al, 2021), managerialism (Rogowski, 2020), social inequalities (Hood, 2023), and the influence of poverty on child protection (Saar-Heiman and Gupta, 2020). Anti-racist practice also needs to be further embedded into how we consider family life and parenting (Okpokiri, 2021), and there needs to be a concerted effort to decolonise child welfare curriculum and raise awareness of cultural competence and humility (Crisp, 2024). Furthermore, social work has an established history of feminist academics who challenge the gender norms in families, society and practice (for example, Dominelli and Campling, 2002; Fawcett et al, 2005; Wendt and Moulding, 2016; Noble et al, 2024). Child welfare should use a wide range of critical thinking to inform how we approach kinship care rather than just attempting to slot in kinship care as a step-by-step procedure to be ratified and trained on.

Putting thinking into practice, child welfare practitioners, researchers, and families need to do two things. Both are difficult but necessary.

The first is to disrupt current narratives through knowledge, reflection, activism, and everyday conversation. This chapter is unashamedly political and critical. The first step of change must be to ensure that those working in child welfare know the political motivations attached to kinship care because, to stress once again, kinship care can and will be exploited. Broader sociopolitical understandings of managing family life can better equip child welfare workers to undertake more reflexive, collaborative roles with the diverse nature of families in kinship care arrangements (Ferguson et al, 2018). We must focus on the small everyday tasks that must be managed and ensure that society, governments, policy, and legislation treat families with dignity, respect, and fairness. We need to ensure that values and ethics, rather than economic justification, are central to our work – the starting points and the focus every day. Actively keeping this in mind will help ensure that child welfare work focuses on both individual and societal change. It will help us to recognise and negotiate the space and the contradictions in between without losing sight of what matters – a fairer society so that all children can thrive safely.

The second thing we need to do is ensure there is appropriate support and resources to recognise and navigate the critical in-between spaces occupied by kinship care. We recognise these spaces by not being persuaded by top-down arguments but by starting bottom-up from the experiences of those in kinship care and finding out what truly matters. The starting point must be the middle of the 'circular debates' diagram in Figure 2.2. What is the value of kinship care for children?

To meaningfully answer this question, appropriate time and space are needed for learning, reflection, and discussion. Tick-box approaches to gathering views are not enough. If kinship care can be exploited, as explored later in the book, so can the gathering of children's views by policy makers, practitioners, and even researchers. Knowing a child's and potential caregivers' likes, dislikes, wishes, and desires is helpful but insufficient. The vital part of assessing need and support is to debate how they navigate the pushes and pulls inherent in the world around them. Assessment, support, and collaboration should provide space for families to consider and discuss managing the sociopolitical and geopolitical tensions inherent in family life and society. For these meaningful and complex discussions to happen, time is needed to build rapport, go at the families' pace, and provide the least intimidating spaces for them to discuss the political, economic, and social realities. This means that child welfare practitioners require the right working conditions.

Finally, there is also an opportunity to influence how other child welfare systems function. Having argued that complex family relationships such as kinship care cannot easily integrate into existing legislation or oversimplified notions of family duty or government responsibility, it also seems appropriate to re-evaluate how current global processes align with the core values of social work, child welfare, childhood studies, and family life. A fresh approach to and method for understanding the lived experiences of families in kinship care from around the world might serve as a model for other child-centred work, such as work on foster care and adoption. It is time for other child welfare systems to learn from kinship care and how it adapts to global and local politics, as opposed to kinship care unsuccessfully adopting their more established but often rigid problematic practices.

Conclusion

Kinship care occupies a unique and complex space within child welfare, intersecting personal family dynamics, societal norms, and broader political agendas. This chapter has highlighted how kinship care is often leveraged for its economic benefits, especially during times of financial strain. While governments may promote kinship care as a cost-effective alternative to state care, this approach can sometimes overlook the intricate needs of children, families, communities, and society, as can taking a blinkered approach to the development of norms and excluding the influence of neoliberalism and risk.

The next chapter zooms into the debates surrounding the concept of child permanence. It critiques traditional viewpoints of permanence while advocating a fresh perspective that emphasises children's experiences of kinship care. It also discusses how nurturing emotional connections and a sense of belonging can give children the stability they need to flourish in a safe environment.

3

Valuing permanence for kinship care

> It doesn't matter if you don't live with your mum or your dad, but that you live with people that actually care about you and know who you really are. I don't know. I think it just kind of gives you like a freedom to be like you want to be. So, nothing really matters. I guess it doesn't really matter as long as you're just happy within yourself and there's people around for you.
>
> Megan, child research participant

Navigating the complex, broader political debates surrounding kinship care is crucial. Focusing on children's lived experiences within these family arrangements is equally vital, if not more so. This chapter explores the concept of permanence for children in kinship care, emphasising their need for a sense of belonging, security, and confidence in their current and future care arrangements. While drawing on international practices, the primary focus is on the meaning of permanence for the children in kinship care in England who participated in the 'What matters to children living in kinship care' study.

The chapter first explores the origins and development of the concept of permanence, including its various forms – physical, legal, and emotional. The second part examines research on kinship care and its alignment with the principles of permanence, focusing on the safety and wellbeing of the children involved. Finally, the chapter summarises previous findings and propose new perspectives for practice, questioning whether the traditional concept of permanence adequately addresses the needs of children in kinship care.

The origins of permanence and its significance for kinship care

The importance of permanence for all children

The Children Act 1989 was pivotal in embedding the notion of permanence into English legislation, ensuring that all children, regardless of their living arrangements, are provided with a stable and loving family environment. According to the Department for Education's guidance on the Children Act 1989, permanence should offer every child 'a sense of security, continuity, commitment and identity ... a secure stable and loving family to support them through childhood and beyond' (DfE, 2010, p 12). Permanence emphasises the value of a child's place within the family. It is rooted in debates about family preservation, belonging, affiliation, history, heritage, custom, and emotional continuity for children (Boddy, 2017). We all require a sense of permanence in our lives to flourish.

Traditionally, permanence has been rooted in child development and psychosocial theories, particularly attachment theories, such as those proposed by Bowlby (1980). Additionally, there is a human rights perspective. Article 20 of the United Nations Convention on the Rights of the Child specifies that if a child cannot be raised and cared for by their birth parents, the child's permanence must be ensured as soon as possible in a safe and stable family environment. In the discussions surrounding children in 'out-of-home' care, Moran et al (2020) identify the need for continuity and three key factors that are most likely to influence permanence in foster care:

- relationships;
- communication;
- social support.

Despite the theoretical foundations and the clear human rights mandate, research suggests that achieving permanence is challenging. Several intrinsic and extrinsic factors can influence it. These factors include organisational and systemic cultures, social work training and support, and dynamics involving foster carers and birth families. The characteristics and personal values of all parties involved also play a role (Rock et al, 2015). The concept of permanence has also evolved in diverse ways across various countries and jurisdictions due to differing child welfare practices (Pösö et al, 2021).

The importance of permanence in debates about kinship care and child welfare

Regarding kinship care, discussions about permanence, its definition, and how it can be achieved for children vary widely due to the many ways kinship care is conceptualised and practised. Nevertheless, permanence remains a vital consideration when discussing the potential benefits of kinship care (O'Brien, 2012). This is unsurprising because, as previously discussed, kinship care is often viewed in policy, legislation, and research as an alternative to fostering, adoption, or residential care, thus placing it firmly within the child placement arena.

Since the foundational work of Goldstein et al (1979), the concept of permanence has been a central focus in child welfare placements as well as in social work policy and practice (Schofield et al, 2012). Biehal noted in 2014 that permanence has been 'a key goal of child welfare systems internationally for over 40 years' (2014, p 955). And in England the 2010 guidance for the Children Act 1989 states: 'Permanence provides an underpinning framework for all social work with children and families from family support through to adoption' (DfE, 2010, p 2).

Kinship care is often endorsed as more likely to achieve permanence than other 'out-of-home' care alternatives (Winokur et al, 2018). This perceived benefit is one reason why section 22C(7)(a) of the Children Act 1989 mandates local authorities to give preference to placing the child with a relative, friend, or another connected person. *Kinship Care: Statutory Guidance for Local Authorities* reiterated this, although provided a caution:

> many children benefit by being placed with relatives or friends or others connected to them, near their own homes, continuing to attend the same school, living with their siblings and in accommodation that suits any special needs. However, not all these factors are always beneficial for all children, and some will have greater priority than others at different times in children's lives. (DfE, 2024, pp 19–20)

The origins of permanence

Investigating the history of permanence highlights its importance for kinship care set-ups and further examines the relatively recent cautionary advice from the Department for Education's guidance (DfE, 2024). The prominence of the permanence narrative in child welfare has partly arisen to address concerns about drift. Drift refers to the delay in securing long-term care for children. This concept originated among practitioners in the UK and the US (Simmonds, 2014). Historically, child welfare processes in many high-income liberal countries often led to children staying in foster care for extended periods without being returned to their original family unit or placed in alternative long-term care options such as adoption. Children were often placed in what was meant to be short-term foster care settings and then relatively forgotten. Overburdened services assumed these children were more likely to be safe and cared for, so they directed time and resources toward other children deemed more in need.

For a long time, foster care for children was particularly condemned. It was believed that foster care should be considered an intermediate, temporary solution to child welfare concerns. This belief stemmed from the notion that remaining in foster care for extended periods can be detrimental to a child's wellbeing. Epstein and Heymann (1967) initially claimed that only two options exist for parents: a secure placement at home or, if necessary, an adoptive home. A foster placement was not regarded as a long-term care option.

This emphasis on permanent, long-term secure placements for a child's wellbeing was furthered by the Oregon Project (Emlen, 1981), which also cautioned about the dangers of significant drift in stranger foster care. Such concerns led to a push for explicit goal-directed activities to move children out of temporary care as quickly as possible (Brown and Ward, 2012). This emphasised the 'planning' aspect of 'permanency planning', a commonly used term in social work practice (Maluccio et al, 1986).

Eventually, the need for swift, pre-emptive permanency planning outside of fostering resulted in a more defined legislative, policy, and practice framework. Its impact was most notable in the late 1980s, particularly in England, with the enactment of the Children Act 1989. Nonetheless, it continues to hold significance today. For instance, the 2008 Children and Young Persons Act and the Department for Education's care planning guidance (DfE, 2010) mandate an agreed-on permanence plan for all children who are accommodated or in care. Additionally, adoption targets were established and remained in place until 2020 (DfE, 2012).

Another significant turning point for the dominance of the permanence narrative in children's services in the UK was the introduction of a 26-week limit for cases in family court in England, as stipulated by section 14 of the Children and Families Act 2014. This time limit was introduced in response to cases that lasted over a year in court. The aim was to speed up decision-making, reducing both drift and the time children spent waiting for permanence decisions. The 26-week limit also emerged as a response to legal cases such as *Re B (A Child)* [2013] UKSC 33 and *Re B-S (Children)* [2013] EWCA Civ 1146, which raised the bar for adoption and reiterated the value embedded in the Children Act 1989 that remaining within the family must come first.

However, the 26-week limit had concerning ramifications for kinship care arrangements (Hingley-Jones et al, 2020). The reduced time frame often leaves insufficient time to assess or even identify potential carers within the family network. Frequently, birth parents put forward potential kinship carers only later in the proceedings, relatively close to the end. Bowyer et al (2015) note that this could have worrying implications for the quality of care provided to children in kinship arrangements. If the assessment period for kinship carers is considerably shorter than for foster carers or adopters, the approval threshold might be lowered. This raises concerns that children, particularly those who have experienced abuse or neglect, may not receive the robust, safe, and reparative care they deserve and need.

In 2019, the Family Justice Council published *Interim Guidance on Special Guardianship* to address the issue of limited time available for assessments within the 26-week timeframe. The guidance clarified that extensions are available for kinship carer assessments and provided clear criteria for these extensions.

Different categorisations of permanence and their meaning for kinship care

It is essential to now examine how these principles are currently implemented for the children in kinship care who participated in the original research to assess further whether fostering and adoption ideals can align with the experiences of children living in kinship care.

In English legislation, policy, and practice, permanence is typically divided into three clear categories (DfE, 2010):

- physical permanence: the stability of a placement;
- legal permanence: carers have parental responsibility through court orders;
- emotional permanence: grounded in theories of attachment.

In child welfare academia, permanence is often contextualised in a slightly different way. For example, Sinclair et al (2007) distinguished between:

- objective permanence: a placement lasts physically until adulthood;
- enacted permanence: all concerned feel and act as if the child is part of the family;
- subjective permanence: the child feels part of the family;
- uncontested permanence: the child does not feel conflicts of loyalty between their current family and their birth family.

Objective permanence focuses more on time and place, while subjective, enacted, and uncontested permanence refer to how children and their families feel about care. These categories also relate to pre-care experiences and how the children's future following care is envisioned (Samuels, 2009). In this chapter and the remainder of the book, permanence is categorised into physical, legal, and emotional aspects. However, other classifications, such as those by Sinclair et al (2007), are kept in mind and referred to periodically.

Physical permanence and stability

Aligning with the concerns that originally led to conceptualising permanence, promoting placement stability has remained one of the fundamental goals of child welfare (Connolly and Morris, 2011). Historically, countries such as the US and the UK have emphasised physical permanence more than emotional permanence. Physical permanence is easier to measure than other forms of permanence. Emotional permanence was assumed to follow if stability was prioritised. Frequent changes in a child's family arrangements can have detrimental effects on their wellbeing, including negative impacts on physical and brain development, as well as an increased risk of behavioural, social, and academic problems for children (Konijn et al, 2019).

Contentions exist regarding the strong emphasis on physical permanence. Schofield et al (2012) noted that permanence can exist without a continuous placement. Additionally, a child's ongoing placement does not necessarily equate to feeling secure as a family member (subjective permanence). The prioritisation of minimising a child's moves through preferred methods like reunification (for example, in France) can significantly undermine emotional permanence, compromising relationships with foster families and a child's genuine sense of stability (McSherry and Fargas Malet, 2018). The potential overemphasis on stability and fewer moves is especially relevant for kinship care, where a child frequently encounters conflicting feelings about being in various care placements within the same family (Kallinen, 2021). It is not simply a matter of reducing the number of moves within a family to automatically fulfil a child's need for stability or emotional permanence.

Even if a child does desire physical stability, the need for multiple placements often depends on available resources. The impact of inadequate resources was highlighted in the UK as early as 1999, when Sellick noted the increasing challenges local authorities faced in recruiting and retaining sufficient foster carers. It is estimated that by 2026, there will be a shortfall of around 25,000 foster carers in England, with approximately 20 per cent of fostering households leaving the system each year (Oakley, 2021). The cost-of-living crisis, the invasion of Ukraine, and global economic inequalities are likely to worsen this situation.

This lack of foster carers does not simply imply a nationwide scarcity in places such as England. Instead, the foster carer shortage is geographically based, resulting in a lack of carers who can care for specific types of children, particularly those who have disabilities or additional support needs (The Fostering Network, 2024). This shortage and displacement of appropriate carers mean that many children are not matched with their proper care needs or are moved far away from their communities. Consequently, many children find themselves needing to be moved on after a short period in a particular foster placement to one that is a better match.

Due to a shortage of local authority foster carers, local authorities often rely on out-of-house foster care provided by independent agencies. There is reticence to do this for extended periods because it is more expensive (Sellick, 1999). Such concerns greatly influence local authorities' decision-making regarding permanence and practice (Care Crisis Review, 2018). This situation has resulted in an increase in kinship care placements, which, as highlighted in the previous chapter, are viewed as more affordable and more abundant, and are believed to result in fewer moves for children unable to remain with their birth parents (McCartan et al, 2018).

Despite these caveats and nuances, physical permanence and stability remain dominant considerations and solutions for policy makers. For instance, in England, various government guidelines have sought to mitigate multiple placements for children (for example, HM Government, 2018). This includes the MacAlister (2022) review, which highlighted the problem of numerous moves and recommended addressing it with regional care co-operatives. Charities like Children England (Samuel, 2023) have robustly criticised regional care co-operatives, stating that the proposals are unlikely to resolve a dysfunctional market and that the actual marketisation of care placements for vulnerable children is the central issue, both logistically and ethically. They argue that it is immoral for large companies to profit from the needs of children, particularly those who have experienced neglect and abuse.

Legal permanence for children in kinship care in England

Another perspective on permanence centres on legal permanence. Different countries have varying legal systems designed to ensure permanence for children who cannot stay with their birth parents. National attitudes toward adoption, fostering, and residential care often influence the establishment of these legal systems, the specific legal orders that underpin them, and the likelihood of their implementation (Skivenes and Benbenishty, 2022). For example, adoption has long been the favoured choice and gold standard in the UK and the US. In contrast, countries like Denmark, Russia, and Romania use residential units for 'out-of-home' care, while most countries globally favour foster care as a more effective option for children who cannot be cared for by their families.

The following section explores the various forms of legal permanence for children in England, aligned with the circumstances of the children in the 'What matters to children living in kinship care?' study. It evaluates whether current legal orders are adequate for kinship care arrangements.

Adoption orders

The Adoption of Children Act 1926 marked a pivotal moment in adoption history, as it brought much-needed regulation to what had previously been an informal process. It established the adoption order, a lifelong order. In most instances, adoption orders, alongside special guardianship orders, effectively provide children with permanent homes (Selwyn et al, 2014). However, adoption orders are not commonly used for kinship care in England, despite overall adoption rates being higher than in other countries (Harwin, Alrouh et al, 2019). One reason for this is that they legally revoke the rights and responsibilities of the birth family, granting them to the adoptive parents. This irrevocably severs legal ties between the birth parents and the child.

Such severance is considered a significantly more punitive intervention than a temporary placement with a foster family with the hope of returning to the original family unit. There is a misconception that the UK is particularly draconian because it is the only country that enforces adoption without the agreement of the birth parents. This further inflames the controversial debates around legal severance. Nevertheless, this is not the case. Most European nations also allow adoption without parental consent, although only some have implemented this regulation to the same extent as in the UK (Fenton-Glynn, 2016).

As well as concerns about the removal of previous parental rights with adoption orders, there are concerns about the severance of contact with the previous family unit. The Adoption Act 1926 initially prohibited any contact between birth parents and their adopted child, designating the new carers as the child's new mother and father. This historical practice of physical and legal severance has contributed to the reluctance to use adoption for kinship care arrangements (Harwin, Simmonds et al, 2019). Children in kinship care face specific challenges in fully separating from their family members while remaining within the family unit. Additionally, concerns about role confusion and identity issues may arise if a child refers, for example, to their grandmother as their mother (Freeman and Stoldt, 2019).

More recently, a seemingly more palatable option to complete severance has been proposed. Open adoption has gained traction since the 1990s (Gross, 1993). Open adoption involves adoptive and birth families sharing identifying information and maintaining contact during and after the adoption process. This contact may take various forms, such as email exchanges, in-person visits, and written correspondence. Despite its rise, open adoption still lacks a legal definition in England, and birth parents do not possess an inherent right to contact following adoption. The adoption agency and courts carefully evaluate the decision to facilitate continued contact, with the child's best interests at the forefront. Also, in practice, continued contact depends on the characteristics of the adoptive parents (Gorla et al, 2023). Consequently, the enduring legacy of both real and imagined fears of complete legal and physical separation persists, making the use of adoption orders for kinship care less desirable.

Special guardianship orders

Special guardianship orders are the most commonly used orders for establishing legal permanence for children in formal kinship care arrangements in England (Neil et al, 2019). Special guardianship orders were originally intended as an adoption-lite solution to the debates over complete legal and physical severance. They were designed as an order to complement adoption in response to the failed custodianship regime highlighted in the

Children Act 1975 (Bainham, 2007). The Adoption and Children Act 2002 amended section 14(a) of the Children Act 1989 to establish special guardianship in law. The Special Guardianship Regulations 2005 further strengthened the legislation.

Initially, special guardianship orders were intended mainly for cases where a child had formed a strong bond with a foster carer but, due to their age, was unlikely to be adopted. Special guardianship orders were also regarded as an option for children who had maintained strong connections with their birth family, emphasising the importance of not completely severing those ties (Wade et al, 2014). The order allowed for the sharing of parental rights and responsibilities.

For kinship care, special guardianship orders allow birth parents to share legal parental rights and responsibilities with the kinship carer(s). However, a special guardianship order grants the carer the majority share of parental rights and responsibilities. In practice, this sharing of rights and responsibilities means that birth parents must be consulted regarding significant issues in the child's life, such as health and education. Nevertheless, kinship carers can over-rule the birth parents when making final decisions. This power weighting in favour of the new carers is reinforced by the requirement for birth parents to apply to a court to challenge a special guardianship order once it has been established.

Unfortunately, the increasing use of special guardianship orders has not laid the debates regarding severance to rest. This is especially true for those who are sceptical of, or opposed to, anything other than adoption as the ultimate alternative to birth parent care. For example, Narey (2011, np), who authored a blueprint report for *The Times*, is highly critical of special guardianship orders. He describes them as an 'unhappy compromise' that often keeps children in 'dysfunctional environments'. The narrative of a risk society prevails, and Narey subscribes to the simplistic and potentially unethical notion that intergenerational risk is pervasive and irreconcilable within households, particularly low-income households. The implication, whether intended by Narey or not, is that those living in poverty are more likely than others to be risky, unfit, and beyond redemption. Because of this, their children may need to be removed from their birth families because they are perceived as being more likely to require new family care to have better chances to thrive without the risk of harm.

Residence orders and care arrangement orders

Before special guardianship orders, residence orders were often used to secure a child's legal permanence with kinship carers. Like special guardianship orders, they allowed parents and carers to share parental responsibility for the duration of the order. However, this sharing was genuinely equal.

As a result, kinship carers' power to act autonomously was severely limited. Residence orders were replaced by child arrangement orders, introduced by the Children and Families Act 2014. In recent years, there has been a notable decrease in the use of residence orders, primarily due to the uncertainty surrounding parental responsibility.

Supervision orders

The use of supervision orders for kinship care arrangements is subject to ongoing contention. A supervision order imposes a duty on the local authority to 'advise, assist and befriend the supervised child' (Children's Act 1989, s 25a). In kinship care, it is typically used alongside other orders, most notably special guardianship orders (Harwin, Alrouh et al, 2019). There are concerns that supervision orders have served as a makeshift solution when there has been insufficient time to test the suitability and stability of kinship placements, and that the new arrangement will not meet the fostering and adoption standards. As noted earlier, due to Re-BS, the statutory requirement in the Children and Families Act 2014 to complete section 31 proceedings within 26 weeks allows little time for testing arrangements and establishing relationships, particularly when numerous potential kinship carers are identified late in the process (Harwin et al, 2019). Therefore, adding a supervision order to the special guardianship order is a risky and potentially unethical strategy to justify the speedy placement of a child when their wellbeing and relationship with carers have yet to be tested. This concern was also highlighted in the Special Guardianship (Amendment) Regulations 2016.

A serious case review in Derbyshire in 2017 also questioned the value of the supervision order (Myers, 2017). It reflected earlier findings that children subject to supervision orders frequently do not receive the protection they need and deserve. In terms of obtaining local authority support, resources, and monitoring, a supervision order may not be 'worth the paper it is written on' (Hunt et al, 1999, p 351).

Emotional permanence

Emotional permanence is now widely recognised as the ultimate goal in child welfare, surpassing the value of legal and physical permanence. It is a 'sense of permanence which is crucial' (Thoburn, 1994, p 37). Emotional permanence encompasses a child's emotional, subjective, enacted, and uncontested feelings of stability. This concept is crucial for a child's sense of belonging and mutual connectedness, allowing them to feel part of a family (Schofield et al, 2012). Legal standing and orders provide a degree of security, from which a sense of permanence can be established. Time and physical stability of placements can also play a role (Moran et al, 2020).

However, current research clearly indicates that it is vital to think beyond legal permanence and physical stability to find the right match for children's needs. Permanence relies on 'securing the right placement for the right child at the right time' (Boddy, 2017, p 37) rather than adhering to a hierarchy of preferred orders, gold standards, or placement types.

Nevertheless, achieving a sense of permanence is a complex and contested issue in child welfare and permanency literature. There have been, and continue to be, further cyclical debates centred on two broad counterpoints: substitute psychological parenting versus family preservation and support post separation.

Substitute psychological parenting

Goldstein and colleagues (Goldstein, Freud, and Solnit, 1979; 1986; Goldstein, Freud, Solnit, and Goldstein, 1986) encapsulate the concept of psychological parenting in their trilogy of books. They propose that the most effective parental relationships were typically found with biological and what they termed natural parenting. This perspective aligns with Bowlby's belief that young children should ideally remain with their birth parents, particularly their mothers, as this represents the most natural psychological relationship. While Bowlby uses ethology to underpin his attachment theory of child psychology, Freud relies on her father's psychoanalytical instinctual/drive theory, which was in dispute with the Kleinian and Winnicottian object relations perspectives. Simply put, in all these cases and regardless of the explanations, psychological parenting, especially mothering, is considered the most natural, indispensable, and in need of protection.

Goldstein, Freud, and Solnit suggest that one of the most effective ways to protect this vital parenting relationship is for families to be left alone with minimal intervention. However, they also indicate that the state must intervene if parenting is excessively neglectful or abusive. In such scenarios, the best course of action for the courts is to step in quickly. Initially, a brief period of temporary foster or residential care should be considered. Afterward, the child can return, but only if the original psychological parenting link is not further compromised.

If a child's psychological needs cannot be met through temporary separation, it is best for birth parents to relinquish their responsibilities and rights entirely and for the child to be adopted and receive new parenting. There needs to be substitute psychological parenting. This complete separation was thought to be especially important for infants who have experienced birth family failure, as it was believed they may struggle to cope psychologically with shared care arrangements. A new family placement should be pursued as early in the child's life as possible, with a total severance from the previous inadequate parenting.

In an international context, different approaches to psychological parenting have led to varying policy directives for 'out-of-home' care across various countries. For instance, some conservative countries, like France, prioritise family support and quick reunification if a child is removed from their birth parents' care, aiming to avoid substitute parenting as much as possible. In contrast, liberal countries such as Canada, the UK, and the US, tend to favour permanent alternative parenting when birth parenting fails or is likely to fail. As previously mentioned, adoption is generally viewed as the most suitable permanency option for young children who cannot remain in their parents' care. In these liberal countries, there is a lower likelihood of planned reunification.

The psychological parenting narrative in both cases tend to promote an either/or mindset – either staying with the family or completely cutting off ties. It also assumes that foster, residential, and kinship care cannot be considered long-term solutions. Such arrangements fail to meet children's long-term need for substitute psychological parenting.

In England, the Children and Families Act 2014 re-emphasised the notion of complete separation and substitute parenting if birth parents are considered incapable. The Act removed the general duty of local authorities to promote contact for looked-after children, including those placed for adoption. This change was initiated by Narey – who, at that time, was the government's advisor on adoption – to boost adoption numbers and speed up the adoption process. Although Narey did not directly condemn open adoption, in his report for *The Times*, he stated that after the adoption process is completed, adopters should be regarded as the child's 'real and only parents' (2011, np). This narrative perpetuates the hierarchy of placement types that plague international child welfare perspectives to this day (Pösö et al, 2021).

Adoption continues to be touted as the preferred way and the gold standard to secure permanence (Kirton, 2020). For example, in January 2020, the then children's minister sent a letter to all directors of children's services stating that the new government would prioritise adoption as the route to permanence. Another notable instance is the launch of the National Adoption Strategy in July 2021 (DfE, 2021). This strategy, backed by a £48 million investment, aimed to improve adoption services across England by reducing delays, enhancing recruitment, and ensuring high-quality support for adoptive families. The strategy underscored the government's commitment to providing stable, loving homes for vulnerable children, highlighting adoption as a crucial solution.

Birth family preservation

The narrative of substitute psychological parenting and complete separation has faced significant objections. Since the works of Maluccio et al (1986) and Thoburn (1994), the notion of substitute families and total severance has been challenged by scholars such as Biehal (2014), Boddy (2017), Cossar and Neil (2013), and Featherstone et al (2014). These academics agree regarding the importance of permanence for a child's identity formation and the essential role of children's kin networks in helping them understand their past, present, and future relationships. Instead, the debate starts on whether fostering is a valid long-term permanence option, the meaning of children's best interests, and the extent to which these interests are tied to birth family relationships after separation (Kirton, 2020).

Since the Rowe and Lambert (1973) study titled 'Children who wait', the notion and logistics of having only short-term foster care have become almost mythical. Long-term fostering is now accepted as a necessary and valid permanence option. For example, Biehal's (2014) study compared adoption by strangers, adoption by foster carers, and long-term foster care, including kinship care. Where long-term foster care placements were stable, the child's emotional and behavioural development, as well as their educational outcomes, were found to be similar to those of adopted children. Evidence now indicates that adoption may still be preferred, but it is not the only route to positive outcomes for children, and legislation has gradually acknowledged this shift in thinking. In 2015, the Department for Education legally defined long-term foster care, and long-term foster care regulations and guidance were issued as part of updated care planning guidance.

Regarding complete severance from birth families following separation, a BASW (British Association of Social Workers) investigation examined its ethical and human rights implications for UK adoption (Featherstone, Gupta, and Mills, 2018). Key themes that emerged included the impact of austerity on low-income families, the lack of resources, and tight timescales. Ongoing concerns have also been raised about whether the adoption process and the support offered exacerbate class inequality (Gillies et al, 2017). Adoption could, therefore, be perceived as a means to avoid and delegitimise support for poor working-class families. It might be viewed as social engineering aimed at ensuring the dominance and supposed righteousness of the bourgeois, predominantly White, middle class. The BASW inquiry depicted the severance of relationships post adoption between children and their family members as unjust and harmful to both.

The other main arguments against complete severance post adoption are:

- Psychological coping: A child can cope psychologically with multiple caregiving relationships beyond Bowlby's allowance of secondary attachment figures (Cassidy et al, 2013).
- Psychological presence: Birth parents will be psychologically present, whether or not they are physically present (Samuels, 2009).

- Heteronormative requirements: The complete severance stance takes on board particular notions of heteronormative requirements (Hicks, 2005), the norms of the nuclear family, and conservative gender roles, which do not reflect the diversity of contemporary family set-ups (Goldberg, 2019).
- Practical viability: Questions persist about the practicalities of post-separation severance in the evolving social media landscape (Greenhow et al, 2017).

Overall, a robust evidence-informed recommendation suggests that it is often more appropriate to maintain some level of involvement from birth families in a child's life. The Care Inquiry (2013) also endorsed this approach. The inquiry recognised that the care system was failing many children and that often it focused on breaking relationships rather than making them. It has also been demonstrated that initiatives like Lifelong Links provide children and young people with a stronger sense of identity and agency. Lifelong Links aims to establish a supportive lifelong network for children, including past carers, if they wish to participate (Holmes et al, 2020).

Kinship care introduces a different dimension to the debates surrounding separation and certain placements being viewed as the gold standard. Since kinship care arrangements involve separation from birth parents while keeping the child within the family constellation, even logistically, complete severance will be challenging to maintain. Therefore, while they may often be drawn into these discussions, such as in questioning the legitimacy of special guardianship orders, the debates regarding continuity and discontinuity in fostering and adoption may not readily apply to kinship care. This further illustrates the challenge of fitting the square peg of kinship care into the round hole of fostering and adoption, as mentioned in Chapter 2. For this reason, gaining a deeper understanding of what permanence and severance mean for children in their specific kinship care settings, including long-term foster kinship care arrangements, is crucial. Such insights could be obtained through appropriate research, which will be explored in the next section.

Research on permanence and wellbeing for children living in kinship care

Research on legal permanence for kinship care

Most studies focusing on permanence in kinship care fall into two broad categories: examining legal permanence and placement stability. This is because, as previously discussed, they are viewed as more measurable. Research highlighting these two variables is more likely to appease the currently dominating 'what works' ideology, allowing a sense of permanence or emotional permanence to be implicitly implied or ignored.

Furthermore, many studies are comparative. For example, most research investigates how kinship care placements influence legal permanence, such as reunification, adoption, or legal guardianship, in comparison to non-kinship placements (Koh, 2010; Ryan et al, 2010; Koh and Testa, 2011).

A summary of the research on legal permanence and kinship care suggests mixed findings. Some studies suggest that kinship care often causes delays in time in the justice system and can reduce the likelihood of legal permanence. Others suggest that it increases the probability of legal permanence. Ryan et al (2010) examined more explicitly the kinship adoptive experience compared to other non-kinship adoption types. Regarding the legal order of adoption, they concluded that '[k]inship adoptions appear more readily to produce positive outcomes and permanent placements' (Ryan et al, 2010, p 1631). These types of research suggest that adoption with kinship carers is a better option for children's wellbeing compared to adoption with strangers. In this regard, it aligns with the narrative promoting kinship care as the best choice for children while also maintaining the perception of adoption as a gold standard.

Research on stability for kinship care

When considering stability, studies typically examine how kinship care placements influence placement stability compared to non-kinship placements (see, for example, Koh, 2010; Perry et al, 2012; Font, 2015; Delfabbro, 2020; Clarke et al, 2024; Rowlson and Shabbar, 2024). These studies indicate that kinship care placements predict greater stability. Kinship placements are less likely to break down, and children are less likely to experience multiple moves (Koh, 2010). However, it has also been noted that if placements are unsatisfactory, children living in kinship care are less likely to move (Farmer and Moyers, 2008; Farmer, 2010). Therefore, the absence of breakdowns may not equate to the child's happiness or sense of permanence, and other crucial factors may be at play (Sinclair, 2005).

Other studies have found that, in terms of stability, most children do not benefit from being placed with kin (Andersen and Fallesen, 2015; Clarke et al, 2024). Overall, research generally agrees that children in kinship care are provided with as much stability, or sometimes more stability, than their non-kinship counterparts (Winokur et al, 2018).

Research on emotional permanence for children living in kinship care

The research specifically addressing emotional permanence for children living in kinship care is relatively limited. This is somewhat ironic considering that the emphasis on emotional stability is frequently highlighted as one of its key benefits. The studies conducted indicate that children in kinship care arrangements are more likely to maintain family ties, possess a stronger sense of identity, and remain in the same community and school (for example, Broad et al, 2001; Broad, 2006; Burgess et al, 2010; Dill, 2010; O'Brien, 2012; Selwyn et al, 2013). These factors contribute to a child's sense of emotional permanence by providing continuity in their social and cultural environment. Kinship care arrangements can also assist children in maintaining a family history, ethnic identity, and cultural consistency, which are often unavailable in non-kinship foster care (Hunt et al, 2010; Kiraly and Humphreys, 2016). Research comparing kinship care to fostering and adoption has also found that kinship care arrangements are more likely to promote secure attachments and relationships between the child and the carer, as they often share a history and familiarity (Ponnert, 2017). Although valuable, these studies do not focus directly on emotional permanence or discuss it much further than the psychosocial or potential outcomes for when the children become adults.

Despite the proposed benefits, some studies challenge the notion that kinship care universally fosters better emotional permanence. For example, some studies in the US indicate no significant differences in the quality of relationships between children in kinship care and those in non-kinship foster care (Strijker et al, 2003). Others even suggest that relationships in kinship foster homes may be more strained (Chipman et al, 2002; Harden et al, 2004). Additionally, statistically kinship carers are more likely to face financial difficulties, be older, have less education, possess poorer parenting skills, suffer from more health problems, and receive less formal and informal support (Selwyn et al, 2013), and these factors can contribute to heightened stress levels. Elevated stress levels in carers can make it more difficult for the children's emotional needs to be met and for emotional permanence to be felt.

The mixed and sometimes contradictory findings likely stem from the diverse contexts of the researched family settings and the inherent complexity and individual differences within family relationships. Established relationships in kinship care can also be more complex and susceptible to stress than those in stranger foster care arrangements (Sykes et al, 2002) since caregivers and children must not only navigate their immediate family relationships but also renegotiate existing broader family dynamics (Rubin et al, 2017).

Contact for children living in kinship care

The topic of contact is crucial to debates surrounding a child's sense of permanence. As previously discussed, contact remains a contentious issue, particularly concerning a child's emotional sense of permanence, and it can also influence the stability of a placement (Iyer et al, 2020). Article 9 of the

United Nations Convention on the Rights of the Child provides for the right of a child separated from one or both parents to maintain personal relationships and direct contact with both parents on a regular basis, unless doing so contradicts the child's best interests. In England, this is reiterated in section 34 of the Children Act 1989, which stipulates that when a child is taken into local authority care, they must have reasonable contact with any person who has or had parental responsibility prior to entering care.

In kinship care arrangements, children are more likely to maintain relationships with their extended family and have contact with their siblings and birth parents (Rubin et al, 2017). Research suggests that children regard their birth parents as important to them (Burgess et al, 2010; Kiraly and Humphreys, 2013b). However, parental contact for children living in kinship care can often be problematic, distressing, and even re-traumatising for the children (Kiraly and Humphreys, 2013a). This is compounded by the assumption that kinship carers can manage contact without training or support from services (Argent, 2009). Research from 2016 proposes that parental interaction should be replaced with more broadly thought about family contact (Kiraly and Humphreys, 2016). It should focus on the entire family, and the nature of contact should be considered in light of the child's specific situation instead of families receiving arbitrary rules and rulings from the courts or local authorities.

Risk and other factors that impact child wellbeing in kinship care and permanence

Protection and safeguarding for children living in kinship care

Practitioners often worry that a child's sense of permanence in kinship placements can be diminished due to existing complex family relationships, unauthorised contact, and potential collusion with birth parents (Kiraly and Humphreys, 2013a). Concerns are also often raised about whether kinship carers can protect the children from risky family members and, in some cases, violence from the birth parents (Hunt et al, 2010). However, as revealed in the previous chapter, relatively little mention of child safety and intergenerational risk is made in kinship care research, literature, or policy discussions.

A recent scoping assessment of safety in high-income nations by Hallett et al (2021) found that the risk of neglect is greater in kinship care settings than in other types of 'out-of-home' care. However, the risk of sexual and physical abuse is lower. According to the scoping study, there was minimal difference in the rates of emotional or psychological abuse. It was acknowledged that strained family relationships between carers and the birth family were more prevalent in kinship care, which raises the risk of abuse towards carers.

While these general conclusions regarding risk are valuable, other research challenges them. One study, for example, revealed no difference in physical abuse rates (Burgess and Borowsky, 2010), whereas another identified a greater risk of sexual abuse (Litrownik et al, 2003). In summary, although there is limited evidence to support practitioner concerns regarding risk, there is also minimal evidence to contradict them. However, findings do highlight that kinship carers are less likely to be monitored or report situations. As such, risks for children and their families are more likely to be hidden from professionals.

The physical, mental, and emotional wellbeing of children in kinship care

The last consideration regarding permanence specifically for children living in kinship care is the connection between positive emotional permanence and outcomes for children. Most UK research indicates that children in kinship care achieve developmental outcomes that are equal to or better than those of their non-kinship counterparts (Farmer and Moyers, 2008, p 200; Sacker et al, 2021), although they are twice as likely to experience long-term health problems or disabilities that limit their daily activities (Wijedasa, 2015). Additionally, research has found that children in kinship care exhibit fewer mental health issues (Holtan et al, 2005; Winokur et al, 2018) and behavioural issues (Conway and Hutson, 2007), and have less educational needs (Farmer and Moyers, 2008). Kinship care can also help reduce the stigma and trauma associated with separation (Messing, 2006).

Despite these findings, Farmer et al (2008) demonstrated that children still face stigma from their peers due to the family arrangements. Furthermore, those in kinship care have reduced access to services (Winokur et al, 2018). Consequently, lower usage of medical, mental, and educational support services may not necessarily indicate better wellbeing. Kinship carers may also downplay behavioural difficulties for fear of the children being removed from their care. This concern could further hinder access to and the undertaking of assessments (McCartan et al, 2018).

How could permanence and kinship care be better considered?

As demonstrated in this and the previous chapter, one of the main challenges is that, in research, legislation, and policy making, permanence for children in kinship care can quickly be positioned in the same space as permanence for children in adoption, fostering, and other child welfare placements (Skoglund and Thørnblad, 2017). This narrow view of kinship care as a child welfare technology, rather than as a distinct form of family living, presents numerous challenges. For example, while focusing on efficiency, outcomes, and effects helps outline the broader context, it is not particularly useful for making local policy recommendations, providing individual assessments, or determining if a specific family should undertake kinship care. Like much of the 'what works' literature, placement-oriented kinship care research and thinking tend to generalise and obscure the specific family context and downplay the complexity and diversity of familial relationships (Andersen and Fallesen, 2015).

This can be challenging for child welfare practitioners. It can generate spurious and simplistic assumptions, such as the belief that children in kinship care will likely meet their permanence needs by remaining within their family culture. While this may hold true for some children, as powerfully described later by the children in this book, it is not true for all. Consequently, the initially proposed values for child welfare, such as promoting a child's safety and sense of permanence, can be lost. Attempting to include kinship care in standard child welfare services in research, legislation, and policy can overlook the everyday intricacies of how families function. Instead of focusing on the how, it can concentrate on the characteristics of what families are and what outcomes they can provide.

A study by Ferraro et al (2022) emphasised this confusion surrounding causality. They found that once research considers the characteristics of children and caregivers, the effects of kinship care on behavioural and emotional wellbeing are not significantly different from the effects of non-kinship foster care, although the effects slightly favour kinship. Additionally, the Nuffield Looked-after Children Grown Up Project (Sacker et al, 2021), which compared health and social functioning outcomes among kinship care, foster care, and residential care, found that children in kinship care fared better regarding behavioural and emotional outcomes. However, it clearly warns that kinship care should not just be seen as a panacea: 'These outcomes might be a consequence of the early life experiences that led children to be in care and/or could be consequential to their experience of the care system' (Sacker et al, 2021, p 7).

Another issue with the research on kinship care is that many studies do not use theories, but instead focus on empirical outcomes. When they do integrate theory, it typically aligns with dominant discourses of human development and socialisation, such as attachment. Despite the known importance of applying theory to practice and centring assessment on the views of those with lived experiences, very little data describes children's experiences, and broader sociological, political, and historical contexts are often dismissed as irrelevant. This leads to research, assessments, and support that are both partial and biased. Permanence, kinship care, and the wellbeing of children must always be situated within their social-political-historical context, as has been done in this chapter and Chapter 2 on kinship care support.

Social-political-historical considerations are particularly vital when it is often recounted that stability, permanence, and wellbeing are 'better, or at least as good' as for children in kinship care compared to those in stranger foster care (Winokur et al, 2018). This can be misconstrued to imply that these children do not have the same level of need (Rubin et al, 2017), which can also lead to inconsistent service provisions not only between local authorities but also often among practitioners (Farmer and Moyers, 2008; Selwyn et al, 2013; Brown et al, 2019; Kinship Care Parliamentary Taskforce, 2020; Schoenwold et al, 2022). Additional factors such as the higher likelihood of poverty, isolation, carer stress, and ill health, along with complex family relationships, indicate that these kinship children and their families are likely to require more support than those in foster placements, not less (Selwyn et al, 2013). Without appropriate support, it becomes more challenging for the carers to meet the needs of the children. This will impact the child's duration in the placement and their sense of permanence and wellbeing. Therefore, it is sadly ironic that 'financial assistance and other support and services provided by child welfare agencies are skewed against kinship carers' (Owusu-Bempah, 2010, p 92).

Conclusion

Physical, legal, and emotional permanence significantly impacts a child's wellbeing. The importance of permanence is well documented in research and literature, but its effects vary depending on the child's and family's circumstances, which evolve over time. The debate between maintaining connections to past relationships and opting for complete severance will persist, influenced, no doubt, by scandals and political rhetoric. It is crucial to approach these permanence discussions cautiously, as political power has often swayed historical debates, legislation, and policies rather than relying on consistent research findings. They also typically do not readily apply to kinship care.

Practitioners and policy makers should embrace ambiguity rather than seek certainty when thinking about permanence and permanence for children living in kinship care. While outcomes like placement and legal stability are more straightforward to monitor and theoretically simpler to achieve than emotional permanence, they do not necessarily reflect ongoing wellbeing, especially in the complex context of kinship care. For instance, maintaining contact with past carers benefits many children, but for some, it can cause unnecessary harm. A one-size-fits-all approach, dictated by fixed legal orders, fails to capture the dynamic and sometimes turbulent nature of family relationships, particularly in families dealing with trauma and conflicting feelings about each other's risks.

Research on kinship care is relatively sparse compared to other child welfare issues, often offering only general insights into its benefits. The mantra that kinship care placements are 'as good as or better than' other options has gained widespread acceptance among policy makers, lobbyists, and researchers. However, promoting kinship care as yielding better permanency and wellbeing outcomes for children, despite being underfunded and under-supported, raises questions about the allocation of resources. Logically, funding, resources, and time should focus on children with poorer outcomes, such as those in foster care, which leaves children living in kinship care and their needs overlooked.

The recommendations for policy, practice, and research align with those from Chapter 2. Rather than viewing kinship care solely as a process or an alternative to state care, it is crucial to explore and acknowledge the nature of familial relationships and the fluctuating sense of permanence for children within kinship care. Research should not only consider stability, legal orders, or generalised wellbeing outcomes but also examine how these children are cared for and how they experience belonging and security within the current political climate. Children's perspectives and experiences must be better understood in their social-political-historical context. Chapter 4 explores an approach to achieving this through child participation.

4

Valuing child participation

> They should listen to children as well because they might have things that they would like to say, and maybe they have things that they'd like adults to hear. And it's not all of the time that adults are properly listening to them.
>
> Kimberley, child research participant

Previous chapters have illustrated the ambivalence surrounding kinship care. It is challenging to fully understand where kinship care lies between a private family matter and a public concern, which depends on values and social-political-historical contexts. It is also difficult, and possibly unhelpful, to compare kinship care to fostering and adoption or to situate children's experiences and outcomes within traditional debates regarding permanence. One option that can aid in better understanding the meaning of permanence is, as Kimberley suggests, to 'listen to children as well'.

In research, this listening can be achieved through a qualitative participatory design. Rather than quantitative methods that examine the 'when', 'where', and 'how many', a qualitative approach is more concerned with the 'why', 'how', and 'in what way'. Most qualitative research involves asking individuals and families about their experiences of things that happen in their lives (Shaw and Holland, 2014). This type of participatory research can provide insights into what it feels like to be another person and to understand the world as they experience it. Indeed, qualitative participatory approaches can effectively give voice to those, such as children, who are often silenced and marginalised (Gilgun, 2015). When placed alongside more positivist quantitative research, it can assist policy makers and practitioners in addressing the specific needs of children and their families (Casas, 2011).

Like kinship care and permanence, participation is not without nuance. Co-production, participation, and the concept of the participatory child are subject to increasing scrutiny (Spyrou et al, 2018). It is multifaceted and can be described as 'messy, fraught, and ambiguous' (Gallagher, 2008, p 404). This chapter highlights the messiness and ambiguities surrounding participation and the obstacles that may hinder participatory research. It responds to calls to better explore child participation's complexities and contradictions (Kosher and Ben-Arieh, 2020). It is not good enough for me to doggedly insist on more child participation in the conclusion of every chapter, and then apply it without considering the intricacies.

The chapter is divided into four sections. First, it explores participatory research, participation, and the fear of getting it wrong. Then, the chapter identifies the legal, practical, and conceptual framing of child participation. It is crucial to examine how both participation and concepts of childhood are understood. Following an analysis of the presence or absence of the child's voice in kinship care research, this chapter proposes a new approach to participation, one that is dialogical and recognises the following:

- Participation is steeped in power relations and an acknowledgement of agency. It is, therefore, also inherently a political endeavour.
- Like kinship care and permanence, participation is often submerged and restricted by monological thinking. Monological thinking suggests that childhood, identity, and participation can only be explained and done in one way or another.
- Participation often focuses on voice, listening, and consultation rather than broader considerations such as agency, place, space, and time.

What is participatory research and participation?

Participatory research and listening to experts by experience suggest that purely top-down research, planning, and policies are both ineffective and inappropriate. Instead, participatory research advocates that local perspectives, interests, and priorities should inform any initiatives by involving the collaboration of those affected by them (Humphries, 2008). Participatory research is also generally viewed as ethically and ideologically sound (Shaw and Holland, 2014).

In some ways, all qualitative research and everyday child welfare practices are participatory. Whether individuals are there to provide data and views or are more actively involved in the design and implementation of research and support, they still participate. To more or lesser degrees, there is always an amount of what is now frequently termed co-production. However, the difference between conventional research strategies and participatory research is that participatory research tries to identify and balance out the power differentials involved from its conception through to its application (Percy-Smith and Thomas, 2009).

The basic principles for participatory research are summarised as follows (Humphries, 2008):

- Participatory research strives to equalise power between researchers and participants. It adopts a bottom-up research approach that focuses on the local historical, cultural, political, and socioeconomic factors as defined

by those who live in the situation. Therefore, those most affected by situations can become empowered, active agents capable of determining the research questions, methods, analysis, and outcomes.
- The knowledge base for research and policies, such as those concerning child welfare, arises from ongoing genuine dialogue between theory and practice, as well as between researchers and the researched.
- Participatory research uses methods that are flexible, creative, and tailored to the needs and wishes of the participants.
- The emphasis is on process as well as outcomes.
- The researcher's or practitioner's role is of facilitator rather than director.

With deeper interrogation, these basic principles very quickly become problematic. They are about how participation should be done, almost like the elements of a recipe, and they unravel with more in-depth explorations of power and knowledge production. For example, for participation with children, adults still hold power about what constitutes ongoing genuine dialogue and when it would be appropriate to initiate it. These adults' opinions are subject to their own beliefs and values, pressures from organisations' policies, and the broader societal view of children. Suppose children are predominantly perceived as vulnerable and innocent. In that case, it might never seem the right time to initiate a genuine dialogue with them for fear of re-traumatising them.

Even if children are perceived as capable and resilient overall, this may overlook a paradox concerning vulnerability, empowerment, and resistance. The children's status as vulnerable enables them to have a voice in research and be lauded by policy makers and practitioners as brave, with the research viewed as valid even though it may produce tokenistic representations of the marginalised, seldom-heard group of children. Children's vulnerability and minority status create opportunities for others who hold power to save them and selectively grant some empowerment (Butler et al, 2016). This raises questions about whether uneven power differentials have truly changed that much.

Children's involvement in research, policy, and practice is nestled within broader perspectives regarding children, childhood, empowerment, philosophy, politics, ethics, and social science research methods (Heinsch et al, 2020). Children's participation becomes even more complicated when we apply it more broadly to the power relations inherent in child welfare work, child protection, 'out-of-home' care, and kinship care. Such complications can mean participation is rarely implemented due to trepidation that it must be done right (Godden, 2017). If not, there is a risk of further marginalising and exploiting oppressed groups such as children.

Such apprehensions, combined with the need for what is seen as the more robust 'what works' evidence-based practice, can prevent social work researchers and practitioners from even attempting participatory practice, and this is reflected in the research. Children who have received social work intervention still report that they do not feel heard, do not influence decision-making, and are often uninformed about what is happening (Bijleveld et al, 2020). This occurs despite the belief of many involved in child welfare that participation can be beneficial for all (Kosher and Ben-Arieh, 2020).

Why should child welfare workers and researchers listen to children?

Despite the complexities of participation, it must be strived for, especially with children. Child welfare practitioners, researchers, and policy makers must listen to children for legal, practical, and conceptual reasons (McCafferty, 2017).

Legal

In recent decades, listening to children has gained increasing support in child welfare research, policy, and practice (van Bijleveld et al, 2021). Incorporating children's views aligns with the values and practices embedded within children's rights discourses. For example, Article 12 of the United Nations Convention on the Rights of the Child grants children the right not only to express their views but also to have those views taken seriously regarding 'all matters affecting' them (United Nations General Assembly, 1989, np). Ensuring their perspectives are heard is particularly crucial for children who have been subject to abuse and neglect within their families (Moran-Ellis, 2010).

In England, the Children Act 1989 mandates that practitioners must consider children's wishes and feelings. It is said that this is their right, enhances democracy, and is essential for their protection (Sinclair, 2004). Children's involvement as a means of protecting them is also found in many influential government documents, such as England's influential *Working Together* report (DfE, 2018). Also, in her review of the child protection system, Eileen Munro (2011) stresses the importance of listening to children. However, she acknowledges that this is not always straightforward and that workers do not consistently listen to the child's voice (see also Winter, 2010). This concern was reiterated in the MacAlister (2022) review.

Gathering and taking seriously children's views in all matters affecting them does not just include day-to-day child welfare practices and service delivery. The Convention also clearly states that children's participation rights must be integrated and applied in policy making. It also includes children's right to have their views heard in research (Skauge et al, 2021).

Overall, in the UK, such legislation and guidance propose that social work practitioners, local authorities, and policy makers should focus on giving a voice to children and young people receiving services (Lansdown, 2010). This is particularly the case for those in foster care (Nybell, 2013). Initiatives that have attempted to do this include the Children's Commissioner for England's annual survey of care leavers and those in care. Also the Children's Commissioner for England conducted one of the most extensive surveys of children's views, published in 2021. The Big Ask survey ran for six weeks and, as the Commissioner keenly emphasised, attracted a 'record-breaking' more than half a million child participants, including some in local authority care (Children's Commissioner, 2021, p 52).

A challenge with the Big Ask survey is the potential for bias in determining who might and would be able to complete the questionnaire, particularly as it was undertaken in the immediate aftermath of the COVID-19 epidemic. There are also concerns around the disparities in access caused by digital poverty (Holmes and Burgess, 2022). Also, there are doubts about whether it was designed alongside children. Lastly, many recommendations were similar to the then-unpublished Independent Review of Children's Social Care (MacAlister, 2022). For example, one recommendation was to establish more 'Family Hubs'. It is questionable whether the children themselves explicitly referred to family hubs as a means to provide better access points for families to receive help. It seems unlikely that they would have come across or used that phrase.

Local authorities also run children in care councils so that they can hear the views of children who receive services. However, these small groups usually have minimal impact on decision-making (Wright et al, 2006). Some local authorities have also devised their own surveys for children receiving services. These are not publicly available, but generally, they are 'poorly devised, very long and with potentially upsetting questions that are conceptually confused' (Selwyn et al, 2017, p 366).

All the examples discussed show that, while ensuring child participation is often considered necessary and good practice in legislation and national policy making, logistical and ethical challenges frequently arise when attempting to implement it.

Practical

Despite legislative and rights-based mandates, child welfare practitioners, policy makers, and researchers often fail to facilitate meaningful child participation. This is unfortunate because, in practical terms, child participation holds both instrumental value in terms of service outcomes and intrinsic value rooted in concern for wellbeing (Skauge et al, 2021).

Instrumentally, child participation in child welfare research, policy, and practice will likely make support more effective, sustainable, tailored, and democratic. Involving children also has the potential to enhance decision-making processes and outcomes by ensuring decisions are more inclusive and responsive to their expressed needs (V. Barnes, 2012). Listening to children means that service involvement is more likely to align closely with the realities of their lived experiences and what they say matters to them (van Bijleveld et al, 2021). Accountability and transparency can also be improved through child participation, with children given the right to hold decision makers to account.

Participation is also argued to have intrinsic value, which can benefit the participating child's wellbeing (Kosher and Ben-Arieh, 2020). Literature and research suggest that listening to children can enhance their self-esteem and social skills (Vis et al, 2011), promote their wellbeing (Kosher and Ben-Arieh, 2020), and encourage autonomy and agency (Križ and Skivenes, 2017). This, in turn, can motivate the child and shift them from feeling they are just a problem with deficits (van Bijleveld et al, 2021). It has even been found that participation can help children and young people protect themselves from further abuse (Vis et al, 2011). Finally, it is proposed that participation can prepare children for adulthood and active citizenship (Wyness, 2018). An example of this is learning tolerance and respect for others (Ochs and Izquierdo, 2009).

Conceptual

Concepts of participation: ethical or exploitative?

The way participation is conceptualised and valued is one of the most important indicators of how, or if, it will be applied. A challenge with participation is that, like kinship care and permanence, the more we explore it, the more it becomes riddled with apparent contradictions and the need for nuance. Participation is not linear and does not easily fit into strict levels or categories. For example, some, such as Cornwall and Jewkes (1995), have attempted to value participation by measuring its success as either shallow or deep. Hart (1997) also famously describes a ladder of participation, where the most basic level may be manipulative. Hart's paradigm is commonly used yet frequently challenged for its linear approach to graduating from tokenism to full child co-production. Other concerns regarding the ladder include the subjective nature of its application in group settings, which can obstruct the ability to draw general conclusions, and the vagueness of vital details regarding the most employed participation methods (Hagen, 2021).

Simplifying or framing participation in hierarchical and linear terms has other drawbacks. Defining participation criteria can oversimplify and, in my experience, result in haughty comparisons, competitiveness, and zealotry among researchers, practitioners, and policy makers, emphasising that only their specific forms of participation can be deemed valid. This may hinder participation even before it begins. Even if participation does happen, constant critique can dissuade practitioners and researchers from attempting participation again. The hierarchical mindset and subtle finger-wagging can create fear that serious misconduct can be alleged – that the specific child participation undertaken by others is superficial and potentially exploitative (Shaw and Holland, 2014).

These anxieties regarding exploitation remain a central fear for child participation. Spyrou (2011) argues that it should not be assumed that participation overcomes the power imbalances between children and adults or results in more authentic research. Warnings throughout the literature indicate that participatory research may only be used in a tokenistic manner (Holland et al, 2010). Additionally, there is very little evaluation or monitoring to measure the effectiveness of participatory research with children, and even less involving children's views on participation (Kennan et al, 2018). As a result, participation may unwittingly perpetuate the exclusions and injustices it seeks to overcome.

Such grave concerns about exploitation and the abuse of power must not be diminished. Participation is fundamentally political, especially when considering its original primary purpose – the redistribution of power and knowledge production (Arnstein, 1969). This stands in contrast to claims that participatory research ought to be seen as a value-free process and an 'anti-politics machine' (Ferguson, 1994). Approaching participation in an apolitical manner can lead to a loss of critical and reflexive thinking and promote tick-box, yes/no methods (Tisdall, 2017). Apolitical tick-box participation is not only poor practice but also raises ethical and moral concerns. Participants can easily be reduced to a type of basic resource and a unit to be measured.

In contrast, overvaluing and unreflexively elevating participants as powerful redemptive agents can also be unethical. For example, experts by experience can be viewed as empowered, by those 'on high', to show and then, if encouraged, educate others about tackling their own social exclusion. Rose's (1996) theories further argue that participation often shifts responsibility for governance and decision making onto individual capabilities rather than onto society. Participation can relieve society of its duties to address the structural inequalities faced by participants, such as children. It is ethically dubious to suggest that individuals are entirely responsible for shaping their future through voice and choice. It is worse still to propose that marginalised individuals are completely responsible for ensuring the wellbeing of others by educating them or practitioners. This can reinforce social disparities, victimisation, and the burden on marginalised individuals to bear the emotional labour for educating others about their oppression. It implies that those who fail to become agents of change, particularly after they have been granted empowerment from others, only have themselves to blame (Boone et al, 2019). This rhetoric of 'individualisation', which parallels 'neoliberalization' (Brenner and Theodore, 2002, p 6), leads to a culture of 'responsibilisation' (Zinn, 2020). For this reason, Fielding (2008, p 59) speaks about participation's 'deep dishonesty'.

The deep dishonesty of participation is further amplified, considering that co-production is frequently idolised as intellectually and ideologically noble (Canosa and Graham, 2020). Being known to facilitate participation can enable researchers, institutions, practitioners, and providers to gain positive reputations. It has become highly sought after in child welfare to utilise experts by experience. Projects, including 'what matters' PhD studies and books, are more likely to receive funding if they incorporate participation and co-production methods. Practitioners are also more likely to be commended (Humphries, 2008). Citizens, particularly children, are also usually cheaper for projects and institutions than researchers and staff. Participation, therefore, can serve as a cost-effective solution to the complex challenge of social exclusion. Cynically, it may not be about meaningful participation or addressing power dynamics, but rather about being seen to do the right thing in a coincidentally cheaper way.

Concepts and theories of the child and childhood

When considering child participation, it is also essential to consider how children and childhood are theorised. Whether implied or explicit, a particular theoretical perspective of childhood underlies any research or practice involving children (Harden et al, 2000). Hodes remarks that there are often many different contrasting views: 'the diversity of ideas people have about children is as striking as the convictions with which they are held' (1992, p 258).

The diversity of how childhood and children are theorised presents a challenge for child welfare researchers and practitioners, particularly for social workers. Theory matters in social work (Shaw and Lorenz, 2016). Yet, there is not one sole distinctive theoretical or methodological base (Hicks, 2016). The absence of a single theoretical perspective stems from the two main objectives of social work, as highlighted in the International Federation of Social Workers' (2014) global definition of social work. First, social work is about helping instigate individual change. This complex professional activity often overlaps with the roles and values of other professionals, such as those in medicine and psychology. The second objective is to promote social integration, social justice, and solidarity (Lorenz, 2016). Accomplishing these two tasks requires using several theories, some of which may be contradictory.

Despite this tension, when considering children, social work primarily uses conventional models, assessments, and interventions, particularly those based on child development and socialisation (Graham, 2011). This is due to social work often addressing its 'kind of inferiority complex' (Lorenz, 2016, p 456) in relation to other disciplines and professions by typically surrendering to a narrow view of valid evidence and explanations. These emphasise value neutrality, which only specific disciplines, such as psychology and medicine, are thought to be able to provide (Reisch and Jani, 2012). For example, direct work with children often over-relies on insights from attachment theories (Smith et al, 2017). This is especially true when examining loss and a sense of permanence for children who cannot remain with their birth parents.

Attachment theories explore the meaning of events and relationships for children and their inner lives (Thomas and O'Kane, 2000). This helps children to understand what has happened within their family during separation and assists them in building their identity formation (Fahlberg, 2008). However, robust critiques of attachment theory exist. For example:

- Cultural bias: The theory's principles are often based on Western notions of 'good parenting', which can marginalise non-Western parenting practices (Levine, 2014).
- Mythical function: Attachment theory has been critiqued for functioning as a myth in widespread use. Drawing on Barthes' (1973) concept of myth, this suggests that attachment theory can obscure other vital factors in child welfare and development (White and Gibson, 2019).
- Diagnostic mindset: The dominating use of attachment theory in child welfare can promote a diagnostic pathologising mindset that individualises issues and often centres on deficits.

Resiliency-based approaches are another example of the overuse of child development and socialisation theories in social work (Hook, 2019). Particularly during the 1990s, enhancing resilience in children became a sought-after goal of interventions. Resilience emphasises children's capacity to recover from trauma and to demonstrate competence while coping with continuous or cumulative adversity (Bottrell, 2009).

Overall, child development, socialisation theories, and trauma-informed approaches are beneficial frameworks for conceptualising childhood and children, provided they do not become unwaveringly trauma-focused, centring primarily on children's deficits (Graham, 2011). Overusing child development and socialisation theories can also create research and practice that positions children as passive objects. This, in turn, influences social and health policies, potentially limiting them to a perspective that prioritises children primarily as future citizens in terms of human capital. The objective is to shape children into valued, healthy, secure, law-abiding individuals who contribute to the economy rather than become a costly liability. This can lead to the perception of children as service consumers who must achieve predetermined outcomes. This is summed by de St Croix: 'Success for a young person is not about enjoyment, ethics or living their lives for the "here and now"; instead, they should focus almost entirely on their individual future, with every decision a calculated move towards their "outcomes"' (2012, p 4). Focusing only on the here and now aligns, instead, with neoliberalisation social policies that emphasise children as 'becomings' rather than 'beings' (Qvortrup, 1994). Again, it can promote individualisation and ignore the cultural and political aspects of life.

The new sociology of childhood

The new sociology of childhood can challenge the dominant paradigms of child development and socialisation that guide most research and policy in child welfare, particularly concerning permanence and children in 'out-of-home' care (James and Prout, 1997). In the 1990s, the new sociology of childhood began repositioning children as subjects rather than objects of research (Mason and Hood, 2011). Rather than the children in the studies being individualised, this alternative way of thinking centres on the context of children's lives. It achieves this by moving away from traditional views in child psychology and sociology that saw children as passive and lacking adult capabilities. It adopts a more interactive approach, where children do not merely internalise the social world but also engage with structures and strive to understand their culture. Therefore, they are active participants in the world and possess agency. This challenges the notion that children are 'adults in the making' and emphasises children as 'beings' rather than 'becomings' (James et al, 1998).

The new sociology of childhood also emphasises children's own voices as the most reflective of their selves, their lived experiences, and their realities (Graham, 2011). With this paradigm, children's views have become worthy of, if not an essential addition to, research. It accentuates that the best way to understand a child's situation is to ask them. However, this new paradigm has struggled and continues to struggle with the demands of policy, practice, and funding bodies for more evaluative 'what works' research. This issue is particularly evident in kinship care, which is often conceptualised as a public service in policy and research rather than an upbringing by relatives (Skoglund and Thørnblad, 2019). The private world of family, experiences, and relationships is often devalued in favour of knowledge based on its observation as a service (Reisch and Jani, 2012). Children's views in kinship care research remain a secondary, less reliable, and less valid endeavour.

In recent years, critiques of the new sociology of childhood have emerged (Ba', 2021). This is largely due to its tendency to sometimes promote children's voices and agency to the point of fetishism. The new sociology of childhood has faced accusations of replacing the portrayal of the child as vulnerable, dependent, and developmentally deficient with an image of the autonomous, competent, capable, knowing, yet constructed child. Additionally, while the new sociology of childhood gives agency more status in research, it often constructs it as something singular, unwavering, inherently positive, and awaiting discovery. The new sociology of childhood can still assume agency is something a child either has or doesn't have.

To counter this, academics such as Spyrou (2019) and Capella and Boddy (2021) propose reconceptualising voice and participation as relational. This theorises voice, choice, and participation as something we all possess, yet our ability to be put into action depends on circumstances. Agency is, therefore, an assemblage of sorts and the dynamic relationship that happens in between objects and people (Oswell, 2012). Such approaches to conceptualising agency avoid the pitfall of considering it as an 'essential identity, position or characteristic' (Tisdall, 2016, p 365). It moves away from just assuming a neoliberalised construct of human capital, which is something to be unreflexively acquired or not (Ba', 2021).

Another dispute with the new sociology of childhood is that human and non-human materialities are often disregarded in favour of discourse so that the 'new' paradigm can separate itself from the previous biological, psychological, and developmental discourses (Kraftl and Horton, 2018). In simple terms, nature has been substituted with culture, the material with the discursive, and structure with agency (Prout, 2011). The next chapter, which discusses ontology and epistemology, further explores this type of hard social construction.

The last challenge relevant to child welfare research is that in the new sociology of childhood, children are often seen as just 'beings'. Many authors now understand children and adults as both 'beings' and 'becomings'. This perspective not only dismantles adult/child dualisms but also encourages child welfare workers to address children's present and future lives (Uprichard, 2008).

The views of children in kinship care research

This section analyses how these complexities surrounding child participation play out when researching and listening to children living in kinship care. At the time of writing, children's voices have been included in fewer than 30 published international social work studies that focus specifically on kinship care. This number is not substantial given the global prevalence of kinship care arrangements.

These studies differ in their scope, methodologies, and where they took place. For example, one was conducted in Ghana (Kuyini et al, 2009), while six originated from Spain. Only two of these – the studies by Montserrat (2007) and Montserrat and Casas (2006) – were translated into English.

Most studies seeking children's views come from the US (for example, Brown et al, 2002; Messing, 2006; Dolbin-MacNab and Keiley, 2009; Kelch-Oliver, 2011; Tompkins and Vander Linden, 2020), a few are from Norway (for example, Holtan et al, 2005; Holtan, 2008; Skoglund et al, 2022), some are from Sweden (for example, Hedin, 2014; 2012), and one is from Finland (Kallinen, 2021). Additionally, some kinship care child participation studies come from Australia (for example, Hislop et al, 2004; Downie et al, 2010; Kiraly and Humphreys, 2013; Kiraly and Kertesz, 2021), while the remainder are from the UK (for example, Hunt et al, 2008; Farmer et al, 2013; Selwyn et al, 2013; Wellard et al, 2017; Selwyn and Briheim-Crookall, 2023). Overall, the broad findings from these studies indicate that many children were happy in their kinship care arrangements, although many exhibited significant emotional and behavioural difficulties as a consequence of adverse experiences and trauma.

Kinship care research solely examining the views of children

The studies mentioned involve the perspectives of children alongside those of adults, such as carers, professionals, and birth parents. There are relatively few kinship care studies that include the child's voice, and even fewer that listen solely to the views of children (for example, Broad et al, 2001; Aldgate and McIntosh, 2006; Hunt et al, 2008; Aldgate, 2009). The concern is that children's voices on their own are deemed inadequate. Adults' views are often considered more reliable and knowledgeable than those of children (Tay-Lim and Lim, 2013). Therefore, when research combines the two perspectives, adults' views will likely take precedence, and policies and practices may not fully capture children's lived experiences. This highlights the need for more kinship care research that is not diluted or persuaded by adult voices (Pitcher, 2013).

While research on kinship care that exclusively incorporates children's views is guided by diverse objectives, methodologies, and contexts, certain common themes emerge. These are summarised as follows:

- Overwhelmingly, most children are happy with their care arrangements, their lives in general, and their kinship carers. They feel love, care, kindness, and a sense of belonging (Altshuler, 1999; Broad et al, 2001; Hislop et al, 2004; Montserrat and Casas, 2006; Montserrat, 2007; Burgess et al, 2010; Downie et al, 2010; Selwyn and Briheim-Crookall, 2023; Shuttleworth, 2023b).
- Children feel that their caring arrangement are stable, but not necessarily permanent (Altshuler, 1999; Broad et al, 2001; Aldgate and McIntosh, 2006; Messing, 2006; Montserrat Boada, 2007; Hunt et al, 2008; Clements and Birch, 2023). This may be due to the children worrying about the

health concerns of their usually older carers (Hislop et al, 2004; Messing, 2006; Wellard et al, 2017; Selwyn and Briheim-Crookall, 2023).
- Many feel a sense of unresolved loss (Hislop et al, 2004; Aldgate and McIntosh, 2006; Downie et al, 2010).
- Many children believe that kinship carers have old-fashioned parenting styles and are stricter than other parents, and this stifles their independence (Broad et al, 2001; Hislop et al, 2004; Aldgate and McIntosh, 2006; Broad, 2006; Kuyini et al, 2009; Downie et al, 2010).
- Many children emphasise issues related to family relationships and contact with their birth parents, siblings, and extended family. They frequently feel not listened to about these matters (Hislop et al, 2004; Holtan, 2008; Burgess et al, 2010; Downie et al, 2010; Kiraly and Humphreys, 2013b; Wellard et al, 2017).
- Many studies highlight that the children feel stigma about their family life and often tell nobody, or almost nobody, about it (Hislop et al, 2004; Aldgate and McIntosh, 2006; Messing, 2006; Montserrat, 2007; Aldgate, 2009; Burgess et al, 2010; Downie et al, 2010; Selwyn and Briheim-Crookall, 2023).
- Many children discuss financial and environmental stress affecting their families, including overcrowding (Broad et al, 2001; Brown et al, 2002; Hislop et al, 2004; Downie et al, 2010; Selwyn and Briheim-Crookall, 2023).

Notably, in Aldgate and McIntosh's (2006) study, most children were in contact with a wide range of relatives, many of whom remained in contact with their siblings who did not live with them. The children generally made no distinction between siblings, half-siblings, and step-siblings, all of whom were often equally important to them.

There have also been a few valuable retrospective studies capturing the views of those who were in kinship care but are now adults (for example, Dolbin-MacNab and Keiley, 2009; del Valle et al, 2011; Wellard et al, 2017; Cudjoe et al, 2019). The findings suggest a lack of resources after the caring arrangement officially finishes. Poverty, unemployment, and cultural and religious beliefs also cause difficulties for both carers and the children. The research also shows that kinship care can provide both benefits and difficulties with contact with siblings and birth parents. The participants also appreciate that kinship care can provide continuity of family stability and closeness. While these studies reinforce findings from other child perspective research, they concentrate on the impact of kinship care on where the participants are as adults. As they are retrospective and dependent on adults' memories and contexts at the time of the research, this may lead to views that are more adult-centric and less able to capture how the participants navigated their lives when they were children (Bell and Bell, 2018).

All the findings mentioned provide a good scope of kinship care's benefits and challenges; however, they often give limited attention to the how regarding permanence. For example, many children felt that their caring arrangements were stable but not permanent. This does not fully explain the child's feeling of permanence. It also does not show how the children managed their sense of permanence and navigated the space between stability and a sense of permanence. The children were also happy, but again, this does not, aside from hypotheses and inferences, provide insight into the relationship between happiness and a sense of permanence or stability. Different studies cite various reasons, depending on their research paradigms and a priori views. This means that researchers often only combine correlations with causes, turning possibilities into probabilities and then into facts and certainties (Alderson, 2013).

Many of the studies mentioned indicate that children often do not feel heard and require more opportunities to express themselves. This underscores the value of child participation research. The fact that children feel unheard is concerning, but research must go further than just stating this claim. When researching and listening to children, it is essential to be mindful of the previously discussed debates around childhood, rights, and agency. This is especially true for social work research and practice, where it is crucial to understand a child's sense of permanence and identity and ensure that children are not just seen as passive objects. It is not enough for studies to end on an '*upbeat note*', stating children need to be given voice in the future (Lesko and Talburt, 2012, p 280, emphasis added). Children also need to be seen as active in constructing their lives in the present. They are making do and getting by (Crosby et al, 2012). As such, researchers and practitioners should also be concentrating on what the children are currently doing to meet their own needs and how they are currently navigating permanency within their family lives. Researchers should be listening to how the children are utilising their agency and how they are helping to construct their own lives. Child welfare practitioners should view how children are currently doing kinship care and encompassing permanence.

Children in kinship care arrangements views in broader studies of looked-after children

Another way the views of children living in kinship care have been sought is through more extensive general studies on children in local authority care, including comparisons of different placement types. Several literature reviews have compared children's perspectives regarding their care experiences (for example, Dickson et al, 2010; Wood and Selwyn, 2017; Selwyn et al, 2018). Similar to the previously mentioned studies, only broad conclusions can be drawn about these children, particularly those in kinship care. The children, again, expressed that they were generally happy in the care arrangements, emphasising the significance of relationships with their family and the wider community. However, many would have preferred to have remained in the care of their birth parents if possible. The children also wished to be more involved in decision making. When researching permanence in these broader studies, the children expressed a need for stability in their placements and a sense of belonging. They also desired an understanding of their life stories. The UK survey for *Our Lives, Our Care* (Selwyn et al, 2018), which examined the subjective wellbeing of 2,263 looked-after children (18 per cent were in kinship care), also highlighted the importance of pets.

One of the most relevant studies for this book, by Biehal (2014), includes children in kinship care within broader placement comparison research. She gathered the views of children in kinship care alongside those in foster care. The study also directly examined a child's sense of permanence. It employed a range of theoretical perspectives, including attachment, developmental, socialisation, and sociological understandings of family. The children in the study revealed the many ways they perceived belonging. The interplay of past and present experiences, mental representations, and relationships shaped these perceptions. The study illustrates how the children in statutory placements actively enacted their sense of permanence.

Throughout this and the previous chapters, it has been reiterated that there are significant challenges in incorporating kinship care into broad placement studies and comparing it to other 'out-of-home' care arrangements. To summarise, these challenges are:

- It's like fitting a square peg into a round hole (Dill, 2010). Children in kinship care arrangements have a different demographic profile compared to those in other 'out-of-home' arrangements. Even the term 'out-of-home' care is not an accurate description for many of these children. They also do not fit the ideals of permanence associated with foster care and adoption and have different experiences and relationships with their families, child welfare practitioners, and the state (Connolly et al, 2016).
- Favourable starting points lead to favourable outcomes (Koh and Testa, 2008). It is difficult to say with certainty that kinship care alone is the reason for generally more favourable outcomes (Dorval et al, 2020). Alongside attempts to smooth over and aggregate the vast, complex, interweaving differences between placement types, selection bias is inherent in placement studies. Placement types will be selected based on availability and accessibility for the research and in practice. If a child or a family is perceived as more challenging, if housing is unsuitable, if kinship care is more culturally aligned with certain traditions, or even if

there is a limited number of foster carers, this will impact where a child is placed and will skew the data. Unequal selection and representation of the type of care pose challenges for existing research (Xu and Bright, 2018).
- Who decides what outcomes matter? The premise of the debate over whether kinship care is better or worse than other placement options typically operates on the evidence-based framework of 'what works for kinship care as a service'. This is in the hope that child welfare policy can tailor more effective practice. This often-rigid framework frequently prioritises what adults, carers, child welfare workers, and sitting governments believe matters to children. Again, it tends to focus on the 'what' rather than the 'how', rarely acknowledging a child's agency. As a result, this surface approach often overlooks the underlying political dimensions of child participation and kinship care.

Monological thinking

The critical point of this chapter is that child participation often fails to be genuinely participative and collectively empowering due to monological thinking. This concept, along with the challenges it presents, is reiterated throughout this book in various forms. For instance, monological thought may view kinship care as either a placement service or a natural, cultural, family arrangement. Additionally, monological thinking may suggest that permanence can only be achieved through substitute parenting or by maintaining lifelong connections with past carers and care experiences.

For child participation, monological thinking tends to recycle old arguments with little resolve (Graham and Fitzgerald, 2010). From these monological viewpoints, issues are perceived in binary either/or terms. Examples of monological thinking regarding child participation arise from treating children as identical to adults or as distinctly different from them (Punch, 2002). Depending on whether children are seen as similar or different from adults, they can be considered either at risk, vulnerable, and lacking agency or as completely agentic and potentially risky (Lefevre et al, 2019). Children can also be viewed as either negatively affected by exclusion or negatively affected by inclusion, and it is often assumed that children either want to participate and share their voice in research or they simply do not (Bijleveld et al, 2020). Also, child participation research might be seen as either truly transformative or merely tokenistic (Holland et al, 2010).

Further investigation reveals that monological thinking influences child participation in four main ways: children can be treated the same as adults; children can be treated differently to adults; children can be treated only as vulnerable; and often oversimplified concepts of voice, consultation, and listening are applied. These points are now elaborated on further.

Being treated the same

One challenge of monological thinking is the tendency to treat children as though they are adults. Methodologies that reflect the new sociology of children frequently over-valorise children. As previously discussed, children can be fetishised for being active, agentic, competent, knowledgeable, and intrinsically aware (Abebe, 2019).

Academics such as Hammersley (2017) argue that children should never be considered as being as competent as adults in research. He is cautious about them even being regarded as co-producers. Hammersley suggests that treating children as equals in research fails to acknowledge that social research is a specialised activity that only a small percentage of adults, and even fewer children, can conduct. Therefore, he advises that genuine co-production is neither possible nor advisable. Rather than the children, the researcher must be accountable for methodologically robust, ethical, and meaningful research.

Treating children the same as adults can also minimise their individual differences and fail to acknowledge existing inequalities (Tisdall, 2012). The biases and prejudices inherent in society may not be considered (Fitzgerald et al, 2009). For example, a child typically needs a specific status to contribute to conversations about their lives. An extroverted, able-bodied, White, male, middle-class, educated child from the Global North is more likely to be able to access participation and be more capable of speaking up. Viewing children as the same overlooks the need for equitable social systems and the significant self-determination and agency required for children to advocate for change. It implies the existence of a fair and equal society, a notion heavily challenged by social work, sociology, history, and indeed the present.

Being treated as different

On the other hand, children can be treated as different from adults. This approach is the most common in child welfare work (Bijleveld et al, 2020) and the social sciences (Horgan et al, 2017). It aims to consider varying competencies, skills, and abilities. However, being treated as different can also lead to children being treated as immature. As Qvortrup (1994) suggests, they are treated as 'becomings' and not yet adults, rather than as 'beings'. This means their ability level is often evaluated based on age and proximity to adulthood. For example, participation and citizenship are often not recognised for children under 13 years old (Horgan, 2017). Younger children, who have little chance to influence decisions in their daily lives, are frequently overlooked (Lansdown, 2010). Additionally, there is a belief that young children may engage in participation with unrealistic expectations because they are too young to know, oversee, or understand their situations

(Bijleveld et al, 2020). Consequently, children, especially younger ones, can be viewed not only as different from adults but also as inferior.

Being treated as vulnerable

Another example of monological thinking is how children are often viewed as especially vulnerable compared to adults (Meehan, 2016). Focusing only on vulnerability and trauma leads to anxiety and caution about involving children in research. As explored in later chapters, other people's views of children solely as vulnerable victims have posed a consistent challenge throughout this study. This aligns with the emphasis in social work on protectionism rather than on empowering children (Kennan et al, 2018). There exists a fear that participatory involvement may re-traumatise children who have been subject to challenging and even abusive experiences.

Such wariness is evident in the lack of participatory social work practice with children (Bijleveld et al, 2020). Vis et al (2011) found that case managers fear burdening children and want to protect them from discussing painful experiences. Additionally, research indicates that social workers are less likely to involve children and let them participate where their case is classified as one of abuse, neglect, or domestic violence (Križ and Skivenes, 2017). There is also a perception that, due to their vulnerable status, working with such children and including them as research participants is a laborious ethical nightmare (Maconochie, 2013). Regardless of the reasons, wholly paternalistic and deficit views of children's capacities, common in social work and child welfare approaches, leave little room for children's agency, competence, potential, or a more inclusive understanding of the diversity inherent in their family lives (Graham, 2011).

A simplistic focus on voice, consultation, and listening

Monological thinking regarding child participation often reduces nuanced ideologies and behaviours to simplistic words and definitions. For example, in England since the Children Act 1989, legislation, White Papers, and local and national policies have highlighted the obligation to guarantee children's participation. However, in these documents and regulations, children's engagement is often limited to being described simply as 'voice', 'consultation', or 'listening' to children (Canosa and Graham, 2020).

Another example is the United Nations Convention on the Rights of the Child, which also prioritises determining children's views. Focusing on views can imply an over-focus on voice, which may often only be considered legitimate when expressed verbally or in writing. However, alternative modes of communication, particularly for children with disabilities, must be acknowledged (Tisdall, 2012). Also, note that the term 'voice' is singular.

However, people rarely provide standardised, consistent information when communicating with others. When speaking, individuals inevitably demonstrate uncertainty, hesitation, and indecision. This is particularly true when individuals such as children disclose deeply felt concerns related to physical self-image, death, pets, and attachments to missed parents. They attempt to navigate contradictory thoughts by summarising and expressing their inner thoughts, mirroring their internal monologue. Relaying views involves condensing, truncating, omitting details, using symbols, using unresolved truths, and so on.

People also have many voices and 'inner conversations' before deciding which ones to act on, if they are permitted to act. This is like everyday reflexivity (Archer, 2012). Therefore, the child's voice does not exist in isolation. Listening to voices and silences should primarily be regarded as a relational act within the research encounter (Meloni et al, 2015). This book and the research it is based on do not speak to a child's isolated voice, and much less to their collective voice. Instead, it presents patterns of responses over time between the children and the world around them, including with the researcher. The focus is on their often-conflicting voices and how they navigate competing demands, views, and needs from both themselves and others. They, like everyone, are continually navigating their agency alongside how they are perceived, or feel, either different or indeed the same as others. Again, they are making do and getting by.

The terms consultation and listening are also problematic. Most legislation and policy mandate such actions. However, rarely is there a specification of how, when, or even who should be involved. Additionally, neither term indicates that any action must follow consultation or listening. Therefore, despite good intentions, social work participation does not always involve children in decision-making or influencing change. For instance, Križ and Skivenes (2017) found that 40 per cent of English social workers adopted practices and views that can be considered tokenistic and non-participatory. Therefore, consultation and listening can be, and often are, treated as one-off tick-box events rather than ongoing processes (Boone et al, 2019).

Dialogical participation

Some authors now suggest that it is time to move beyond the constructs of listening, voice, collaboration, and children's participation associated with the Global South (see, for example, Fitzgerald et al, 2009; Graham and Fitzgerald, 2010; Cheney, 2018; Abebe, 2019; Facca et al, 2020). These authors propose that participation should not be confined primarily to rules, procedures, and institutional design, nor should it focus solely on difference or equality. Instead, there should be an emphasis on participation as a process of ongoing dialogue in various spaces. It should not be a monological process, like following a recipe, but rather a thoughtful, relational, and dialogical one that involves children from the very beginning of the debates. A dialogical approach does not dwell on an endless discussion about whether a child can or should participate. Instead, it advocates for engagement through a process of mutual recognition, interdependence, and respect for children and their views and experiences. This is similar to sociology's dialectic approach (Craib, 2000). Being granted permission to participate no longer centres on the perception of difference or similarity between children and adults, as they are both. Rather, ethical considerations relate to how participation can be an inclusive process that explores how people navigate between such seeming dichotomies – how they navigate the relational and seemingly contradictory spaces inherent in family life and society.

The notion of participation as an inclusive space to 'navigate between', extending beyond just 'voice', is not new. Lundy's (2007) 'Voice is not enough ...' conceptualises the considerations necessary for participation, as shown in Table 4.1:

Voice: what is it, and who can have it?

Dialogical participation does not conform to the simplistic notions of competence commonly echoed in much legislation and policy. Instead, it suggests that all humans have the capacity to engage from birth when they can reason, analyse, and express complex experiences and decisions. Incompetence, dependence, and vulnerability are not criteria for inclusion or exclusion. Instead, they inform the conditions of the spaces where participation occurs. It promotes a 'person-friendly' process rather than just a 'child-friendly' one (Punch, 2002). All participants, regardless of age or role, are supported in the most appropriate ways. A dialogical approach does not ignore children's voices or prevent them from being heard due to ardent notions of protection. Instead, it takes the view that 'rather than protecting children and young people from research, we need to protect them through research' (Lundy, 2007, p 935).

Table 4.1: Lundy's model of participation

Voice	So that all can express their views safely, verbally, and nonverbally
Space	For social processes to promote intergenerational reflexivity
Audience	Views must be acknowledged and listened to
Influence	Views must be acted on, and it must be an ongoing process with opportunities for feedback

Source: Based on Lundy (2007)

The dialogical approach taken in the study and book incorporates both protectionist and participatory viewpoints to determine how child participation takes place rather than whether it should. This approach is essential, particularly for children in kinship care. As highlighted in previous chapters, there are ongoing tensions between families' self-determination and children's protection from further harm by remaining within them. A dialogical approach understands, acknowledges, and explores these tensions with the children themselves.

Space

Creating appropriate space for views to be formed is the key to dialogical participation. Space is created to promote adult–child relations and facilitate joint problem-solving among people of all ages and abilities. It becomes an intergenerational encounter within relational spaces (Canosa and Graham, 2020). These 'communicative action spaces' encourage children to become part of the discussion, adding different pieces of knowledge while pursuing a shared goal (Percy-Smith, 2015). The use of spaces draws on Habermas' (1985) theory of communicative action, the system, the public sphere, and the lifeworld. Mannion suggests these 'spaces are part of the action, and very consequential in the forms of behaviour they afford and the emergence of the identities that inhabit them' (2009, p 333). Children's participation is reframed with dialogical participation as providing the space for the meaningful exploration of the dynamics of child–adult relationships and reflections at a specific moment in time.

Audience and influence

Often unintentionally, many participation projects involving children may promise respect, listening, and future changes that cannot be fulfilled. A dialogical approach seeks to guard against this by suggesting that both adults and children are wary but honest about the aims, motives, and sponsorship of research and participation. Values such as honesty, listening, and reflexivity form the starting points (Kennan et al, 2018). Nevertheless, it would be naive, idealistic, and possibly even hypocritical to claim that such an approach to dialogue is free from power dynamics. Participants remain subject to cultural, social, legal, and political discourses that both enable and limit what they can and cannot say. Children's social location must be acknowledged as subordinate to that of adults. There must be continuous questioning regarding how those involved should be involved. As demonstrated in the 'what matters' study, there need to be constant check-ins and clarifications.

The continuous exchange of knowledge should involve not only those directly participating but also other structures that seem removed from the act. This is done through ongoing knowledge sharing. Such a dialogical approach draws on traditions from participatory action research (Kemmis and McTaggart, 2005) and resembles Pawson and Tilley's (1997) teacher–learner cycle, explored in the next chapter. Learning and action provide space at the individual level, in terms of recognition, as well as at the interpersonal level, through dialogue with others. It also happens at the systemic level, encompassing the perspectives and responses from services, organisations, and practice.

With such open debate and negotiation, there will undoubtedly be conflict and disagreement. Participation is not an easy process. However, disagreement should not be shied away from; instead, it should be accompanied by empathy towards those with whom we have formed trusting, caring relationships (Kennan et al, 2018). Without conflict, compromise cannot be achieved. Furthermore, without genuine compromise, meaningful, lasting change cannot happen for the good of the child and society. The question then becomes what constitutes good and who has the final say? Is good purely subjective and reliant on who has more experience, and should values even hold a place in empirical research? Here is where participation, even dialogical participation, can run into substantial issues, particularly when making generalisations. This will be explored in the next chapter.

Conclusion

Child participation, especially with children in kinship care, often shows a significant gap between the intention to listen to children and engaging in the actual practice. Kinship care research that manages to include children's perspectives frequently presents generalised findings, many of which can struggle to focus on a child's agency and what they do in the present. Additionally, research can often take perspectives reflecting individualistic, neoliberalised childhood and child development theories. This creates an incomplete and often distracting picture wherein children's views of kinship care are typically secondary to adults' perspectives, or they are compared with those of children not in kinship care arrangements.

The aim of this chapter is not to criticise previous informative and robust kinship care studies or to discourage child welfare academics, practitioners, or policy makers from engaging in or attempting participatory practices. There are already enough competitive comparisons regarding achieving children's participation, and new methods of participation should continuously evolve within their social-political-historical context. There is always room for new approaches and progress. Instead, the chapter's purpose is to emphasise that meaningful participation includes the recognition of the politics and power dynamics involved. It also involves an awareness of the complexities and tensions associated with enacting agency, particularly when various factors, including our own beliefs, society, funders, and political contexts, can constrain it.

An approach based on dialogical participation can help us realise the validity of children's views with a critical awareness of power differentials, inviting active citizenship. This is an ethic and process that can move past simplistic, never-ending monological debates over whether children are different or the same. It offers a deep understanding through generational perspectives, mutual responsibility, and dialogue in spaces (Abebe, 2019). Dialogical participation embraces the politics of participation by becoming part of it. It allows for the mindfulness of resources and inequalities by ensuring that appropriate relational spaces are created according to capacity rather than (in)competence.

Combined with the need to build and maintain emotional relationships with participants, participation should incorporate constant reflection, time, energy, awareness, and emotional effort to ensure an ethical and meaningful encounter within a relational space. Such emotional labour is seldom described in participatory research accounts. Instead, it is often considered more appropriate to outline, step by step, seemingly apolitical recipe-like processes at the expense of exploring the political and emotionally challenging aspects of participation (Lenette et al, 2019). The next two chapters aim to address this by elaborating on the 'what matters' approach, which employs critical realism, values, reflexivity, and creative methods to establish an ethical and robust foundation for listening to children. Chapter 5 begins this discussion by reflecting on philosophy and the value of pets.

5

Valuing a 'what matters' approach

> Well, I'd say it matters to be good, be nice, and, erm, also help others to be good and nice.
>
> Jordan, child research participant

This chapter introduces a new type of 'what matters' approach for research and child welfare. Grounded in Sayer's (2011) *Why Things Matter to People*, the approach combines dialogical participation with critical realism. It employs philosophy, creative dialogical participatory methods, and theory building to illuminate the underlying values that guide our everyday actions. Values hold great significance in our lives. Pursuing the values that matter to us can literally be why we get out of bed in the morning.

Critical realism is a philosophical endeavour, and this chapter is philosophical in nature. While many may feel that philosophy is irrelevant to child welfare practice, policy making, and research, it is vital to consider what exists in the world (ontology) and how we know about it (epistemology). Philosophy connects the abstract to the everyday. It facilitates the application of theory to practice. It lets us contemplate the reasons for different experiences while prompting reflection on structure, agency, and power. Therefore, as all philosophies should be, critical realism is also a political endeavour. Philosophical thought should initiate impactful and political reform. It can allow all those concerned with the welfare of others to acknowledge and confront the stark realities of a world increasingly divided by social injustices, inequality, and polarised debates. Philosophy enables us to pose the right questions, judge explanations based on their merits, and guide us toward the most appropriate, moral solutions.

This chapter delves into the complex yet indispensable philosophy of critical realism. It describes how critical realism navigates a middle space between positivism and interpretivism. Critical realism does this through the stratification of reality, using theories and evaluation cycles and judgemental rationality, and uncovering the values that matter. Then, the chapter shows how a 'what matters' approach can help with childhood research, dialogical participation, child welfare, and social work. Lastly, the philosophy and methodology are applied to the everyday by revealing the mechanisms that mattered in the 'What matters to children living in kinship care' study.

The philosophy of social sciences

Without thinking about what data means and represents, a researcher cannot proficiently or ethically give sound implications or recommendations from their findings. For example, it has been previously found that having pets benefits many children in foster care and kinship care (Wood and Selwyn, 2017). Also, almost all the children in the 'What matters to children living in kinship care' study had pets in their homes. The children would talk incessantly about their pets and joyfully showcase them as positive, important influences in their lives.

Although most children in the study had pets, this does not suggest that most kinship care arrangements worldwide also have pets. The sample is too small to make such a generalisation, even when combined with previous research. The findings also do not necessarily mean that children should only be matched with families who have pets or that local authorities should buy pets for families in kinship arrangements. First, common sense suggests that it is not the pets that are the key here. Second, a moral judgement has been made suggesting that pets are universally beneficial. However, this is not the case for everyone, and some pets can be challenging to care for. Third, in practice, not all families are able to accommodate a pet. Some family members may be allergic, or the family may lack the finances, time, or space.

What is genuinely interesting is the role of pets and the value they bring to the lives of many children. They evoke emotional and physiological responses. These are hopefully positive responses, such as pleasure and the release of oxytocin, rather than anxiety and histamines. There is also something fundamental in the relationships with pets that adds to the wellbeing of the children. Pets really do matter. Pets have meaning for children, although this is not just about how children think, talk, and construct pets. Pets are real and exist whether or not our minds acknowledge them. Also, the UK culture of including pets as part of the family influences how we include them into our lives and homes. Philosophical thinking helps us to synthesise all these considerations. It enables us to contemplate how people, their social structures, and their contexts can be construed, described, fitted together, and, most importantly, meaningfully supported. It allows us to reflect on the general principles underlying the diverse aspects of life and helps us discern what reality is and how to explore it.

Positivism, interpretivism, and critical realism

Positivism

Positivism is a philosophical theory asserting that the most reliable scientific knowledge is derived from empirical evidence, such as experiments and observations. Positivist research is often regarded as highly practical, as it seeks to negate personal bias and study clear tangible outcomes, typically through comparison (for example, comparison of placement disruption rates). It can also be executed on a large scale. Critical realism rejects positivism's over-emphasis on prediction, measurement, and quantification. It suggests a situation or behaviour is not 'meaningless, [even] if we cannot falsify or verify it empirically' (Bhaskar, 1989, p 28). Data does not need to define situations and behaviours into existence. Additionally, while they can guide explanations, measurements are deemed inadequate by critical realists in explaining the underlying nature of phenomena. Positivism is said by critical realists to often conform to hyperrealism (Alderson, 2016). Hyper-realism refers to an over-belief in reality. It suggests that reality can only be defined by the number of things that can be seen and counted, which can then lead to generalisations and recommendations derived from them.

When there is an over-belief in reality, complex situations are often treated as objective yes/no facts that fit into a binary analysis. This mimics monological thinking. Explanations then claim the 'what' as definitive facts. However, researching in this manner does not fully explain the 'why' or the 'how'. Critical realists argue that stopping a level of analysis at this level of observation and description confuses correlation with causation. It may also lead to unfair, simplistic, and potentially bigoted categorisations of groups through essentialist determinism.

Essentialist determination has already been alluded to in this book. It is a belief that infers that certain groups possess specific characteristics that determine their behaviours, situations, and needs. It moves away from trends towards fixed differences (Pilgrim, 2023). Taken to extremes, this could imply, for example, that racially minoritised children could incorrectly and unjustly be condemned as more challenging or less emotionally resilient due purely to their ethnicity. Research only through positivist, quantitative, and similar empirical methods can easily lose the person through the process, the problem through the scientific technique, and the most important questions through data and regressions.

Social constructionism and social constructivism

It is recognised that qualitative understandings, often viewed in opposition to positivist methods, as described in the previous chapter, are also necessary for research and practice, especially for child welfare. For example, listening to the experiences of those in kinship care is vital for a fuller understanding of what it means for family life and achieving a sense of permanence (Messing, 2006). However, the challenge for many qualitative and participation methodologies, including dialogical participation, is that they rely on the notion that knowledge, and therefore truth, is socially constructed (Canosa and Graham, 2020). It proposes that, in contrast to direct observation, reality primarily emerges from human meaning-making (social constructivism) in conjunction with collective consensus (social constructionism). As Guterman notes: 'Although both constructivism and social constructionism endorse a subjective view of knowledge, the former emphasises individuals' biological and cognitive processes, whereas the latter places knowledge in the domain of social interchange' (2006, p 13).

This suggests gathering views about the world is crucial, and the benefits of social constructionist and social constructivist perspectives are that they can enable researchers to uncover and analyse the social processes and interactions that shape knowledge about how reality is understood, offering a deeper understanding of how societal norms and beliefs are formed. The approaches can also foster mutual collaboration and group unity by creating and accepting shared ideas within society, and they encourage critical thinking by challenging individuals to question and analyse the underlying assumptions and power dynamics that shape societal norms and knowledge (Burr, 2015).

Distinctions are often made between hard social constructivism and social constructionism, and soft social constructivism and constructivism. The hard perspective argues that all knowledge and reality are entirely constructed through social processes and interactions. It posits that there is no objective reality outside of these social constructs. Essentially, it takes a more radical stance, suggesting that everything we know and understand is a product of social agreements and interactions. The soft approach is less extreme, acknowledging that while social constructs predominantly shape our understanding of reality, there is still an objective reality that exists independently of human perception. It recognises the influence of social processes on knowledge but does not deny the existence of an external reality.

Social constructivist and social constructionist perspectives are frequently adopted for child participation. These perspectives, particularly the hard variety, infer that there is no 'grand narrative', but rather little subjective narratives that need to be collated and listened to (Lyotard, 1984). There is no one big understanding of the world. Instead, there are smaller ones which make up a whole. However, this can lead to everything becoming subjective (Guterman, 2006). It is as if there is no absolute truth, and that is the truth. Therefore, hard social constructivism and hard social constructionism have their own grand theory that paradoxically rejects all grand theories.

Putting such an oxymoron to one side, there is an issue that is even more problematic. If everything is subjective and there can be no one truth, there can be no moral judgment (Benton and Craib, 2010). This harks back to Winch's political relativism. Social constructivism and social constructionism can promote a refusal to judge between different cultures and experiences. They suggest there is no one correct way to live. Taken to extremes, social constructionism and social constructionism propose that all our lives and truths are just different, and we need to acknowledge and celebrate them all for what they are. No one culture, no one way of living, is better than the other.

On the face of it, this may seem like an ethically or morally sound sentiment. However, on further reflection, this abyss of relativism cannot be correct. If it were true that no one way of living is better, this would provide no normative base from which child welfare and social workers can act (Taylor and White, 2016). As discussed in Chapter 2, child welfare relies on norms to assess support and risk (Sayer, 2017). For example, we know it is wrong that most kinship carers live in financial hardship. We know that this is not a good thing. We understand this by making comparisons and moral judgements. We cannot just accept poverty, inequality, suffering, abuse, and harm as differences in lifestyles and leave it like that. Postmodernism, social constructivism, and social constructionism can fail to address what is right and wrong. It can let people, society, everything, and everybody off the hook. This could mean there is nowhere to turn, and all that is left is powerlessness and apathy. The one thing child welfare workers, researchers, social workers, policy makers, politicians, and society should never be is apathetic. The question for all of us should always be how social justice is achieved, not whether it should be.

There are also issues with social constructivism and social constructionism regarding representation. How is it possible to generalise from a sample of individuals who are said to represent kinship care if there are no absolute truths? The hope would be that the children's experiences and situations would all be similar enough to make meaningful inferences. However, previous chapters have shown that children and children in kinship care are not a homogenous group, nor are kinship care or experiences of permanence.

Even if one could homogenise the needs of those in kinship care arrangements worldwide, further technical difficulties regarding the authenticity, reliability, and validity of the research would remain (Humphries, 2008). For example, it is argued that participation privileges the older, louder, and more emotionally literate individuals over those who do not conform (Holland et al, 2010), with numerous participation methods reflecting White middle-class communication norms (Vandenbroeck, 2006). Participants in research may also discipline themselves to conform to expected norms. Children, in particular, may try to appease the researcher, their carers, social workers, or society. The pressure to behave well and as others expect is especially true when tasks are often highly managed by researchers and practitioners who rely on schooled obedience and focus (Holland et al, 2010). Social constructivism and social constructionism can often struggle to tackle these problems of generalisability and social inequalities. Instead, it could be said that it may permit them through its principles of multiple childhoods, truths, and narratives, and its overemphasis on the social (Hammersley, 2017).

The middle path of critical realism

Critical realism is gaining increasing acceptance and recognition within the social sciences, child welfare, and social work (for example, Kjørstad and Solem, 2017; Houston, 2022; Houston and Swords, 2022; Murphy, 2023). Critical realism provides a structured way of thinking that helps consider how everything interacts. Critical realism moves beyond pure empiricism and positivism while rejecting hard social constructivism and social constructionism. It dismisses the tendencies of social constructivism and social constructionism, which often frame social realities predominantly as discursive or linguistic actions (Bhaskar, 1993). It posits that reality cannot only be reduced to 'ideas people have' (Jessop, 2005, p 42). This would suggest that there is no reality without language. For critical realists, this is known as the epistemic fallacy, which conflates ontology with epistemology (Bhaskar, 1998). Reality is conflated with the knowledge of reality. Reducing everything to the subjective in this way is hypo-realism, an under-belief in reality (Alderson, 2016). As such, purely social constructionist and social constructivist thinking can make connections between research data, implications, and recommendations appear tenuous at best.

Critical realism combines the positivist's search for an external reality and the interpretivist's understanding that all meaning associated with that reality is socially constructed (Oliver, 2012). It suggests, like some soft social constructivism and constructionism, that there is a social reality whether or not it is directly experienced or observed. Therefore, reality, such as pets, exists independently of human knowledge, the mind, or thought (Morton, 2006). However, how we know about pets also impacts their meaning for us. Furthermore, ontology – what exists in the world, such as pets – always transcends epistemology, which is how we know about pets (Archer et al, 2013).

While critical realism challenges constructivist and empiricist research as ultimate ways of knowing, it does not altogether reject them. By not adhering to the dogmatic idealism of either in their age-long debates on how to view the world, a critical realist perspective is said to combine both in a more structured way. It takes a middle path, which helps analyse, explain, and validate critical social science by drawing on the strengths of positivism and interpretivism and overcoming their limitations (Archer et al, 2013). Critical realism deals with the generalisation and representation gap head-on through retroduction and the emergence of mechanisms, allowing researchers to make more meaning out of data. It does this also through the stratification of reality.

The basic tenets of critical realism

The stratification of reality

Critical realism proposes three levels of reality, a perspective that can assist in explaining the world around us (Bhaskar, 1993). Social reality is understood as stratified systems with objects connected through causal relationships (Morton, 2006). This is highlighted in Figure 5.1.

As shown in the diagram, the actual level encompasses all events, regardless of whether they are ever experienced, like the tree trunk blocked by the wall. The empirical level occurs when the actual becomes experienced, like the branches being in view. Traditionally, the empirical level is where science investigates phenomena. Finally, the real, the unseen root, is where underlying mechanisms generate events and can instigate change for the entire tree. While it is essential to acknowledge both the actual and empirical levels, the real is what critical realists are most concerned with – finding these hidden mechanisms that generate certain phenomena, such as leaves on a tree or the relationships in family life in kinship care.

Mechanisms

Mechanisms are 'nothing other than the ways of acting of things' (Bhaskar, 2008, p 14). Bhaskar proposes a process called retroductive reasoning to identify them. Retroduction is a 'mode of inference in which events are explained by postulating (and identifying) mechanisms which are capable of producing them' (Sayer, 1992, p 107). It takes a step back from the surface

Figure 5.1: Tree diagram of three ontological levels: empirical, actual, real

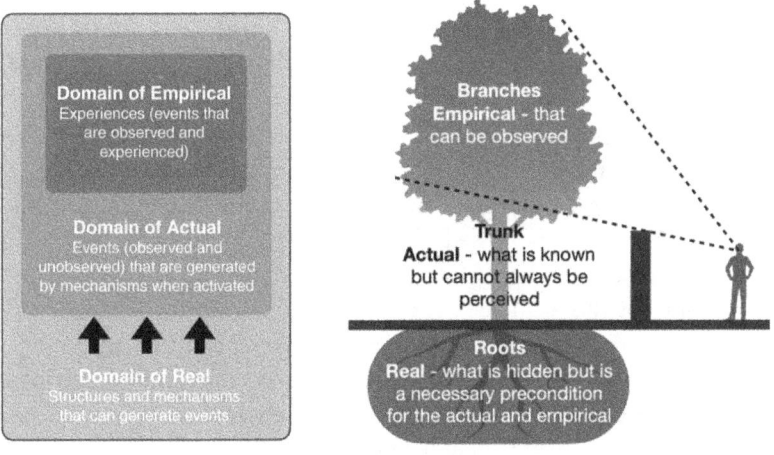

Source: Adapted from Walsh and Evans (2014, p e2)

level of events to identify what must be for events to occur. For example, a child must have experienced disruption to be placed with new carers. Seeing and examining the world in this way moves beyond the flat actualism of the empirical and actual levels, where many positivists, constructivists, constructionists, and interpretivists can remain (Bhaskar, 2008). Without focusing on the mechanisms, the empirical is just presented as fact, and the root causes can be missed.

Mechanisms can belong to the psychological (for example, mental structures, schemas, unconscious processes and memory, object relations, and attachment styles), the social (for example, ideologies, social classes, and modes of production), and the physical (for example, atomic, chemical, and biological structures). To explain further, an example of a psychological mechanism in kinship care is the drive for permanence – this is referred to in previous chapters and other research. Examples of societal mechanisms may be patriarchy, structural racism, neoliberalisation, and the mounting managerialism in social work. A biological mechanism could be the child's release of oxytocin when near their carer. It should be noted that, like the tree's roots, these mechanisms cannot be directly observed, although their impact can be.

Contexts, outcomes and causation

The contexts in which the mechanisms are placed are relevant. It is like the soil for the roots of the tree. For kinship care, contexts, such as the time a carer spends with a child before placement, may impact whether the sense of belonging mechanism is activated. The context will also affect *how* it is activated. Mechanisms are not reliant only on the context, but on other mechanisms too. All these different mechanisms may contradict, act in opposition, or enhance. Very simply:

outcomes = mechanisms + contexts

(Pawson and Tilley, 1997)

This ideology opposes the successionist view of causality that says A leads to B, and so on. Instead, it suggests what is known as 'generative causation' (Bhaskar, 2008). As such, 'causal laws must be analysed as the tendencies of things, which may be possessed unexercised and exercised unrealised, just as they may, of course, be realised unperceived' (Bhaskar, 1989, pp 9–10). The meaning of this is further explored when examining Archer's (2012) interpretation of reflexivity, but the quote highlights a fundamental point of critical realism: everything is fallible. There are many ways of knowing. Despite reality's existence, different people will always interpret it differently. Fallibility is true of researchers, policy makers, and practitioners, even if they are positioned as kinship care experts or write books about kinship care and listening to children. Therefore, findings, theories, and implications must be placed under a web of expectations that cannot be taken as absolute (Archer et al, 2013). There can only be speculative emergent properties and tendencies, even though they are based on something that exists and is real (Bhaskar, 1989).

Judgmental rationality and the realist evaluation cycle

Despite the caveats of tendencies and everything being fallible, it is still possible to generate explanations. Just because all knowledge is fallible does not mean all knowledge is equally fallible (Sayer, 1992). Bhaskar makes it clear that in no way are 'all beliefs equally valid in the sense that there are no rational grounds for preferring one to another' (Bhaskar, 1986, p 72); otherwise, we might descend to the abyss of relativism that holds that there are no truths, in the same way social constructionism and social constructivism can (Taylor and White, 2016). While reality can never be known with absolute certainty, it can be described as better or worse, and have more accurate or less accurate accounts (Hartwig, 2007). This is known as judgmental rationality.

Plausible explanations are derived by trying out the ideas most compatible with available evidence. Knowledge and theories cannot be created from nothing. Science as a social process depends on adapting prior knowledge. In other words, existing hypotheses and theories from past experiences, literature and research are used to try and explain what is happening in the actual and empirical and to help identify and explain the mechanisms. Critical realism is said to be theory-driven but not theory-led. Theories help us understand what might be happening, but they must not wholly dictate the direction of the research (Fletcher, 2017).

This critical realist notion of using and developing theories was furthered by Pawson and Tilley (1997). They devised a realist evaluation process or cycle:

1. Use observations, previous findings, and theories to identify the tentative contexts (C), mechanisms (M), and outcomes (O).
2. Hypothesise how the CMO configurations might fit together.
3. Test out and observe the potential configuration while looking for any other CMO configurations.
4. Through analysis, conclude on what works for whom and in what circumstances. and update the theory.
5. Return to the beginning, with updated theory and data to identify new tentative contexts, mechanisms, and outcomes.

This process helps apply theories to empirical scrutiny. Through experimentation, the possible mechanisms and contexts that are hypothesised affirm either that the theories are adequate or that the theories require adaptation. Theories may even need to be abandoned altogether. Theories are, therefore, judged on their explanatory power. Whether they take us away from explaining what is happening or take us more deeply towards helping us understand the real depends on the adequacy of the theories and concepts adopted and how they are used (Sayer, 2011). This also allows for a steady accumulation of findings over time and promotes methodological pluralism and pragmatism. It also encourages new research to add onto previous research as part of a larger worldwide research cycle that happens over time.

'What matters' valuations

Is/ought dichotomies, facts versus values, normative claims, and doing the right thing

Along with the concept of judgmental rationality, critical realism suggests that individuals and collectives can change society and the world around them. This belief is essential for both child welfare practice and participatory research. This power to transform is why critical realism has the label critical. It is a critical theory and a political endeavour. By extending the ideas of Marx and other Frankfurt School thinkers, critical realism asserts that human subjects are real beings who navigate the world through social interaction. Through this, emancipation, or indeed oppression, can occur.

As noted in the previous chapter, participatory research can unwittingly perpetuate oppression instead of emancipation. Dialogical participation has been proposed to help this. However, everything and everyone is fallible, including social work researchers, like me, who have ambitious ideas about kinship care and child participation. Therefore, how can we ensure that our research leads to emancipation rather than oppression, even when using dialogical participation? How can we ensure we are not inadvertently confirming and imposing our own biased beliefs and values?

This is known as the 'is/ought problem'. Following David Hume (Norton and Norton, 2006), a dominant philosophy is the separation of facts from values – separation of the 'is' from the 'ought'. This separation proposes that value-laden 'ought to be' claims should not be formed from the descriptive value-free facts of what 'is' and vice versa. To do so could be deemed unscientific and biased, and for a long time, it was assumed that researchers should not let their beliefs and biases influence their work. For instance, ethnographer Hammersley (2017) argues that researchers and academics should strive to be value-neutral and objective in their work.

While this is/ought (fact versus value) separation has long been defended in the social sciences and philosophy, it is impossible to maintain or support complete non-valued objectivity in the practice of child welfare or research on it.

First, there is a simple and logical reason for rejecting the separation. To make the argument that 'ought' cannot be derived from 'is' is itself a normative claim, a belief, and an assertion of a value. By its own rules, a scientific 'is' claim cannot be proclaimed on an 'ought' belief. This is like the paradox of a grand theory that rejects all grand theories.

Second, all research questions begin with asserting at least one subjective value. Researchers propose projects due to their concerns about what they feel matters. This is similar to the way you chose to read this book because you may be interested in better ways to support kinship care, permanence, child welfare, and research, and you want to understand the value of listening to children. Or you may be reading this out of obligation, kindness, friendship, or love for the author. These are also values – ones which I very much appreciate. But no matter the nature of the reason, there is at least one reason: you have made a valuation. Placing values on acquiring knowledge happens even when researchers or book readers are unaware of such assumptions or fail to make them explicit (Sayer, 2011). It is vital to remember and remind ourselves of the values that guide us. For example, social sciences and social endeavours are not, and should not be, value-free (Bhaskar, 2008). Social research must endeavour to make political change, and child welfare must be politically active. The overarching aim of research, policy making, and practice is to instigate positive change for individuals and society. Structural inequalities and harmful behaviours associated with oppression should be identified and challenged (Houston, 2001).

Third, separating facts from values implies that value judgements are not made through facts or can threaten the objectivity of facts. This is incorrect. To explain further, here are a few examples:

- Although the statement 'UK kinship carers are more likely to live in financial hardship than non-related foster carers' is a fact, it cannot be read or researched without a value judgement. We automatically consider, subconsciously or otherwise, whether this is acceptable and whether this fact is worth changing.
- Within the statement 'many children are in kinship care arrangements because they have been abused', there is a value judgment, a normative claim, and an opinion about what abuse is. Abuse may be slightly different in different cultures. In a sense, it is a subjective word. Nevertheless, the term abuse is also not arbitrary or meaningless. We cannot just dismiss the statement because it contains a subjective word. Smacking children may be accepted in some cultures, yet it causes various degrees of harm, whether or not it is deemed normal. Although the statement includes a value judgment, it does not mean the abuse is not a fact and should be ignored – quite the opposite.

- Less value-laden statements, such as 'most children are in kinship care arrangements because their birth parents cannot look after them', are less accurate than those that mention abuse. They could even be seen as dismissive of the suffering of the children and a form of gaslighting.

The more one imposes an artificial distinction between fact and value, and the 'is' and 'ought', the more one is removed from the actual world of people, practice, and the things that matter most to people (Sayer, 2011). It confuses the things of logic with the logic of things. The 'no is from the ought' argument is about logic. It concerns the rational relations between statements. However, values are often about emotive states of being and the drive to flourish rather than suffer.

Why 'what matters' matters

In *Why Things Matter to People*, Andrew Sayer (2011) reiterates that we all operate from the middle ground between the 'is' and the 'ought', which cannot be separated. It is what drives us. It is what life or 'life-force' is all about (Sayer, 2019, p 261). For better or worse, we are suspended between things as they are and might become, and things as we need or want them to become (Sayer, 2011). By deciding what is acceptable, we continuously judge what is good or bad, continuously making evaluations. Then, we decide what to do based on what we think is best. This is because while we have capabilities, we also have vulnerabilities, are dependent, and have needs. We depend on our health, environment, and relationships with others. We also know and have all experienced that if actions, the environment, and relationships can enrich our lives, they can also damage them. We can flourish or suffer, which is also shaped by luck and coincidence. Also, we can both flourish and suffer simultaneously, or flourish and then later suffer, or suffer to flourish. This, again, is a move away from simplistic monological thinking and instead navigates the spaces in between.

Such considerations between the 'is' and the 'ought' make our relations with the world one of care and concern. Our decisions and the decisions of others mean something to us, and we typically have various feelings attached to them. These valuations can be about little questions like what is best to have for dinner tonight. They can also be about larger ones, such as whether we would like to have contact with someone who has subjected us to harm. We use experience, future concern, reasoning, and morality to move between the states of lacking and the states of fulfilment and flourishing. This everyday jostling to provide a better future is why we care about things. This is why things matter and why some things matter more to us.

Sayer proposes that moral judgements, values, and evaluations are in the scope of reason. He argues that reason is different from rationale.

Rational thought is deemed logical, objective, and without emotional thought. On the other hand, reasoning is often considered to use emotions, normative judgements, and valuations. Placed in the context of common patriarchal stereotypes of sex and gender, men, who apparently are and should be emotionless, can often be accused of being irrational. Conversely, women are more likely to be told they are unreasonable and over-emotional in their decision-making (Sayer, 2011).

Sayer, as all of us should, condemns such archaic assumptions. He proposes that, regardless of gender, we are prone to making reasonable judgements over rational ones. Using values and emotions provides the foundation for many of our actions. Reasoning and valuation motivate people more than logic or rationale. Deciding what matters most causes us to do what we feel needs to be done. As such, our valuations of what matters are linked to the generative mechanisms innate to universal human nature. To be clear, the definition of innate here is not necessarily blind instinct or biological or essentialist determinism. Innate also involves past and future temperaments, potential and emerging capabilities, and ever-changing contexts. It is vital not to slip into monological nature versus nurture, either/or thinking.

Valuations, then, can be seen as the potential causal mechanisms sought by critical realists. This understanding can be put another way using Archer's (2012) notion of reflexivity and inner conversations. She utilises Bhaskar's (1986) transformational model of social activity and proposes that our actions are influenced, but not determined, by social structures at all levels, including society. These everyday social interactions surround us, including those with family, law, religion, class, and the economy. Such structures may pre-exist specific human actions, but humans also reflexively monitor and can alter the social world. We are never completely passive and without agency, even if we decide we should not or cannot do anything. Doing nothing is still doing something and can sometimes be the best course of action. Through this process of reflexivity, humans can choose whether or not to individually or collectively exert influence over and change the relatively enduring yet evolving structures around us. This occurs through our inner conversations about our personal concerns and how to realise them in a society that is never entirely of our making or choosing (Archer, 2003). We then decide whether to confront social structures or endure them. We consciously and subconsciously choose our battles depending on what we value most.

For Archer, one crucial role of research and possibly any worthwhile conversation is to draw out these inner conversations and the thoughts that bounce in between whether to engage in action or inaction. Outing these complex, value-laden inner conversations allows researchers and practitioners to analyse human reflexivity and individual reasoning. They are the sought-after mechanisms that drive us. Furthermore, a person's explanations of thoughts and actions are significant because such inner conversations 'have powers that can be causally efficacious in relation to himself and to society' (Archer, 2003, p 14). By asking participants and those we work alongside to reiterate their reflexive thoughts, we may challenge any false consciousness they hold. We can help empower others to take another perspective, rethink what matters, and make further changes. Raising and finding out reasoning can not only be a guide to the sought-after generative mechanisms but also can lead to individual and societal change.

Embodiment

A final and relatively new addition to Sayer and other critical realists' thinking is the importance of embodiment (Nellhaus, 2017; Sayer, 2019). Again, this highlights the rejection of radically opposed either/or dichotomies such as the mind and body or culture and nature. Several mechanisms and processes operate at different levels and interact differently. Bodies are neither simply cultural products nor unalterable. Changes to the body occur depending on what causes them and where they are happening. For example, thinking, past knowledge about movement, and physical experience, established in a supportive environment, can all lead to neuroplasticity in the brain. The idea of neurogenesis is even more remarkable, as it suggests the adult brain can grow new neurons (Gage, 2002). Body, thought, and experience are linked.

To put this into the context of participation, a child cannot articulate complicated feelings properly until they have learned a language to an appropriate level. We cannot just dismiss the capacity to think in the abstract as having nothing to do with the body. Everything interacts. Significant interactions exist between the conscious and the subconscious, the psychological and the physiological, the body, brain, mind, and the environment. For example, the body holds trauma (Kolk, 2015). Such connections can operate almost unnoticed in the flow of the everyday. However, they can also be mobilised deliberately as a form of therapy, with in-depth, focused research or personal reflections about what matters.

The practicalities of realist research

In summary, employing a critical realist, needs-based conception of social beings has value. This perspective views actors not only as causal agents and self-interpreting meaning-makers, but also as needy and dependent beings with an orientation of care and concern about things. It presumes children are humans capable of flourishing or suffering. Need here is used as a shorthand that covers lack, want, and desire and includes culturally acquired or emergent needs. When someone says what something means to them, it shows a value-led evaluative relation to the world – a valuation. When children describe what something means to them, it cannot be merely glossed over as a subjective expression of their feelings; it is about something. It concerns their embodied wellbeing or ill-being, relationships, attachments, and commitments to others. It is about concern. Therefore, finding out what matters is about providing space for reflexive thinking and outing conversations. It is about discovering the mechanisms and contexts that can lead to the desired outcome, which, for child welfare research, is ultimately for children to safely flourish in their family lives.

Due to this idea of ongoing knowledge production from gaining what matters from various perspectives, critical realist research tends to use mixed-method approaches. Critical realist research typically uses statistical analysis to ascertain patterns and regularities in empirical phenomena and then qualitative research to probe for deeper explanations (Alderson, 2013). Critical realism takes a both/and approach by utilising empirical research to map out the issues, contradictions, and broad context, as the first half of this book has done. However, there is also recognition that those who experience the situation must remain at the heart of any matter, which is why the second half of the book is just as vital. Facts are important and so are feelings about facts. Bhaskar states that 'actor's accounts form the indispensable starting point of social enquiry' (1998, p xv1). Bhaskar insists that this will help stop explaining behaviour in terms of essentialist determinism. It will be less likely to unjustly label particular groups as having specific problems.

Critical realism also proposes that studies should be undertaken in the open world rather than in a lab or by excessively controlling variables. It is deemed impossible to control all the conditions in the empirical completely. It is deemed unfeasible, especially in the social world full of seeming contradictions, to control all the variables and undertake comparative studies in a closed system (Pawson and Tilley, 1997). Trying to mitigate and regulate environments through methods such as randomised controlled trials is therefore regarded as having limited reliability or validity, especially for social science (Fives et al, 2015). Some also deem it unethical to withdraw help and services, even for scientific or long-term gain.

How critical realism assists child welfare, kinship care, and child participation

How critical realism assists child welfare practice and research

As demonstrated in previous chapters, child welfare, the safe flourishing of children, and child participation are complicated endeavours, especially when they centre around the politics and practice of kinship care arrangements and permanence planning. Child welfare, and especially social work, need more than one analytic perspective to capture the complexity witnessed in practice. Therefore, child welfare is often portrayed as something that utilises multidisciplinary perspectives. It continuously navigates the tension between the individual's capacity for personal agency and the social, economic, political, and other contextual factors. Critical realism welcomes this both/and approach. It allows child welfare practitioners to recognise not only the social factors – such as poverty, neoliberalisation, racialisation, gender, and social exclusion – but also the psychological and biological 'individual' problems – such as anxiety, depression, and substance misuse.

Social work also must be not only explanatory but emancipatory. Like critical realism, it must be critical. Social work's principal task is instigating change while adhering to a particular set of values and ethical practices. This can be done by promoting certain individual behaviours. Change can also occur by exposing any harmful underlying ideologies of influential stakeholders and 'false consciousness'. Critical realism's attention to morality and values provides direction for social work's value-led practice. It confronts the abyss of relativism by advocating for judgmental rationality, stating that not all beliefs are equally valid, such as the belief it is right to beat a child, and some things are not just culturally inappropriate but morally wrong. Critical realism attempts to explain and ethically value phenomena rather than just describe phenomena. Critical realism does this in a way that leads to 'consideration of right conduct and the good life' (Houston, 2010, p 74). It allows for a normative view and judgments of when things are unacceptable. It is also careful not to prescribe to supposed separate dichotomies. Such principles align with social work's central tensions of care and control, protection versus rights, visions of emancipation, and whether the oppressed can also be the oppressor (Oliver, 2012).

Critical realism's stratification of reality can also help pinpoint where appropriate changes and interventions need to be made. For example, it may seem a suitable approach to stop any contact between a child and their birth parents if it seems to upset the child. However, this approach to the issue remains on the actual and empirical levels of reality, like the branches and trunk of the tree. The hypothesis relies on a surface-level explanation. It does not look at the root causes of why the child is upset. It does not look at why the physical presence of the birth parent causes upset. It does not address the real, the underlying mechanisms, and the underlying issues. It may be that the child wishes to have positive relationships with their family members, including their birth parents. Stopping contact may, therefore, actually work against the child's need for positive relationships, as family tensions may become more fraught. It keeps things on the actual and empirical level. Instead, an intervention needs to identify what mechanisms are occurring – whether they include a positive attachment, positive affiliations, a sense of belonging, a sense of safety, and so on. When these have been identified by retroduction, the particular contexts can be determined. For this example, it may be necessary to think of contact differently – without relying solely on face-to-face interactions – rather than stopping contact altogether.

Finally, the idea of fallibility and constant re-evaluation is helpful for social work. Not only does this align with social work's often-utilised Assessment, Strategies, Planning, Intervention, and Evaluation model (Sutton, 2006), but also critical realism describes a social world with multiple opportunities for change by rejecting linear causality. Generative mechanisms are neither determinative nor all-explaining. It is, therefore, helpful for thinking systemically and reflectively and working with uncertainty, which are central tenets of all social work (Munro, 2019).

How critical realism helps childhood studies

Critical realism ensures that real, living, embodied children are present in the research. It does not promote one monological viewpoint over another. It recognises that agency is relational and attempts to explore how it is enacted in the present. It sees things in the dialogical. This is despite the long history of children being perceived a certain way and relentless discussions about whether children should be subjects or objects of research, are passive in their lives or have agency, and should be seen as different or the same as adults, or as 'beings' or 'becomings'. It notices sociological approaches and the various beliefs and discourses of childhood. However, critical realism does not collapse being into knowing. It does not fall into an epistemological fallacy. It acknowledges that bodies and suffering matter and are not ignored through cultural or political relativism.

It must also be remembered that children, the parenting of children, and their wellbeing are all emotive subjects. Alderson (2016) argues that research with children is not only value-informed but value-saturated. Its entire goal is to show how children can flourish. Critical realist research does not ignore this. It advocates that values, emotions, and reasoning play a significant part in any study and all life that involves children.

How does critical realism help with studies on kinship care?

As previously discussed, one of the main challenges of kinship care research is its tendency to homogenise kinship care as one thing with solutions that will apply to all situations. This can also be encouraged by arguments for parity between kinship care and non-related foster care (for example, in Sir James Munby's 2019 speech at the Coram permanence event). Critical realism can help navigate such tensions. It does this by treating kinship care as a context that affects and is affected by mechanisms. It does not pretend that all contexts are the same, but can advocate for what kinds of contexts can allow for the emergence of desired outcomes by activating preferred generative mechanisms. Taking a critical realist approach to kinship care research means that the starting point would be an evaluation not about what works compared to other situations or 'placements', but rather about how it works, for whom it works, and under what circumstances (Pawson and Tilley, 1997). Breaking down kinship care as both a practice and a concept into mechanisms and understanding the role of morals and ethics means that lobbyists no longer have to utilise comparative arguments. Particular children's rights and needs, and the meeting of these, are judged on their own merits.

Critical realist research adds to the current research on kinship care, which usually conforms to traditional research notions of evidence-based practice, and many studies are primarily quantitative and atheoretical. Critical realism, emphasising the plurality of methods, allows quantitative and qualitative research to be seen together. They are both required and helpful, although some more than others. Therefore, the limited body of kinship care research can be examined in terms of judgmental rationality and an ongoing realist evaluation with continuous cycles of research and reflection.

How critical realism helps dialogical participation

The critical realist notion of fallibility is crucial to making participation more ethical and democratic. It can ensure everyone takes appropriate responsibility rather than pointing the finger of blame. It does not rely on individualism or cause unnecessary responsibilisation (Alderson, 2013). Also, while fallibility does not necessarily allow us to get to the ultimate truth, it at least acknowledges there is one. This sceptical honesty will enable us to at least strive towards truth rather than dismissing findings or seeing them as conclusive facts. For example, because of their changeable nature, participants' accounts must never be accepted as straightforward evidence. They must always be subject to theories regarding the mechanisms at play and the real underlying structures that shape such constructions (Cruickshank, 2007). Such questioning happens regardless of whether the participants are children or adults. Whether or not there is a belief that children are different or the same as adults in terms of their competence, reliability, and so on, such debates ultimately serve as distractions. No human has absolute control, power, or knowledge of reality. Reflexivity is, therefore, the key here, remembering that researchers' knowledge is also fallible. While the researcher may have expertise and authority regarding methods, knowledge of broader contexts, theories, or even outcomes of an action, these must also be open to scrutiny, criticism, and corroboration.

Critical realism, therefore, fortifies the process of dialogical participation as an ethic and a process. This ethic has the realisation that we depend on each other to form our views and to survive. We all, therefore, have responsibilities towards each other. This is due to our neediness and vulnerability. We also all have theories of the mechanisms at play, even if adults, including researchers, can feel that they are more able to articulate and speculate about them. We can all speculate on why things are as they are. This leads to participation being an 'I'll show you my theory; you show me yours', akin to Pawson and Tilley's (1997) proposal for realist evaluations. It lays the ground for participation being more than a one-off event and about dialogue. Participation becomes about the dialogical and the debates, the meeting in the middle, outing the inner conversations, and collectively navigating the relational space between the 'ought' and the 'is'. It is about not being persuaded by the monological or certain actors claiming authoritative knowledge.

Finally, it must be remembered that Bhaskar and Archer highlight the transformative potential of human agency. Focusing on structures rather than events enables us to address the root causes of oppression, but also such consciousness-raising is a crucial strategy for tackling it. Dialogical participation and the sharing and critique of knowledge are the first steps to social justice and having a positive impact. Under a critical realist lens, empowerment becomes less about an individual endeavour and more about a collective one. When critical realism is paired with dialogical participation, child participation can only be viewed as political, something emphasised as vital in the previous chapter.

The values that matter to the children living in kinship care

To ground the philosophical and methodological into the everyday, this section introduces the values highlighted by the children in the 'What matters to children living in kinship care' research. These values emerged through discussions with the children about what mattered to them. Together, as discussed in the next chapter, we developed theories using methods such as walking tours, photo-elicitation, drawings, and drama. It was essential to move beyond the surface of observed facts and experiences, the actual and empirical domain, to investigate what lies beneath in the real domain. As Norrie notes: 'Switching perspectives from the "extrinsic", descriptive and explanatory viewpoint to the intrinsic, first-person standpoint [when] we can see this moral sentiment is a first order capacity relating to what it means to be human ... at the core of human agency' (2009, pp 220–1).

To access the mechanisms in the real level of reality, the children were encouraged to be reflexive and make valuations of their lives rather than just provide descriptive answers (Easton, 2010). For example, instead of accepting descriptive answers such as 'pets', follow-up valuation questions were used, such as 'What do you think makes a good pet?' This encouraged the children to discuss the values that mattered for their lives to go well, as highlighted in Figure 5.2.

Figure 5.2: Values that mattered to the children who participated in the 'What matters to children living in kinship care' study

Many may see the diagram as the findings of the research. However, this is just the start of the findings, not the end. It is crucial to reflect on what such themes and insights really mean. It is vital to look at all values in conjunction and notice the spaces in between. These values are interesting, not because they suggest that children in kinship care need these things to have a good life. The purpose is not to focus on making large generalisations or for carers and social workers to aim for or to show these things without reflection. It is not about merely separating the 'ought' from the 'is'. Nor should the responsibility just rest on individuals. The reason why these values are interesting is that many of them seemingly contradict each other. How is it possible to feel special if you believe in fairness? How is it possible to obtain privacy if a goal is to also share with others? These values highlight not only what matters but also the seeming contradictions that are navigated in family life and relationships.

Further analysis of the values that mattered to the children living in kinship care

To further analyse the children's insights, abduction and retroduction were used in the research to identify the underlying generative mechanisms (Danermark et al, 2019). Abduction is also known as theoretical redescription. It uses inference to explain the phenomenon through interpretation and recontextualisation, using theories to help explain. As explained further in

Chapter 6, these theories were relayed back to the children and explained so they could understand and relate them to their lives. Throughout the collaborative process, theories could be changed, eliminated, and supplemented with new ones (Gilgun, 2015).

Retroduction was also used. To recap, this is the 'thinking backwards' from outcomes and effects to causes (Houston, 2010, p 82) so that findings do not just stay in the empirical or actual. The findings were relayed again to the children in the relational spaces we created through dialogical participation. The identified mechanisms were correlated with the children's views to ensure representation across the sample. Further abduction was then used to confirm explanations.

This back and forth, this realist analysis, was never a defined separate stage of the research process. It was not a case of trudging out and labelling a few themes, values, and mechanisms identified with the help of artificial intelligence or a computer software package. Instead, it was an ongoing reiterative process, with the children's help, of placing nuggets of information within their broader context. Alongside ongoing collaboration and reflexivity, this gave the children's insights relevance and rigour (Syed et al, 2010). Therefore, the quotes used in this book represent all participants, no matter their age, stage, gender, ethnicity, or status. They represent the underlying generative mechanisms that emerged and were discussed with all the children.

The central mechanisms for children living in kinship care regarding their family life and permanence

For the study, the mechanisms of 'connection/separation', 'recognition/(mis) recognition', and 'care and protection/independence and risk' emerged as tentative underlying generative mechanisms, as highlighted in Figure 5.3. These prominent strategies for the children emerged as the values that matter the most to them. They were core to how the children were doing family life and permanence in their kinship care arrangements. These mechanisms are the ways of being, thinking, motivating, and doing, and they are subject to potential activation through the contexts and conditions around them. These mechanisms were crucial for the children in kinship care arrangements in making family life work.

Although these mechanisms are distinct entities, they interact with each other. Food is an excellent example of this. Food was a significant topic of conversation with the children in the study. It is an everyday issue that is central to everybody's lives. Talking about food is an easy way to relate to one another, and a way to show concern without being too intrusive. This is similar to how European adults often talk about the weather (Iversen et al, 2022). Also, cooking a child's favourite food demonstrates care, connection,

Figure 5.3: Three central mechanisms that emerged from how the children in the study managed family life and permanence

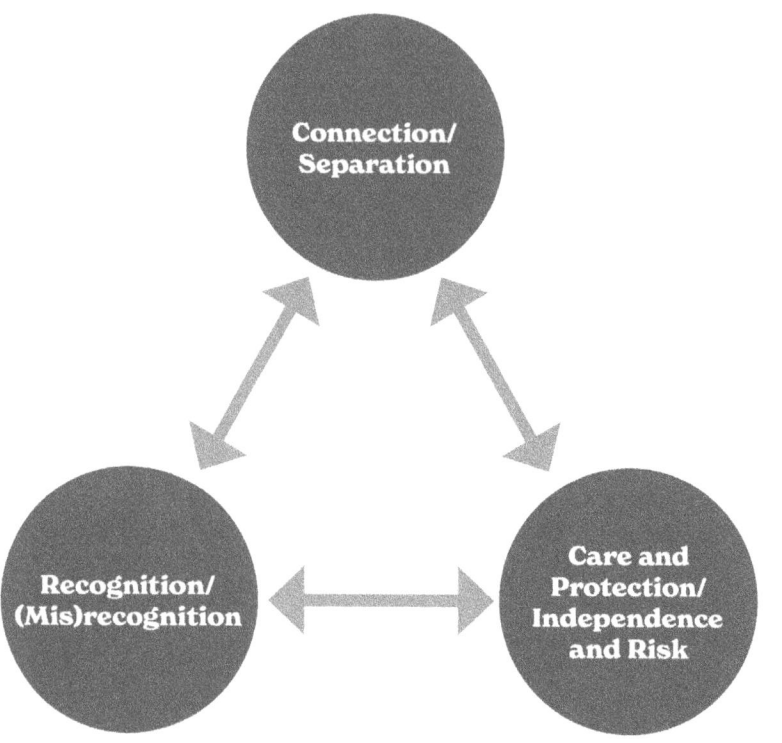

and recognition of their individual likes and dislikes. The children also spoke about how food marks celebratory events when family and friends come together, spend time with each other, share family and cultural recipes, and talk about the past, present, and future. Shared meals are social encounters in which values, emotions, and each mechanism play their part (Rees et al, 2012).

Conclusion

Integrating critical realism with dialogical participation into a 'what matters' approach offers a robust framework for understanding and improving child welfare practices, particularly for children in kinship care. This approach uses the strengths but also addresses the limitations often found in both positivist and interpretative methodologies. It acknowledges the importance of underlying values, social structures, and the material realities influencing children's lives without reducing everything to either primarily a language game or an obsession with prediction, quantification, and measurement.

Instead, critical realism's emphasis on the stratification of reality and the identification of generative mechanisms provides a deeper understanding of the complexities involved in child welfare and family life. It moves beyond surface-level observations to uncover the root causes, underlying mechanisms, and motivating values that shape experiences. This new approach can broaden our theoretical understanding and has practical implications for policy and practice, guiding us toward more effective and ethical interventions.

Ultimately, the 'what matters' approach provides a powerful tool for addressing the challenges and complexities of child welfare, kinship care, and permanence. It enables us to ask the right questions, make informed judgments, and collectively develop theoretically sound and practice-relevant solutions. Through retroduction, judgemental relativism, collaboration, and its ontological stance, critical realism allows researchers to get closer to the real and, with that, the truth. It enables an ethically charged social scientific truth claim, but one that is fallible and, like the participants' viewpoints, open to scrutiny, criticism, and corroboration. It helps stress the central role of participants' knowledge, agency, inner conversations, and valuations. This is particularly useful for those, such as children, who are usually labelled as 'not as good as' and whose voices are not readily heard.

For the 'What matters to children living in kinship care' study, the values that mattered to the children living in kinship care emerged as the mechanisms of 'connection/separation', 'care and protection/independence and risk', and 'recognition/(mis)recognition'. Before delving deeper into what each mechanism means, the next chapter further grounds the 'what matters' approach into practicalities and practice, and provides recommendations for its application.

6

Valuing ethics and 'what matters' participation approaches

> Grandma reminds me of who I am. She says I can do anything if I work hard and as long as I put my mind to it.
>
> Kimberley, child research participant

This chapter explores the essentials of ethical practice, introduces creative methods, and highlights the reflexivity essential for a dialogical 'what matters' approach. It draws on methods used in the 'What matters to children living in kinship care' study and suggests additional ones. While technical details about the research mechanics are available in my PhD thesis, this chapter takes a more reflective approach, connecting ethics and theoretical research concepts for the everyday practice of professionals in child welfare.

Social science researchers must acknowledge their positionality when undertaking research. Positionality refers to the contexts shaping a researcher, including viewpoints, approaches taken, self-identifications, experiences of marginalisation, and personal and professional privileges (Massoud, 2022). Acknowledging positionality is also necessary for child welfare practitioners (Chapman, 2023). It is crucial to recognise power relations and engage in meaningful reflexivity. Also, if, as previously argued, successful child participation encourages reflexivity among children by asking them what matters to them, it would be negligent and possibly hypocritical for us to avoid the challenging work of engaging in reflexivity ourselves.

I begin the chapter by exploring my positionality and promoting the need for ongoing reflexivity. A discussion on the ethics of research and practice follows this. It proposes that engaging children in conversations about ethical practice enhances ethics. Issues of consent, assent, confidentiality, anonymity, and accessibility are addressed within the context of research and child welfare practice. Critical realist and dialogically participative methods are again suggested to manage and mitigate assumptions and biases. Manzano's (2016) interview approach is highlighted for its collaborative, reflexive, and ethical nature, providing insights with relevance and rigour (see Syed et al, 2010). The chapter also shares methods such as Kitbag, child-led walking tours, photovoice, role-play, and checking in through words and pictures. These can be used in practice and in research to help spark everyday meaningful reflexive conversations with children.

Positionality

Critical realism advocates that participants' and researchers' values and reasoning play a significant part in any study. How a researcher sees the world impacts how they collect data, how they analyse it, and what they see as the purpose of research. It influences what they think is right or true. Ontological and epistemological assumptions of social science researchers – how they believe the world to be and how they believe we can learn about the world – should be stated (Longhofer and Floersch, 2014). Acknowledging one's own positionality is also vital. Such awareness is essential for qualitative research (Subramani, 2019) that is value-informed (Longhofer and Floersch, 2014) and theory-driven (Pawson and Tilley, 1997). It is vital for social work research, especially when researching children and families (Featherstone et al, 2014) and the febrile territory of family life for children in kinship care.

Previous chapters lay out the ontological assumptions that guide this book. They discuss the current tensions and monological debates surrounding kinship care, permanence, and child participation. These can cause ambivalence in child welfare research, practice, and policy making. It has also been shown that kinship care research is partial regarding the monological approaches taken, often neglecting children's views.

This book's epistemological assumptions are that children's views are invaluable for child welfare and kinship care. It is a child's right to have their family life experiences heard, but this also adds a new perspective to child welfare practice where permanence is the goal. By accessing children's experiences, we can gain a more attuned understanding of their family lives.

Regarding my positionality, I am a middle-class, White-presenting, half-Ashkenazi, half-English, cis male who is British, Reform Jewish, Queer, and approaching 50 years of age. I have lived in the UK for most of my life and hold a liberal egalitarian, mostly centre-Left standpoint regarding politics, social justice, social work, critical reflection, and anti-oppressive research. I am a registered social worker and an early-career social work academic and researcher with a PhD, an MSc, an MA, and a degree in psychology and drama.

I believe that removing children from their birth parents should only be a last resort for their safety and wellbeing. Families, individuals, and society can change, and social work's fundamental task is to help instigate positive changes (International Federation of Social Work, 2014). Regarding kinship care, my experience and knowledge suggest that local authorities and governments must appropriately support the whole family's needs. However, this is often not the case. I consider that risk is inadequately thought about, particularly when proposing kinship care as a panacea for removing children from their families. I also believe that families have valuable knowledge of their own experiences and situations, and their views should be included in all assessments, policy, and legislative changes. I often use critical realism in my thinking, although I do not label myself a critical realist. Finally, although I am close to my teenage nieces, I do not have and do not want children, which impacts my understanding of children and childhood.

My identities and beliefs are intricate, interconnected, and mutually supportive, although sometimes seemingly contradictory. I regularly utilise the intersectional approach commonly employed in social work (Mattsson, 2014). My identities and beliefs change in importance based on experiences and the environment, influencing my desire to reveal or conceal them. I have benefited from the advantages of possessing specific identities, beliefs, and traits, but I have also encountered marginalisation, victimisation, and violence because of them.

Ide and Beddoe (2024) propose that thinking about one's own positioning, power dynamics, status, and experiences is one of the first steps to undertaking reflexivity. Therefore, announcing my positionality may help to show that I am, at the very least, at the beginning stages of being reflective, insightful, and aware of my biases. However, this performative act also makes me vulnerable both personally and professionally. Others may not agree with how I have positioned myself or the labels I have provided. Using the word 'cis' remains controversial (Esacove, 2024), as does promoting my ethnicity as a half-Ashkenazi 'White presenting' Jewish person (Rubin, 2019). Even the word 'Queer' rather than 'gay', 'same-sex attracted', or 'homosexual' may evoke anger and discreditation from others (Butler, 1993). Some people may be dissatisfied that I hold centrist political ideals instead of being part of the radical far Left who are prepared to protest with a raised fist against neoliberal capitalist indoctrination that fuels social inequalities. Therefore, I am worried not only about receiving criticism for claiming my positionality but also about the potential devaluation of my work, professional reputation, and very personhood.

Reflection and reflexivity

Trying to be aware of my positionality and its impact requires reflexivity (Ide and Beddoe, 2024). Reflective practice and reflexivity are now widely accepted as necessary in contemporary social work (Watts, 2019). However, reflexivity remains a contested term (Subramani, 2019). Therefore, I use the definition put forward by Archer (2003), whose morphogenetic approach is often used in critical realist social work literature (for example, Houston, 2010). This has a more interactive outlook regarding structure and agency. Archer defines reflexivity as something that 'emphasises the autonomy of human agents, with interior thoughts that belong to them alone, but also that such agents reflect upon themselves in a relational fashion, in relationship to others and society' (2003, p 123).

Reflexivity is a complex, confusing, challenging, and emotive process. It involves constantly thinking through how agency and structure interact, highlighting what we can do, should do, will not do, and are powerless to do. This can cause a swirl of thoughts, emotions, and anxieties, sometimes keeping us awake at night. This is an example of engaging in reflexivity whether we wish to or not. The key is that it is not necessary to resolve the conflicts. It is not necessarily about privileging one position over the other. Instead, it is about outing the inner conversations by writing them down or talking about them. It is about confronting and acknowledging all the different actions and structures that push, pull, and position us. This is why reflexivity must be collaborative.

Overall, I try to achieve reflexivity through supervision, a research diary, physical activity, attending conferences, and input from children, families, peers, practitioners, students, and relevant organisations, such as the initial study's collaborating organisations, Kinship and CoramBAAF. Many of them are 'critical friends', as defined in feminist social work research by Appleton (2011). Through ongoing discussion, they challenge my work and help ensure its integrity.

Ethical practice

Ethical practice is aligned with protecting people from unnecessary suffering. It must be seen as an ongoing, complex collaborative process and as the foundation of any research design (Hugman, 2009). Research can influence creating and sustaining discourses, practices, and institutions, such as social work, which can benefit but also harm society (Yip et al, 2016). Bourdieu (1999) has even suggested that all research is a form of symbolic violence.

Unethical social work practice can perpetuate social injustice and harm (Wiegmann, 2017). Therefore, ethical awareness is also vital for child welfare and social work practice (Akhtar, 2013). Ethical awareness in my PhD research involved using Butler's (2002) code of ethics for social work research and applying the principles of the ethics of care, such as respect, integrity, and justice (Tronto, 1994). As a social worker, I also adhered to social work values (BASW, 2021), which require professionals to respect subjects' moral autonomy through honesty, competence, and informed consent.

The 'What matters to children living in kinship care' study aimed to implement ethically responsible procedures. For example, before meeting the children, the study design was submitted and approved by my university's ethical review process. This was with the understanding that, like child participatory practice, any ethical statement is only a starting point, should be considered the minimum statement of values, and is always provisional.

Additionally, ethical concerns for the study were addressed using a dialogical approach. The children were included in the conversations around the power dynamics between them and adults. The dialogical conversations about ethics happened at the very start and throughout the research. Many of the themes that the children and I discussed related to how much say children should have regarding their lives and who had a responsibility to keep them safe. We also discussed how others can perceive them as either vulnerable or able, and as potentially risky, troublesome youths (Lefevre et al, 2019). The children were instrumental in planning consent, assent, anonymity, and confidentiality. Including children in these conversations about ethics and power throughout every interaction can be applied in practice.

These processes aside, one of my primary concerns was that I actively encouraged the children to talk about their complex and often challenging lives. Was I trauma-mining them for my gain? The children provided me with research data, a PhD, and some kudos, and they enabled me to begin my academic career. This raised serious questions about my integrity, a value that greatly matters to me, and whether I was ultimately exploiting the children and their narratives. Was I engaging in the same behaviour that I had previously critiqued in others?

To attempt to mitigate this and ease my conscience, I considered financial payments and gifts for the children. Unfortunately, some literature warns that these can be counterproductive in equalising power relations (Zutlevics, 2016). Instead, I ensured that the children kept the photos they took for the study. I relied not only on previous research and articles, but also on my experience as a social work practitioner. Child welfare professionals should exercise caution when giving children unauthorised money or gifts in exchange for engagement. While this may be well-intentioned, it could contravene standards, such as those of social work practice (Social Work England, 2019), and it could even be perceived as a bribe in confrontational situations, such as in court. On reflection, it may be helpful next time, in line with dialogical participation, to ask the children how they wish to be compensated for their time, efforts, and disclosures.

Aside from the photos, the other benefit I offered to the children was a commitment that listening to them would have a meaningful impact on others and possibly even on them. A fundamental ethical principle of any research is that the participants do not disclose personal information for no reason (Alderson and Morrow, 2020). Effective and meaningful sharing of the children's views and the implications was a crucial part of the study and has been my focus for the last few years through presentations, podcasts, short films, book chapters, practice guides, journal articles, and this book. I have fought hard to make their views as accessible and impactful as possible by using various mediums. With the assistance of funders such as the Economic and Social Research Council, publishers like Policy Press, and publications like the *British Journal of Social Work*, we have managed to make as many publications as possible free and open access.

Gatekeepers, consent, and assent

In child participation research, gatekeepers are the people in the children's lives who are not being researched but provide access to those who are. They are vital as the intermediaries between the researchers and the children. In research, these are usually the people in the participants' lives with legal responsibility for their safety and wellbeing (Clark, 2011). In child welfare practice, they can be adults with parental rights and responsibilities or schools, health workers, and legal professionals. Gatekeepers are never neutral. They always have their own pressures, priorities, aims, and interests for the children and themselves (McFarland and Laird, 2020).

It is often assumed that gatekeepers must be sought for informed consent if a child is under 16 (Shaw et al, 2011). There are many debates around this, usually centring around perceived capacity and vulnerability. As proposed in Chapter 4, this perpetuates monological thinking. The debates also consider legal obligations such as those derived from the Gillick ruling (*Gillick v West Norfolk and Wisbech Area Health Authority* [1986] AC 112). The ruling states that if a child is under the age of 16 and is considered 'Gillick competent' – with 'sufficient understanding and intelligence' – they can restrict their parents from accessing their medical data. Such case law is not intended for research but may be applied to it. The debates will continue, but the fundamental principle is that consent must always be carefully considered. There may not be a definitive legal duty to obtain consent, but there is undoubtedly an ethical one (Robson and McCartan, 2015).

For the kinship care study, I gained permission from at least one person who held parental responsibilities and rights, alongside gaining permission from the children. As is typical for qualitative social work studies, I sought the children's informed assent, and the gatekeepers' consent was provided (Shaw and Holland, 2014). Assent and consent are words that are often used interchangeably, but they have distinct meanings. Assent is more about expressing agreement, while consent is more about granting permission.

Not only did the children provide assent, but they also signed their own consent forms. The children devised their signatures, as many had never been asked to sign consent forms. Although this was not legally necessary, it framed the study's collaborative approach and helped ease the power differentials between the adults and the children. It also demonstrated to the children that their views were significant and central to the study. This inclusion method can be beneficial in practice, particularly when children observe that their carers frequently need to sign documents and question why they are not considered important enough to do the same.

In line with the entire ethical approach for the study, gaining informed consent and assent was as much a process as an event. It did not just happen at the start of the study but continued throughout. Consent and assent were part of an ongoing dialogically participative process and more than just a set of procedures (Shaw and Holland, 2014). It was never assumed that the children were obliged to complete the research because they signed a form. Periodically throughout each session, children were again asked for their verbal assent. There was also an ongoing awareness of cues that the children were no longer comfortable or reluctant to relay further information. We devised a stock phrase: 'I don't want to talk about it'. And they were shown how to stop the recording device. It was vital that the children did not feel unnecessarily pressured and that they understood that the session could stop any time they wished.

Child welfare practitioners can also undertake to foreground this awareness by continuously checking in. Ongoing discussion around consent and assent are crucial components of child welfare practice. They ensure that children, families, and adults are given as much agency as possible to make ongoing informed decisions about the services they receive and whether they want to or feel safe enough to provide their views.

Confidentiality and anonymity

Maintaining the confidentiality of personal information and the anonymity of participants is crucial for research and practice, although an absolute assurance cannot be achieved. This is especially true if a child discloses information about them, or others, being at risk of significant harm (Wiles et al, 2008). In such circumstances, it is recognised that supervision, organisational guidance, and local government regulations are crucial, and national standards of conduct must be adhered to (Collingridge and Curry, 2020). The potential for breaking confidentiality and anonymity must be clearly explained to those we work alongside. Also, individuals and families must be assured that if confidentiality and anonymity are broken, they will be informed about the process as it happens (Segal, 2023).

Throughout the dialogical process, the children and I, and, if necessary, the carers, discussed and negotiated issues around confidentiality. For example, many carers frequently wished to be informed about the private concerns of the children under their care. They ultimately wanted to know what had been discussed. This can be an issue in practice, and other researchers have identified it as a concern (see, for example, Kirk, 2007). Therefore, at the first meeting, we all sat down and I clarified that any information provided would only be disclosed to the carers if deemed absolutely necessary. On further discussion with the children, most said they wished to let their carers know what was discussed anyway, as they did not want to keep secrets.

Anonymity was also negotiated with the children. All the children chose their pseudonyms, which enabled them to feel a level of agency and ownership. A few children wished to become famous through research; as Sydney said: 'Yeah, but people are going to see me in the big report, though, and be like, "Hello, Sydney?" [Pause] Yay. Will I be famous?' Rather than flatly denouncing this or suggesting this may be an unrealistic expectation of our study or a subsequent book, I used a 'what matters' valuation question, asking why fame mattered. We then discussed the benefits and drawbacks of celebrity. Sydney eventually decided she would be content if her family and friends, people she cared about, knew who she was in the study rather than strangers who she concluded might say negative things about her.

Safety for home sessions and mobilised research and practice

Critical realism advocates that research should be undertaken in an open system. It considers that a closed system, where variables are controlled, is impossible for social science. Therefore, the sessions, like most child welfare practice, took place in the family home and, for the walking tours, the child's community. To help the children feel as safe as possible, at least one carer who held parental responsibility was present when we met in the family home. Doors to rooms were left open to safeguard against allegations. When the children showed me around their neighbourhood, permission was sought from the carers, mobile numbers were swapped, and we were always in public view. At the beginning of each session, it was discussed that the children's carers would try not to overhear, but they may inadvertently do so. Ensuring confidentiality and the safety of both the social worker and the individual requires careful consideration and sharing of information in advance, particularly when the experiences can be emotional for all involved (Cook, 2020).

Providing information

The vital points of the information provided to the children involved in the research and their families were:

- the aims and methods of the study;
- that their participation was voluntary;
- their right to withdraw from specific questions or, indeed, the whole study;
- the meaning of confidentiality and anonymity;
- that I had a Disclosure and Barring Service background check and permission and letters from my university.

I conveyed this information through multiple mediums, such as the project website, information sheets, emails, telephone conversations, and visual methods. It was recognised that there had to be appropriately tailored information, in different forms, for various individuals with a range of needs and developmental stages (Beresford, 1997). Presenting the information in these ways did not replace discussing it with children before starting each interview or activity (O'Reilly and Dolan, 2016). Repeatedly talking about the aims of our discussions also helped us maintain focus.

These different methods of relaying information and reiterating the intent of time spent together should be applied to practice. It should never be assumed that children automatically understand what is happening and what will happen just because it has been discussed once or because you have shown them a sheet of paper. Information can be relayed to children and their whole family through talking, information sheets, and age-appropriate books, films, YouTube videos, and other social media (Lefevre, 2018).

Defining ourselves and our role

One significant challenge I have faced when transitioning from being a practitioner to a researcher was determining how to define and present my professional identity. I am proud to be a social worker and do not wish to erase this as part of my identity. Also, research suggests that if the researcher has been introduced as a trusted professional, carers are more likely to provide consent (Cree et al, 2002). However, many families who have had social work intervention have not had positive experiences with social workers. Many approach social workers with trepidation and bias (Bekaert et al, 2021). For kinship care, some families no longer wish to have social workers (McGrath, 2021). Nevertheless, I had to be transparent about the study being social work research that addresses social work practice.

After months of consideration and possible overthinking, I decided that calling myself a social work researcher would be the most honest reflection of my role. Positioning myself this way was not without difficulties and may have been futile. It did not seem to matter how I labelled myself. Instead, how others labelled and positioned me seemed more important. Often, the families prescribed a role regardless of how I had introduced myself. Harmony said: 'So then, you're a social worker? It's OK. Like, I've had good ones and bad ones.' Additionally, positioning me as a social worker rather than a researcher, several carers would approach me after I had seen the children, seeking legal or practical guidance. As the research progressed, this decreased, as I remained resolute in labelling myself as a social work researcher. with an emphasis on researcher, I also managed to distance myself by referring the families to other services, such as legal and health services and the Kinship advice line. Ironically, signposting and ensuring a multi-agency response is a core social work task (Morris, 2008).

Timetabling and flexibility

Setting up meetings and sessions and engaging with children involves a lot of physical and emotional labour (Groundwater-Smith et al, 2015). For the research, I ensured I would visit a maximum of two families in a day. This space enabled me to maintain focus and be present throughout my meetings. A four-month gap between sessions with the children also allowed me to reflect, analyse, collaborate, and align potential theories before discussing them with the children. These gaps were in stark contrast to my practice, where I would often have three or more children to visit each day and short timescales for assessments. It has been shown that such intense daily workloads, which entail emotional labour, can lead to poor relationship-building and engagement (Winter et al, 2019). Therefore, organisations, managers, society, and social workers must be mindful of the emotional labour involved in child welfare practice and provide space for reflection, but this should be balanced with how children experience this practice. Again, an open, honest, dialogical conversation is best practice.

Despite my enthusiasm for and commitment to the study, this was not always returned by the carers. I became aware that the research was often yet another external demand and yet another appointment to schedule in the family diaries (Cree et al, 2002). I spent much time reminding some families about plans and renegotiating them. Also, while gatekeepers have a positive function in protecting children from potentially anxiety-producing visits and research, they can use their position to censor children or stop them from engaging (Goredema-Braid, 2010). This protectionism is especially true for children living away from their birth parents, many of whom are likely to have experienced abuse and neglect (Kirk, 2007).

The gatekeepers and the families may also have experienced inadequate services or resources due to cutbacks. They can become weary of professional research and sceptical about the benefits of social work (Cree et al, 2002). Equally, the gatekeepers may coerce the children into participating so that the adults can put forward their concerns through the children (Harden et al, 2000). A patient, empathetic, and flexible approach, with consistent communication, is required for research and practice, and all experiences should be acknowledged by discussing the issues when they arise (Leigh et al, 2020).

Collaborative theory building

As alluded to in the previous chapter, a 'what matters' approach to child participation includes theory building along with children. Theories were embedded in the research sessions. I found that just as researchers and practitioners learn from an encounter, so should children and families. Shared learning exemplifies research and participation with children rather than on children. It also ensures that researchers and practitioners do not depend on the prevailing developmental, psychosocial, or socialisation theories, which may not accurately reflect the realities of children's lives.

The children were keen to let me know if the theories that emerged did not fully apply.

Manzano (2016) provides a helpful interviewing sequence to allow for theory building. This interview structure became the foundation of the study's planning. I now use this in practice to assess potential kinship carers. Manzano's sequencing employs the principles of critical realism's teacher–learner cycle (Pawson and Tilley, 1997) and dialogical participation (Facca et al, 2020).

Manzano (2016) suggests three critical realist qualitative research design phases:

- Phase 1: Theory-gleaning interviews. Exploratory questions are asked about the participants' experiences and valuations.
- Phase 2: Theory refinement interviews. Less standardised and more tailor-made questions, derived from previous answers, are asked.
- Phase 3: Theory consolidation interviews. The interviewer and the participant revisit the theories and consolidate them with further insights. These either 'inspire/validate/falsify/modify' hypotheses (Pawson, 1996, p 295).

Although children should theory-build alongside the researcher or practitioner, it was still essential to maintain overall control in the interviews. Researcher and practitioner knowledge and experience mean they are experts in the processes involved and in how and in what context issues should be investigated (Pawson, 1996).

Professional expertise must also be balanced with the children's expertise in identifying the issues that matter to them most. My general attitude is now that of a competent professional willing to learn from others but also an 'amiable incompetent' (Abbott and Sapsford, 1998, p 112). I hope to present myself as someone friendly, purposeful, and intelligent but also as someone who lacks specific knowledge about lived experiences and is open to being told certain things.

By combining Manzano's (2016) interview sequence and dialogical participatory methods, the primary task of the first phase of the PhD research sessions was walking tours. For the second phase, we used photos the children took to elicit conversation, maps, and role-play. For the third phase, we used symbols and pictures to see if we had represented all that mattered to the children.

Different methods for child participation and theory building

This section looks at tools and methods that can be used for each phase of Manzano's interview sequence. Although their use has been proposed in this sequence, different tools can be used at various stages of the researcher–child and practitioner–child relationship. The priority is ensuring that engagement and various communication approaches can be attempted (Ruch et al, 2020). The children themselves can be excellent guides in teaching us new ways and methods of listening. If only as a matter of participation's founding principle, children's insights should inform how child participation is thought about and undertaken.

Collecting data and information about people's lives requires professionals to be flexible, adaptive, and ready to accommodate the unexpected (Greig et al, 2007). It is essential to be mindful of the different ways that people communicate. Participation with children must be person-friendly rather than dividing methods into child-friendly and adult-friendly. Participation must attend to the various abilities and needs, whether participants are adults or children (Punch, 2002).

Phase 1

The first phase of interviews, the theory-gleaning interviews (Manzano, 2016), aimed to determine the outcomes the children wish for their family life. This is akin to Pawson and Tilley's (1997) 'outcomes = mechanisms + contexts' model, discussed in the previous chapter. Central outcome-focused valuation 'what matters' questions for kinship care research with children were: What matters to you? What makes a good family life? What makes a good parent? What makes a good social worker?

We also discussed the moral orientations and values that the children deemed essential for leading a good life. This allowed an examination of the 'ought/is' for the children (Sayer, 2019). For example, one of the study questions asked the children what they thought their family motto should be.

Kitbag

The Kitbag was not used in the research study, although I have used this tool since and found it invaluable for setting up the relational spaces required for dialogical participation. When practitioners and researchers meet with children, the primary goal is to establish a trusting, respectful relationship and create the calmest, safest space possible, where everyone feels present. It is vital to build a rapport (Dianiska et al, 2024). This is often more challenging than it may initially seem. Children may already have had many different professionals and adults in their lives. It can also be difficult for the professionals, who likely have had many conflicting thoughts going through their heads that day and many different priorities to address.

Kitbag is a multisensory, person-centred resource that helps centre young people, children, and adults so they feel better placed to talk about their feelings. Further information can be found at International Futures Forum (nd). As shown in Figure 6.1, the Kitbag has different objects bound together in a soft cotton wrap with a ribbon. It contains calming oil, presence cards, feelings cards, a talking stick, three-minute and one-minute timers, animal cards, a wonder journey relaxation and exercise booklet, and finger puppets.

The development of Kitbag was informed by research on psychological capacity. Psychological capacity is the ability to manage our psychological responses to being stressed, troubled, or overwhelmed (Hannah, 2008). Kitbag is designed to help people cultivate the mindfulness, resilience, reflection, and inner resources required to navigate today's uncertain, complex, and demanding world more effectively. It allows children, and adults, space and time to work at their own pace while encouraging them to work physically, emotionally, mentally, and behaviourally. It should be seen as more of a cultural intervention than a therapeutic one. It promotes holistic self-care and self-help and can help create more compassionate, caring, and responsible communities in homes, schools, and workplaces.

One of the main benefits I have discovered about Kitbag for initial meetings with children is that it is tactile and offers third objects for interaction. This grants permission for children to not have direct eye contact and pause, distract, and focus the conversation as they wish (Mannay, 2015). The Kitbag promotes play and curiosity alongside adults, and I also often interact with the contents, making power differentials less uneven. Lastly, the calming oil and the timers can promote mindfulness and encourage the users to feel present.

Figure 6.1: Kitbag contents

Source: Image from International Futures Forum (nd)

Child-led walking tours

In the study, we also used child-led tours, where the children take the researcher on a guided walk of their environment. There are now various types of child-led tours, including walk-along interviews, which were used in the research study and are among the most valuable types of child-led tours for practitioners (Veitch et al, 2020; Horgan et al, 2023; McFadden et al, 2023). The method used in the study was an amalgamation of the docent method by Chang (2017) and the more conventional participatory walking interview suggested by Emmel and Clark (2009). Chang (2017) proposes that the participant is the expert who escorts the researcher around areas that are important to them. This allows the participant to choose where to go and how to get there. However, as proposed by Emmel and Clark (2009), it is vital for child participation that a researcher or professional maintains overall accountability for the encounter and takes responsibility for the safety and wellbeing of the children.

For the study, we negotiated beforehand where the tour would be. The children were asked to show me what mattered to them and where they would like to take me for the walking tour. This had the following advantages:

- Although this had to be negotiated, the children primarily controlled what was shown, the walk's length, and the route followed (Emmel and Clark, 2009).
- The children did not have to maintain eye contact, which can be intimidating for many (Trell and Hoven, 2010).
- The tours allowed for natural pauses, such as when opening doors and picking up objects. This diminished some of the awkwardness of silence and allowed the children time to think before they spoke. They were also less likely to focus on what they felt I wanted to hear.
- The tours provided a sense of connection between the environment and the body. It afforded a greater embodied action than just voice and gesticulation (Evans and Jones, 2011). The children literally showed me how their spatial practices are embodied and experienced.
- We did not lose sight of the real, the material, or the reverent (Bhaskar, 2008a). The children often showed me precisely what they were talking about and why it mattered to them.

For practitioners, child-led walking tours are not necessarily viewed by organisations as a time-efficient way to access a child's family life. This reluctance is despite research indicating that the practice of new mobilities in social work, such as having discussions during walks or vehicle rides, can encourage engagement with children and their families (Ferguson, 2009a; 2010b; 2010c).

Phase 2

The main aim of the second phase of theory building was to refine theories and themes (Manzano, 2016). Topics discussed in the Phase 1 sessions provided further direct questions and conversation themes.

Visual methods

Visual methods are becoming recognised as valuable and innovative approaches for research and child welfare practice (Clark and Morriss, 2017). They can also be helpful as part of digital methods. Digital methods and the ethical practices surrounding them are still in their relative infancy. However, following the COVID-19 pandemic, digital methods have provided new opportunities for creativity, accessibility and engagement (Thunberg and Arnell, 2022). For practice, while virtual social work should not replace face-to-face interactions, which are often a more inclusive and sensory experience, a hybrid flexible approach that includes the virtual and real can be beneficial (Pink et al, 2022).

Visual research methods are based on a visual element, such as drawing, photos, mapping, videos, paintings, and so on, to engage participants. For the research, they provided an innovative way to collect information and helped the children communicate in a manner they may have been familiar with, making the process fun and engaging. Nolas and Varvantakis (2017) also speak to the impact of visuals, which can be powerful when showing findings to others. They can provide insight into complex, emotional, and sensitive issues that can be difficult to vocalise. Visual methods also help researchers empathise with participants (Clark and Morriss, 2017).

Social work frequently employs genograms and eco-maps as visual tools to illustrate the significance of relationships surrounding children and adults (Rogers, 2017). I used these tools to help discuss sociological theories of family dynamics with the children (Morgan, 2011). The genograms and eco-maps were adapted to focus on the question 'What relationships matter to you?' Genograms, which often resemble simple family tree diagrams (Carter and McGoldrick, 1989), were particularly useful for children who preferred structured representations. Older children tended to favour them. In contrast, eco-maps offered a more flexible approach, allowing the children to creatively depict their relationships using drawings and movable objects, such as LOL Dolls (Hartman, 1995).

During our research sessions, many children were naturally drawn to the pens, paper, and stickers used for creating genograms and eco-maps. They often picked them up while we were talking and used them to doodle or create pictures to help express their thoughts. For instance, when asked 'What makes a good social worker?', some children chose to draw and annotate their answers. Engagement with these visual tools was just as useful as the visual depiction itself (Turnell and Essex, 2014).

Photovoice

Photovoice is often confused with photo-elicitation (Clark and Morriss, 2017). Photo-elicitation simply inserts photographs into research interviews as a talking point to stimulate conversation (Dockett et al, 2017). For photo-elicitation, photos represent talking points and do not need to be taken by the participants. In contrast, with photovoice, the participants have an active role in taking and interpreting the photos. This is said to reveal deeper understandings, beliefs, values, and meanings. Initially developed by Wang and Burris (1997), photovoice was explicitly designed to involve individuals from marginalised segments of society.

Photovoice allowed me to see parts of children's lives that otherwise may not have been visible. It can be a persuasive means of communication, enabling the participants to explore and reflect on the often taken-for-granted things in their lives in innovative ways (Loeffler, 2005). Taking photos can distance participants from what they are typically immersed in, as things must literally be viewed differently. The photo taken can also act as an extension of memory and as a memory anchor (Shaw, 2020). Overall, the images and actions of taking photos represent an intersection between personal biography, politics, culture, positionality, and aesthetics (Edwards, 1994).

Photovoice also disrupted the typical power disparities of an interview (Goldman-Segall and Goldman, 2014). For example, the children were more able to lead the conversation when producing their own pictures. Using an object in interviews, such as a photo, can aid verbally restricted, reticent, or socially distant participants (Bahn and Barratt-Pugh, 2013). The children also altered the pace and shape the conversation by either remaining on specific pictures or swiftly moving on (White et al, 2010). Photos were held, compared, and turned over. They were objects that could allow a sense of security. In my sessions with the children, I noted how they often talked into the photographs about complex emotive issues. Also, they could avoid making eye contact with me when they were clasping a photo as evidence of what they said. Presenting photos seemed to reduce the strangeness of interviewing because it was like showing a family album or sharing photos on a phone (Tinkler, 2013).

Kolb (2008) recommends four stages to photovoice. First, participants are presented with a question. They then explore the most efficient way to capture images that accurately convey an answer. This triggers a cognitive process, as individuals contemplate before entering the second or active phase, where they take the photos. For the study, the children were provided with disposable cameras ('is this what you had in the olden days?') following the initial meeting. They were simply asked to take pictures of 'what matters' to them. Due to consent and confidentiality issues, and to be polite, the children were told to ask permission from people before taking their photos. We negotiated ground rules and ethical practices before and during the task. After the children took their pictures, the film rolls were sent to me at the university. The photos were then developed.

For the third stage of photovoice, the children opened the pack of photographs at our next meeting and could show me some, all, or none of the photos. This allowed the children to maintain some control over any disclosures or any pictures that they later deemed sensitive or inappropriate. The photographs were then used to generate dialogue grounded in the meaning of their lifeworld. The process provided engagement and empowerment in the research process through the participants' actions and narration. It enabled the participants to become researchers in their own cultures and lives (White et al, 2010). The children in the study spoke enthusiastically about being given an independent research project within the study.

As with all child participation, there needs to be some caution and reflexivity. Using photos in interviews alone does not empower children, and the issue of representation when using photos in research remains a contested issue (Rogers, 2017). As discussed in the previous chapter, participatory methods like photovoice, particularly with children, can adhere to hard social constructivism. Therefore, images can be open to many interpretations and 'truths', particularly if the interviewer is the person making interpretations. It has also been argued that taking photos is not just about capturing representations but also about 'compressed performances' (Pinney, 2004, p 8). This is especially true with photovoice, where participants show and then talk about what is shown (Hodgetts et al, 2007). Therefore, ongoing reflexivity regarding positionality, bias, and the methodology used to collect and interpret information was crucial when employing photovoice (Dockett et al, 2017). I spoke to many of my peers and the children about the benefits and challenges of using and interpreting photos.

Drama and role-play

Role-play and other drama activities can also be used to engage children. These were not initially included in the study design. Their inclusion was an excellent example of the reflexive and dialogical participatory research approach that developed with collaboration. In the first interviews, one of the themes that emerged was how the children viewed themselves and how others viewed them. I attempted to explain the basic tenets of recognition theory to the children (Honneth, 1996). As such, I asked the children in the second interview: 'How would you describe yourself?' and 'How would others describe you?' They often said, 'I'm me' or used other abstract responses. These are great answers, but I struggled to make sense of them for my research. However, one child, who must have seen the puzzlement on my face, suggested, 'Do you mean how would you introduce yourself?' This seemed a helpful way to ask the children the same question. In a subsequent interview, a child who was incredibly energetic and who I had difficulty focusing throughout the interview told me she loved drama. Therefore, we played a game where we pretended to meet at a party and had to describe ourselves. This kind of role-play re-engaged the child with the interview. The child's suggested participatory method highlights that they are often best placed to know how to communicate and engage with them.

Drama is not often used in social work research or practice, even with basic imaginary play and role play (Shaw and Holland, 2014). It is only traditionally used for training child welfare and education practitioners (McMullin et al, 2023). However, both Wulff et al (2010) and an ethnodrama researcher, Fabian, state that some types of knowledge can be represented 'only through action, enactment, or performance' (Fabian, 1990, p 6). It draws out responses in ways that are tacit, spontaneous, and embodied rather than merely cognitive.

Phase 3

According to Manzano (2016), the final phase of interviews is theory consolidation. Initial findings and analyses were reflected back to the children to ensure we had all listened and understood appropriately (Manzano, 2016). The themes, explanations, and theories still needed to 'earn their way' into the final analysis or assessment and show 'practical adequacy' to provide an explanation (Sayer, 2000, p 43). In line with the realist studies, which evaluate the effectiveness of theories (Pawson, 2013), meaning saturation, rather than data saturation, should be sought (Hennink et al, 2017). It is not necessary for all the children to precisely repeat what is being said by others for a study to be complete. It is more important that the same theories that explain their different views, values, and circumstances keep being inferred.

Reviewing with the child

For the study's final phase interviews, visual methods were used alongside another interview template bespoke to each child. It adapted another tool, the 'Words and Pictures' explanation (Hiles et al, 2008). I showed a picture of themes gathered so far, as shown in Figure 6.2, and then we

Figure 6.2: Images used to elicit words and pictures narratives with the children

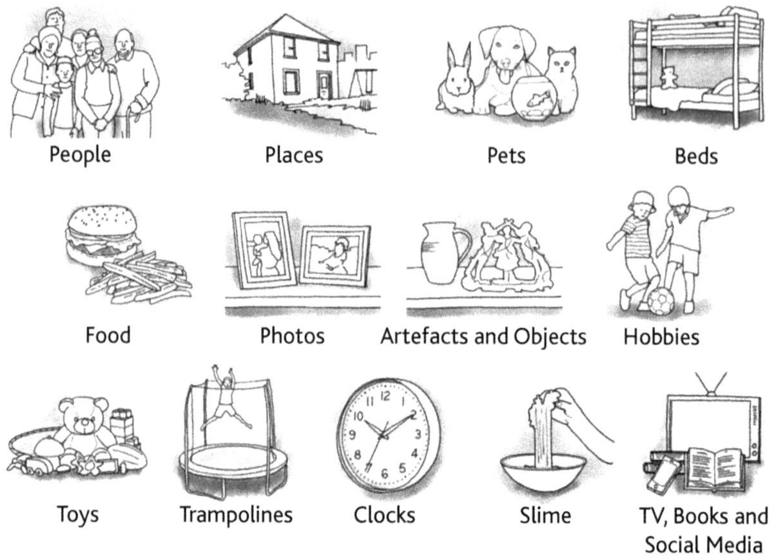

People	Places	Pets	Beds
Food	Photos	Artefacts and Objects	Hobbies
Toys	Trampolines	Clocks	Slime	TV, Books and Social Media

co-constructed a story around them, titled 'What matters to children living in kinship care'. The children usually narrated a day-in-the-life story.

We reiterated different theories or explanations that helped account for why each thing they spoke about mattered. At the end of the interviews, the children were asked a set of questions that explicitly allowed them to have a final reflexive space to explore the inner conversations and mechanisms they had previously highlighted. For example, they were asked 'What's the difference between children and adults?'

Conclusion

Ongoing collaboration, dialogical participation, critical realism, and a 'what matters' approach helped develop the research methodology and task-based methods (which can also be used in practice). This also ensured a continuous critique of the suitability of theories that emerged from the study. It promoted reflection and reflexivity through the continuous rechecking of my positionality. Most importantly, working in partnership helped ground the overall focus of the study. It ensured that I never lost sight of how the research could improve child welfare practice for children living in kinship care. It allowed me to ensure that theories struck a chord with families and practitioners and that the research would mean something and matter. The ongoing collaboration ensured that the children's views became a valuable resource for the methods used as well as having policy and practice implications. As seen in the following chapters, it allowed their perspectives to produce profound insights that address the everyday realities of family life, child welfare practice, and permanency planning for children living in kinship care arrangements.

7

Valuing connection/separation

> Family are part of your life, and you sometimes get to see them, or you don't. You just like, you know that they are there with you, looking out for you, but like not in your house or near.
>
> Danielle, child research participant

This chapter and the two that follow next expand on the existing knowledge of kinship care, child welfare, permanence, and child participation highlighted in previous chapters. They illuminate the perspectives of the children involved in the 'What matters to children living in kinship care' study and illustrate the value of the 'what matters' approach. These chapters explore how three mechanisms that emerged from the children's views interconnect for those living in kinship care. The chapter focuses on the 'connection/separation' mechanism, as shown in Figure 7.1, which demonstrates how children in kinship care understand and navigate the ambivalences of family relationships.

The children's valuation of connection/separation disrupts the static, monological interpretations of family that persist in kinship care and other child welfare research, policy, and practice. These monological perspectives can suggest that family life can only be one thing or another. The first part of this chapter shows how the children in the study conceptualise the fuzzy, ambivalent boundaries and definitions of family life, along with the spaces between absence and presence, as illustrated by the quote from Danielle. The second part illuminates how the children navigate this by sharing time, space, and narratives. The final part of the chapter proposes how child welfare practice can be improved by considering the children's meanings of family. Imposing rigid binary categories on children's family circumstances presents an unrealistic portrayal of their lives. Instead, there needs to be greater consideration of a child's current agency and their ability to define and manage their experiences.

What does family mean for the children?

Presence and absence: The many ways to 'be there'

Most child welfare processes are motivated to enhance the daily interactions between children, family members, and professionals who are, or can be,

Valuing connection/separation

Figure 7.1: Connection/separation – one of the three central mechanisms that emerged from how the children in the study managed family life and permanence

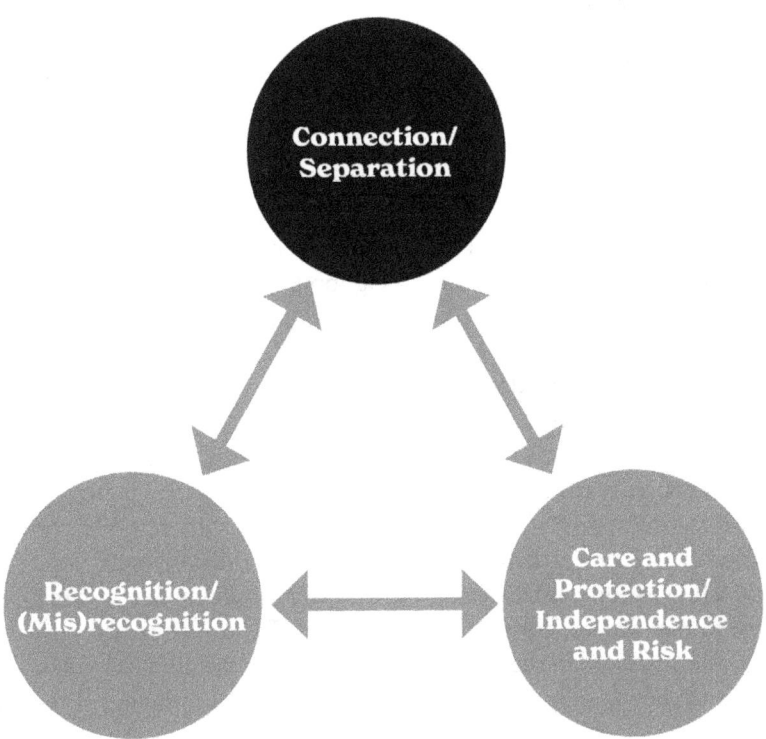

physically present in their lives. For example, documents such as contact plans, parenting agreements, and support plans emphasise physical presence. It is more straightforward to manage and understand what can be seen and easily quantified, or as critical realists may say, manage the 'empirical' and the 'actual'.

Focusing on what can be observed resonated with the children in the 'What matters to children living in kinship care' study. They considered the people around them and how each family member could contribute to family life. The children also thought about the unseen mechanisms and connections and the less readily apparent possibilities and opportunities. They also considered the 'what ifs' and the influence of people not physically there, including their own prospective children. They possessed a more expansive intergenerational perspective that encompassed not only physical presence but also intent and purposeful engagement. Megan said:

> You can kind of tell when someone's from a family where they, like, it's a strong family unit [or] somebody's from somewhere where they, like,

they don't really make any effort with each other. So, I just feel like, for me, if I've always got family around me and I've always got some who will hopefully support me … And I should have somewhere to go if I need to. You never know definitely, but it'll be nice to know that if I have that in the future for my children and stuff, that they can get the benefits out of that as well.

The children also contemplated the influence of past connections, especially the deceased. Death was a topic all the children mentioned in every research encounter. The children felt a strong need to engage in conversations about the death of their loved ones, pets, neighbours, and community members. A reason for this may be that kinship carers are typically older compared to non-kinship carers (Selwyn and Nandy, 2014). Danielle, for example, stated: 'because your life doesn't end. Because if someone dies, you still have their life in your heart.'

One's initial response to their pervasive thoughts about death may be compassion, empathy, and sadness for the children. Engaging in daily reflections on mortality may seem too macabre for children. However, the children showed remarkable calmness rather than distress when discussing death. This relational space between loss/separation and presence/connection appeared manageable for them to talk about. Even if they had never met those who mattered in their family while alive, the children still spoke about them, and they usually celebrated their presence and influence. Erica said:

And this is over there, the shelves. That's our great grandma, our grandma's mum, and we never got to see her. She died when Grandma was seven years old. But, erm, we've seen pictures of her, and Grandma looks like her, and she's very beautiful. And Grandma says we get, she gets her good looks from her, and we get erm … good looks from her as well.

Children's conceptions of absence and presence were also fuzzy for adults who were still physically around daily. This was demonstrated by Thomas, who talked about his current kinship carer having an omnipresence and an X-ray superpower: 'Nanny can see through walls because she knows what I'm doing.'

The children recognised these transitory, in-between spaces in various imaginative ways and, by first acknowledging their existence, regularly created novel strategies to navigate their relationships. Rainbow, for example, learned new skills and formed new routines to keep in touch with her sister after she moved to Australia. Rainbow said: 'Although my sister is not here, I can see her by phone, by computer and by things that she's given to me, like love. And I talk about people that aren't here every day. And I have pictures of them. And this [shows a card], it says sisters will be forever friends. And my sister's fiancé taught me how to ride a bike.'

The notion that the children did not perceive separation and connection in isolation, even when engaging in seemingly solitary activities like riding a bike, appeared throughout all our discussions. Therefore, the children and I discussed a theory that emerged from these experiences, understandings, and management of loss. They had learned to try and navigate the paradox that there is no such thing as total separation, not even in absence, and that others can reside within you, hopefully motivating you and helping you achieve, even when they are not physically present (Leitch, 2022).

The significance of this cannot be over-emphasised, particularly for children who have had numerous carers during their childhood. Separation and loss are prominent features of a child's experiences before and during care (Fahlberg, 2008). There are, however, various types of loss that can occur. Boss (2000) defines two types of ambiguous loss. Type 2 is psychological absence with physical presence, such as experiencing neglect due to parental substance abuse. Boss and others have also acknowledged Type 1 ambiguous loss, where there is psychological presence with physical absence, which is typified when children are removed from their primary caregivers (Samuels, 2009). Under such circumstances, children frequently consider the opinions and judgements of their previous carers, even without any direct contact with them. Children experience the interplay of separation and loss continuously, particularly in kinship care arrangements in which children are removed from a family but remain within it. The children's views demonstrate they are not working with monological ideals of absence and presence, the either/or, but rather working with the both/and.

Returning to in-between spaces of relations

Acknowledging the interplay of relational spaces is why the mechanisms highlighted in this book – 'connection/separation', 'recognition/(mis) recognition', 'care and protection/independence and risk' – include their antonyms, their opposite states. Rainbow talks about her sister being there yet not being there. So does Thomas. This aligns with Bhaskar's conceptualisations of absence and presence. Bhaskar states that there is no way that a purely present being, object, or event can exist without its opposite. For example, a room is made up not only of furniture but also of empty space. Also, absence or negativity always precedes presence and positivity (Bhaskar, 1993). There must be space to put furniture into. Applied to kinship care, children must have the necessary emotional space with their new carers to be able to accept their love and care. The complexities of managing absence and presence must also be acknowledged, as explained by Harmony:

> Yeah, it's important to have pictures of him because ... yeah ... we can't see him anymore. We like to have pictures of him to remember him, erm ... and the last time I saw him, erm, it was actually quite a hard time and sad. And everyone was saying to try and leave it and forget him as best I can. But he's my brother, yeah, and I can't. And erm, so after [my brother's] situation, erm, I remember I used to, like, cut my hands.

The complexities of the both/and when it comes to separation and connection are rarely recognised in the everyday. However, as demonstrated by Harmony, unless these are acknowledged, such as through daily interactions or therapeutic intervention, they can lead to disenfranchisement and manifest in harm, and they may never be resolved (Leitch, 2022).

How the children construct the fuzziness of family life

> We have friends that, like, it's her granddaughter and her ... they're not like our *family* family, [but] family like our extended family. And I'm talking about like great uncles that I see like once every so often. But it's like they're family because, like, they've made the effort to, like, be with us and stuff like that. And they're like [pause] that's all that makes it family. I think if they can make an effort to, like, want to spend time with you and stuff. I don't think for family you actually have to be ... related to you. I just feel like they have to want to relate with you.
>
> Eliza

Children who try to manage the in-between relational spaces of family life rely on the both/and being acknowledged and on their own beliefs of who should be included in their family. They contemplate who matters enough to engage in the challenging task of navigating connection/separation. Sydney said: 'Well, I've got Nan and Grandad, aunts and uncles, Mum and Dad, and Anna [not genetically related] who now lives with us. So, I call her family, because she is my family really. Oh god, I've got so much family, they keep popping in my head.'

The children described an abundance of genetically related family members, non-genetically related family, and those living in family spaces who were involved in their lives and care. They were adamant that all these different people could be family. Sometimes this could become overwhelming. This broad range of people considered family is not unusual for kinship care arrangements (Farmer, 2010). According to the children, those who were not genetically or legally family members, even those not living with the children, could be considered family. Louise said:

So, I'd say my karate sensei is part of the family. So, she'll make jokes about you all the time. So, if you done something wrong, to make a joke out of it, she protects you, she teaches you right and wrong and is always there so ... and very friendly.

Some children, such as Danielle, Purple, and Rainbow, broadened the meaning of family further and attributed familial relations and fraternity to their religious beliefs. Rainbow said:

They can have different blood to me, but God thinks we're a great big family, so like this is just an example .... So, yeah, [my friend] is my sister, but she's with someone else ... I mean, like so, basically, you're my brother but living with someone else, because God thinks we're all a great big family.

The more we made valuations about family for the study, the more complicated defining it became. Each child would have a particular way to distinguish between different types of family. Some would use terms such as proper family versus relatives: Lucy said: 'Well, I have family like I call proper, proper family, the people who I live with, and then, and then everyone else I call relatives because, I mean, they're related to me.'

Others used phrases such as close family versus extended family: Kimberley said: 'Yes, well, Grandma and Erica are my family, but then I have an extended family, like really close friends who were there, who take us out sometimes and, erm, they are always there for us, and I think like close friends are sort of family as well.'

Nevertheless, throughout our conversations, the children encountered inconsistencies in naming various family groups and subgroups. In many instances, this type of confusion became apparent regarding birth parents.

Paul: So, would you say that your birth mum and dad are relatives or family?

Lucy: I probably call them relatives, but then I might call them family. Well, I haven't seen Mummy in ages, and I haven't seen Daddy in ages, so I probably [pause]. I don't know, probably a bit of both.

It emerged that family was ever evolving for the children. The family members' positions were relational, fluid, and ever-changing. The children's classification of family and its members depended on roles, behaviours, and intent. Certain family members would not stop being family if they did not show consistent commitment and affection or keep the children safe. They did not become wholly absent and separated from the family. The children acknowledged this was impossible. Instead, poorly performing family members would be demoted from being considered proper family, close family, or even relations.

Kimberley: I see my, erm, like my aunties and uncles in Singapore, they're like my family as well, and I feel safe for them as well, and they take care of me as well. But my Mum and Dad, I don't really see them as family to me like anymore, because when we go and see them, I don't feel happy and safe with them and I don't feel like comfortable, and I was worried, erm, when I'm there, and I just want to go back home.

Paul: So how would you, what would you call them then, if they're not family?

Kimberley: Erm, I just called them Mum or Dad. Sometimes, I call them [N – mum's first name] or [B – dad's first name]. Cuz sometimes, when they make us upset, and I don't really see them as proper family to me, so sometimes I just call them [N] and [B].

The way family can shift and undergo change shows that the children understand family as something people do rather than something people are (Morgan, 2011). It moves away from idealised understandings of family often held in society and child welfare policy and practice. Williams (2004), in his influential book *Rethinking Families*, alludes to the diversity and fluidity of family practices. Morgan's (1996) notions of family practices support this, suggesting that family is not just a social institution. Family 'represents a quality rather than a thing' (Morgan, 1996, p 186). Rather than family being a noun, family should be viewed as a verb. It is an everyday practice and activity that we do. This sociological interpretation proposes that family should not be treated as a static group consisting of genealogical ties or legal bonds.

Nevertheless, caution must be exercised before endorsing such simplistic generalised suggestions that family simply means different things to different people. Such interpretations imply that family is merely a subjective, changeable social construct based on feelings, values, and beliefs. Instead, thinking in the in-between and using a critical realist viewpoint proposes that family cannot just be dismissed as a language game or a social construction (Bhaskar, 1989). Critical realism suggests that subjective interpretations are combined with a fixed reality independent of the mind and how the children think of family. Even though the children often had wide-ranging ideas about who could be family, they also knew that genetic ties meant that some family members would always remain family members even if you did not want them to be. Zack said: 'Everyone who I'm related to is important to me, even if you hate them. They're still important. Like have you heard the saying that you can't choose your family, but you can choose your friends. Like that.'

This reliance on genetic bonds to be considered part of family, rather than genetic bonds being the only way to define family, was reiterated by all the children. An additional focus on the ontological once again demonstrates the both/and. Genetic relatedness, being part of a household, future relationships, and time spent with others all interact with social and cultural attributes to form family composition. All these things matter. This is significant because more concrete, measurable things, such as the proximity of family members and the number of relations with genetic ties, can be just as crucial for a child's sense of family affiliation as how the children feel about them.

Relationships with birth parents

Echoing previous research, all the children showed ambivalence towards their parents (Kallinen, 2021). As demonstrated by Thomas, the children often had seemingly polarised views about their birth parents, frequently differing from one conversation to the next.

Thomas:	I don't like my mum, but I want her in my life.
Paul:	What about your dad then?
Thomas:	No. He doesn't do anything. He just does something bad and fights.

Later, in contradiction, Thomas spoke about wanting to see his father more.

Paul:	And you think you got them [action figures] from your dad for Christmas? So, how often do you see your dad?
Thomas:	Well, I think I got them from him coz he's a bit nice to me and buys things for me.
Paul:	Cool, so how often do you see your dad?
Thomas:	Well, I pretty much never see my dad. It'd be nice to see him a bit more.

The children often believed their relationship with their parents would change as they aged. They all took a life course perspective and considered their and their family's context, as demonstrated by Rainbow:

They're far away because they used to take drugs from me. Drugs and drink alcohol whilst they were with me, so then I had to be adopted. But I still love them even though they have just been mean to me.

I'll see them when I'm older. Not until I'm 13, and I can do martial arts – pew, pew, pew [pause]. In case they try to force me to drink alcohol and try and put a bag in my mouth, and then I'll pew, pew.

The conversations we had about their birth parents were often challenging for the children.

Paul: I see. So, you still love [your birth parents] then?
Louise: I don't really want to talk about it.

Louise provides a good example of the challenge of valuing birth parents. She illustrates how complex relationships and cognitive dissonance could cause the children to struggle even to discuss their relationships with their birth parents.

Siblings

Overall, the children felt more at ease when talking about their siblings compared to talking about their parents, although their relationships with siblings were still complex. The children spoke about their full siblings, half-siblings, step-siblings, and siblings who were living in the same house but were genetically aunts and uncles. They discussed siblings who had been adopted, siblings they had heard of but never seen, siblings who they were only allowed to see supervised, and siblings of half-siblings. This is despite minimal mention in kinship care literature and research regarding sibling relationships (Wellard et al, 2017). Furthermore, despite widespread commitment within UK policies to the principle of maintaining sibling relationships and research evidence supporting this principle, maintaining these relationships continues to be particularly challenging when children are not in the care of their birth parents (Moran et al, 2020).

The children often viewed sibling relationships as beneficial, because they felt they had a shared experience. The sibling relationships often predated their current family care arrangement and reduced the intensity of separation. Children with siblings were more likely to have others who could empathise with them and their situation. Siblings also gave them a sense of identity and groupness (Davies, 2015). Erica said: 'Kimberley, she really loves me, and she cares for me, and she, like, wherever we go or whatever we do. And we understand each other and sometimes talk in bed about, like, what's happened to us. And if grandma's not there, she protects me.'

Siblings, however, do not always get on, and their relationships vary according to personal and social factors. Therefore, the children displayed a spectrum of feelings toward their siblings. Siblings were affectionate, concerned, and responsible towards one another. However, there was also often hostility, rivalry, and even violence towards each other. Jake said: 'Yeah, I only like talking to [my sister] because when I actually see her, she actually just says "go away, you stupid, you bum head". And so sometimes, I kicked her by accident, like a Power Ranger.'

Rainbow liked that she had no siblings living with her. She understood that having siblings might have taken away some of the parental attention she received.

Rainbow: I'm happy to be the only one with my mum and dad.
Paul: So then why does it matter that just you lives with your mum and dad?
Rainbow: I like it because I get to spend time with them, whole weekends.

Punch (2005) proposes that children often acknowledge the legitimate authority of their carers when they consistently demonstrate their responsibility towards them and their ability to care for them. However, she suggests power dynamics among siblings are more contentious and prone to disagreement, often involving bargaining and physical force to achieve desired outcomes. Navigating these power relations can also depend on factors such as age difference, development, and the sense of responsibility that children may possess for each other. Zack said: 'Say you have a little brother, like, like siblings give you a responsibility, and it makes you a good person to look up to and things like that, like a good role model to some people.'

Overall, the children showed that having relationships with siblings can be an effective way to learn the complexities of socialisation and how to navigate complex ambivalent relationships. Siblings can also help with a sense of belonging and continuity and can prime a child for collective responsibility.

Pets

> Well, I would say that it is a family because you're sleeping with some pets, you stroke pets, you get to feed pets, which is the best thing about them. So basically, I would say that they were included.
>
> Jordan

Family members did not have to be human. According to the children, pets can also be family members (Cain, 1985). As previously mentioned, except for one household, all the children in the study had pets. One of the main reasons the children said pets were valuable was because they provided company while not talking back. Harmony said:

Because people can then go tell other people what you said, and they can also use it against you later. Like, you don't expect people will do things like that, but they do. And pets are just there for you. Like animals and dogs – like, they're just there for you.

The children also indicated that pets are a shared possession and responsibility, serving as a focal point to signify how the family unites (Sussman, 2016). Many would insist that pets help them develop responsibility and prepare for future caregiving obligations. However, when directly asked whether they fed their pets, cleaned out the dwellings, or took them for walks, most confessed they often did not fulfil these duties. Lucy said:

Well, I do try to look after them quite a lot, but Grandpa looks after them more because it's a bit too early for me to take them out. But I like the dogs because they're really nice and friendly. I love training them and stuff, and going on walks of them when I can, and growing up with them, and watching them get told off by Grandma.

The children often described pets as being calming family members who provided consistency and commitment. Kimberley said: 'I'd have a dog or a cat, and it's kind of like comfort or like a little friend, and it might not leave your side.' In this way, pets were part of the family that could provide them with care and even, as explored in the next chapter, a sense of permanence.

A growing sense of family

Despite all the various explanations of what constitutes family, all the children desired to feel part of a broader family. This is usual for children in kinship care arrangements (Biehal et al, 2010). One of the most illuminating and unique themes that arose from the children's valuations of what constitutes family was that it is ever-growing and developing. You could never lose family. Sydney said:

Yeah, I don't think, I don't know how you really lose family. [It is] in the galaxy man. But erm, I did get more family, which was my baby cousin. That was only one person. And then I'll get more and more, and more and more, and more, more, more, more family.

Eliza even suggested that a growing sense of family is one of the benefits of kinship care:

Well, for me, most people that I need, even if they're not like directly related to me, they're like, for me, they're still like family. So it's like, it's kind of not compensation, but it's like I've got so many other family members, so it kind of makes up for the fact that I don't have the, like, original house unit.

This further demonstrates that while the children felt a sense of loss due to their situation, this was accompanied by a sense of gain as they recognised that they would have multiple familial relationships throughout their childhoods and beyond. They illustrated how loss and gain, absence and presence, and connection and separation are not strict binaries. Instead, the children navigated the positives and negatives as they understood them on a continuum.

How children navigate family life

Sharing

> Yes, because it's important to go to different places because you can see the environments, erm, sometimes you can learn new things and you can see new things. And, erm, it's fun because sometimes, like when we went to Singapore, you can meet new people, or people that you have heard about but not seen before. And, erm, it was fun to do these things with Grandma and Erica.
>
> Kimberley

The second part of this connection/separation chapter elaborates on how and why children construct and differentiate between family members. It also demonstrates how they and others navigate the fuzzy boundaries of family life through sharing. The children often spoke about how sharing is intrinsic to a sense of family. This need to share experiences, narratives, time, and space was highlighted when all the children, like Kimberley, reiterated the importance of family holidays (Lehto et al, 2009). They also mentioned the sharing of pets, plants, time, and resources. They spoke about having a shared understanding of narratives and identities. Sharing events, responsibilities, and experiences is fundamental to positive family functioning (Freistadt and Strohschein, 2013). It helps build bonds and attachments, leading to a better sense of permanence in the family (Mayall, 2002).

Sharing space

The children often spoke about the use of space. An example of this was sharing a room with siblings. Child welfare practice and policy debates remain about whether sharing rooms is appropriate. In English legislation, the

Housing Act 1985 states that children over the age of ten of the opposite sex should have their own bedrooms; otherwise, this is considered overcrowding. Research by Bacon (2016) proposes that a child's bedroom is a haven where they can move away from dominating adult control, and depending on cultural expectations, it is usually established as a private space, preferably not to be shared. However, the children in the 'what matters' study were seemingly ambivalent about this.

Paul: What's it like sharing a room?

Purple: Erm, it's sometimes nice. It gets a bit crowded because Danielle always takes up most of the space. Although sometimes if you share a room you get to, like, to speak to your sibling at night-time, and also, we get to like play games together.

It was more important for the children that various spaces were available depending on the tasks they needed to carry out and their moods. They appreciated areas like living rooms where the whole family could be together. Nevertheless, they also valued spaces that were distinctly their own, such as a preferred chair in the living room or at the meal table. The children also appreciated space to be alone. Eliza said:

Yeah, because I share a room, and I don't ever feel like I don't have anywhere to go and just, like, build my own. So, I don't think it's necessarily about needing to have your own room. It's just like needing to know that there is somewhere that you can go if you need to be alone or whatever.

The children demonstrated that they were adept at managing their space in the home, mainly when they wanted to be alone to achieve privacy, agency, ownership, or restoration (Costa Santos et al, 2024). While emphasising the child's agency is crucial, it is also essential to highlight that inside the home, this is primarily facilitated by adults (Michelan and Correia, 2014). It is typically limited by household rules and adult supervision. It must be remembered that children's agency is a 'relational dynamic' (Spyrou et al, 2018, p 6) and children are interdependent with their context, including their family relations within the home.

Despite these boundaries, children would navigate these relational spaces to experience connection/separation. Beds are a good example of how shared and private spaces were often on the both/and continuum for the children. When describing what makes a home, most children in the study would look at their beds and refer to them. They were vital parts of their family lives.

Paul: When you're in your home, do you feel different than when you are in other places that aren't your home?
Rainbow: Yep, because my bed is sooo comfy, and the other beds seem like this floor [wooden floor]. And see how hard this floor is [stamps on the floor]. It's that hard.

For many children, beds helped them maintain a separation from the world and the worries around them. However, at the same time, beds also helped the children not feel alone, neglected, or wholly detached from others. For example, Unicorn wished her brother would not disturb her when she wanted to sleep: 'Sometimes, at bedtime, when I want to be on my own, my little brother comes in, and he just plays, but I don't want him to because I want my personal space when I'm in my bed.' Despite her assertion that she wanted to be alone when asleep, Unicorn also insisted on sleeping with over ten toys on her bed. These soft toys were given to her by her birth parents, her grandparents, and other family members. She also had to have a night light to avoid feeling scared and shut out.

Jake gives another example of managing the intricacies of both separation and connection and how navigating this tension is played out with the use of beds:

Jake: And sometimes when I wake up in the middle of the night, I always go into that bed [Jake takes me into his grandparents' room to show me some blankets on the floor next to their bed].
Paul: Why do you come and sleep in here?
Jake: 'Cos sometimes, I always wake up in the middle of the night. So, and I can't get back to sleep, so, 'cos my bed's uncomfortable. Because my bed's not the comfy one.

It is unlikely that the floor was physically comfier than his cabin bed. It is more probable that he felt more emotionally comfortable and comforted being near his grandparents. Many of the children reiterated this specific need for comfort when sleeping. They spoke about the importance of being able to sleep in your kinship carers' bedrooms when scared or worried. They wished to feel connected even when engaging in a seemingly solitary activity, such as sleeping.

Gardens were also important places where the children felt both connected and disconnected at the same time. Eliza said:

I feel like if I go to the garden, I'm out of the house, but I'm not like away from everyone. So, it's nice for me to just cool off, or think, or just going to sit and chill. But I'm not like detaching myself. But I also feel like it's a place where everything. Like, if you want to have people around and stuff and just have a good time, you can go and the garden and stuff.

Overall, spaces, places, and the use of the environment symbolised, and helped the children manage, the dynamic push and pull of relationships in their family lives. These everyday uses of children's spaces can be seen in ways that confirm and challenge their sense of affiliation, connection, and family functioning (Thornock et al, 2019).

Sharing time

> You don't have to do things with people. You can just, like, be with them … like watching a film could be one of the most specialest things in the life.
>
> Zac

The concept, or rather the context, of time permeated throughout the sessions. Pets, plants, people, and objects were often introduced by name, and the child put a time stamp on how long they had been in the family. Time was very much relative or, rather, relational to others. Lucy said:

> I don't know why, but I took a picture of the clock. I don't know why time is really important to me. Like sometimes I get worried if I don't know what the time is. I just really like having a clock. So, I don't know why. It just makes me feel kind of safe.

People often need to know the time to feel safe (Forman, 2015). Having some control and knowledge over what is to come is vital. Power differentials are inherent in using and understanding time. Critical time studies show that control over time is a hierarchical power and governance medium. Time plays an essential role in social methods of inclusion and exclusion (Halberstam, 2005). For example, time is often allotted for children. This can include free time or time for parental contact. Therefore, if time is not used compassionately and efficiently, it can symbolise precarious and chaotic lives (Yuill and Mueller-Hirth, 2019). Children may feel that they are returning to chaotic care or inadequate care.

The children in the study discussed needing routines (Selman and Dilworth-Bart, 2024). This allowed space for matching rhythms and time-dependent events with other family members (Siippainen et al, 2023). For example, Louise discussed the importance of having a movie night with her carers every Friday. Louise said: 'Which is where we have cocktails and nibbles on a Friday night. Which is a child's, a kid's movie. Yeah. And then a buffet-type meal with cocktails, well I have mocktails. So.'

However, carers and the children do not necessarily have to do the same activities. For example, the children often inferred the need for mush time (Baraitser, 2013b). Mush time is when family are together, not necessarily in the same room, but in the same place, such as in the house. Another example is when family members are on holiday at the beach. During these moments, each person's rhythms seemingly match, even when one person is listening to music, another is playing on their phone, and another is reading a book. Purple said: 'So we are normally doing quieter things after dinner, like homework or here on the computer.'

Children and adults use time as a commodity. However, as Megan stated, time is just as valuable if it is spent alone or with only one other person engaging in activities they enjoy.

Megan: That it can be quite difficult being a child, and that they just need like time with people, but time alone as well. Because every Sunday with Nan, well we go to church and it's just like [pause]. We're just alone with Nan, and then Grandad can be here and have time on his own [pause]. And it's just nice to be with just Nan and like just Grandad sometimes. Like there are some days when we go out fishing. Fishing at like the beach and stuff now. It's like, he's got passion for it, and it's just nice to see him happy.
Paul: OK, do you like fishing as well?
Megan: Not really. It's alright [laughs].

The children were active in the mobilisation of time and space. They were not just passive recipients of family life being done to them. The children emphasised the importance of reaching a consensus over how time is spent together. If family time was compulsory without negotiation, this would often cause frustration. They did not like to feel forced into spending time in specific ways, and they did not like it when rhythms did not match. For example, Kimberley and Erica expressed frustration that their birth father spent time on his phone and seemed bored when he was meant to be engaging with them during contact. They were also frustrated when they met with their mother. Erica said: 'We don't like it when we see her. She makes us upset. She says things about what we don't want her to say about the past and things we don't want to talk about.'

Spending time connecting with mutual consent and recognition seemed more important than the activities undertaken. Spending time was essential to attuning to each other's feelings and desires (Baraitser, 2013a). It is crucial to building an affinity and a sense of belonging. Nevertheless, rhythms should ideally match. There should also be a consensus from all parties about whether the time is spent focussing on the present, the past, or the future. Consensus and consent are particularly relevant when considering social work interventions such as life story work or relationship-based practice.

Sharing narratives

The children mostly used 'we' when telling stories and decisions that affected them. This inclusive 'we' can be seen as a discrete and economical way of expressing feelings of belonging and collaboration (Kachel et al, 2018). When placed in the context of family, which the children said was often large and in flux, 'we' can signify an attachment that shields against further feelings of potential rejection and loss.

The children also shared traditions and stories about their relatives, including their birth parents. Eliza said:

> So, every summer, we are part of the carnival. Like we always do something, so we've all been carnival queens, and then it was Danielle's year this year. And it's like a family tradition, and I think my mum was it as well. But it's just kind of, like, we used to do it with my mum and my dad, and my sisters. And then my sister stopped coming, and then we still carried on and then my mum and dad stopped, but it's like we still go.

Finally, the children relished stories and photos about their journey with their current family unit. Danielle pointed to photo on the fridge and said: 'That's the first morning we were here. My grandad couldn't fit in. He went to the loo, and when he came back, there's no room [laughs]. We always laugh at that.' It is important to note that both Eliza and Danielle are reiterating that even in absence, there can still be presence.

Photos

Photos were material objects that helped the children remember and recognise their family lives but were also actively used to help manage shared family narratives (Chambers, 2021). The children possessed many photos in their rooms, on their phones, and in their houses. This allowed the presence of those people in their lives who they had a connection with. Photos allowed psychological connections to continue even in people's absence. They also gave the children some control over remembering important events and people. Eliza said:

> Because it's like in that moment if you get a picture that's like, you've got that moment now forever. Like, I'm a really sentimental person,

so I just feel like if you get a photo of that moment, nobody can really take it away from you really.

The way the photos were displayed indicated the children's feelings towards them. For example, Harmony managed her feelings towards her mother by taking control of her physical photographic presence:

> Erm. And then I do have pictures up there, but I decided to, like … oh … hide [points to a picture of her mum]. OK [laughs]. So, I have pictures up there. Let me get them down … a picture of my mum, but I always get an argument with her, so I don't really like to bring them out. I just. Yeah, that's why it's behind that, and I turned it round.

Harmony is once again demonstrating the remarkably nuanced ways in which children actively mobilise and navigate absence and presence. Her navigation has many layers, including her use of a photograph and her attempts to partition and impose negative consequences on her mother by restricting her presence both physically and mentally.

Memory shelves, memory boxes, and transitional objects

Like photos, many children had memory shelves, boxes, and ornaments they associated with people and events that mattered. Again, these were a way not only to control such connections, but also to link the past, present, and future. Kimberley said:

> Like the whole shelf, it's like memories because we went to Singapore, and that's Grandma, Grandma's mum, my great grandma. And [my sister] Erica got me that, and I got her that [points to ornaments]. And I used to do gymnastics, and I won this shield because I was working hard and achieve lots of things in gymnastics. And Grandma got these lights, and it lights up. And, erm, so some of these ornaments, like, erm, I sometimes like to sit on my bed and just look at them, because when I look at them it makes me like happy. And erm, it's sort of like memories to me, like good memories. It makes me feel like more calm, and it takes a bit of worries off my mind and stuff. And it makes me think about Erica. Like happy memories of Erica and myself. And of Grandma and her mum. And sometimes I just sit on the bed, and I just like, erm, look at it. And sometimes I talk to my great grandma, because talking to her is, like, nice.

The children engaged in life story work (Baynes, 2008) of their own accord while sophisticatedly controlling how and when it was done. Similar to

Harmony turning around the photo of her birth mum, the children had ways to manage objects that sparked more difficult memories. They found ways of managing the emotive space between traversing connection and disconnection. Eliza said:

> And this is why it's like … it used to be like a coping box, and it's got like memories from my old primary school. Like the last, like, the cardigan that my mum gave me. And stuff like that. And it all goes in a box rather than on the shelf because I kind of like, I put it away a bit. And I tried to turn it into a positive thing. Kind of like, I can, I can still look in it, but now every time I feel like I open it, I have to add something else to it that was good. So, it's like when I go on the school trip, I can open up the box and I can look at all the other stuff. But I have to put in like the good stuff, like first, so that that that stays managed. So yeah. It's just 'cos I know it's there. So, it's like nothing has been ignored kind of thing. But I feel like obviously there's no point in dwelling on things, but you can remember them, because it might, like it was still a part of your life, it's still happened. But I just don't think dwelling on it is very helpful.

Eliza highlights a key concern about not dwelling on the past, but rather moving forward in her life. This was reiterated by all the children, who did not shy away from remembering challenging events and people. A vital aspect of using remembering is that it should help the child feel ultimately optimistic about the present or help them progress. Erica said: 'It's OK to think about bad memories but we have to feel safe to do that.'

The children and I spoke about toys and other things being transitional objects (Winnicott, 1953). Unicorn, for example, used badges on her school bag that were given to her by her carers. Sydney, who stayed with different family members throughout the year, introduced me to her soft toy, Fairy. She said: 'Fairy is family. I've had her for years. Well, not always this one. But I sleep with her and take her with me wherever I go. And she talks. [Sydney waves Fairy's hand and says in a high-pitched voice] "Hello Paul."'

Toys, especially soft toys, were linked to history and reminders of how they were worthy of care. The toys demonstrated ways other family members could show concern, care, recognition and understanding. They helped manage the push and pull of absence and presence. Some objects were also a way for the children to feel secure and feel that they still had a connection to those important to them. Lucy said: 'Erm, because my other nanny, she gave it to me a long, long time ago, and I really like sometimes when, erm … the Care Bear gets dirty, erm, and Grandma has to wash him, I get really sad, and I can't sleep, because Care Bear's not there.'

The importance of such transitional objects has long been recognised in social work and for children in care. The literature demonstrates that using objects, photos, and toys aids a child's sense of agency and wellbeing (Watson et al, 2020). The insights from the children living in kinship care reiterate their importance. The children often used teddy bears, badges, letters, and clothes as transitional objects. Therefore, it may be helpful to conceptualise memory shelves, memory boxes, and even life story work as object attachment and transitional objects. They bridge the gap between internal and external experiences and create a link between us and the outside world (Winnicott, 2002). These can also provide children who have changed carers a sense of security and continuity, an assortment of familiar sights, smells, touch, and stories (Fahlberg, 2008). They allow a bridge between connection and separation and between the past, present, and future (Watson et al, 2020).

Play

For many of the children, play was a way of negotiating imagination and reality. The children seemed to experience these realms simultaneously, trying, testing, and confronting the two. Therefore, although play had to be fun, it was never frivolous. The children spoke about play having meaning (Linn, 2009). As Sydney explained: 'Because it's fun, and I can do things. And, erm, I use my imagination. Or actually, I have discovered that I do have magic in real life.'

Play was also a strategy to spend time with others. The children preferred games that they could play with other people. Again, a connection was vital for them. Collaborative play also allowed the children to construct and understand their positioning with others and test their power and vision (Chudacoff, 2007). The children used play not only to show how they care for others or navigate the world of adult roles but also to demonstrate that they belong to certain gendered and commercial cultures.

Paul: Why do you have these LOL Dolls?
Rainbow: Well, so I can play with them, and they're so cute. Look. And we do things together ... and I can collect them. And some of my friends have them as well, but I probably have more.

Play is natural yet constructed. It is also freely chosen yet often requires permission and assistance (Clark, 2003). It is powerful and empowering yet can be quickly diminished by other forces. For example, children get told how much screen time they are allowed. As previously discussed, time is also about power relations, predictions, and the consequences of time not being used appropriately (Sharma, 2011). Play has a meaning beyond just its outcome, but also has meaning in its outcome (Linn, 2009). It is not just what can be achieved by play; it is also what is achieved through play. Through play, the children navigated the contradictions in their lives, expressing and working through their inner conversations. They used play to help understand, try out, and mobilise their connections and power relations with the world around them (Cook, 2018).

Books, music, social media, and TV

Lastly, the children also used books, music, social media, and TV to disengage at times but also to engage (Bolshaw and Josephidou, 2022). They were helpful ways to socialise, connect, and be attuned to others and their interests. Social media was particularly significant for older children in communicating with their friends, many of whom did not live in their local neighbourhoods. Books, social media, and TV were used to escape and gain a sense of autonomy. Louise said: 'Erm, I don't know, it's just when I hear music, I just, it kind of takes the control of me as such, and it just means a lot to me. It makes me forget about the outside world.'

While they were part of escapism, music and books still had to have some relevance to their lives. They still had to have meaning. Kimberley said:

> Books are about relating to real life as well, and sometimes it's nice to get stuck in the book and you kind of shut out everything else, and you're like on your own in a different world. And I kind of feel like if there's a main character, then I kind of feel like I'm that person, and I can relate to them. So, I kind of learn, and it helps you a lot in life.

Overall, the children showed that books, music, and social media were ways for them to feel both connected to and separated from the world. It enabled them to actively engage in the process and take some control in how they navigated the space(s) in between.

Practice implications

Recognising how families do

The children's insights showed how they disrupt common, simplistic notions of family in social work policy and practice, which are often used for assessments (Wissö et al, 2019) and are usually based on theories of attachment or socialisation (McCafferty, 2020). Sociological explanations and those from other disciplines, such as children's geographies, are also useful to help recognise and explain the children's lived experiences. Child welfare should use many explanations and theories to help understand family life (Boddy, 2023).

Acknowledging how families do rather than just focusing on what families are (Morgan, 2011) means practitioners and policy makers can be wide-ranging when deciding who should have caring commitments within kinship care arrangements. Carers do not necessarily have to have any genetic relation to the child. The children consider family as practices that are performed, evolve, and grow. Family is not static for the children. Instead, most probably due to their experiences, it changes, as do the roles of the individuals within it, although there is always a genetic connection remaining even when the children or other family members minimise it. The most important thing for these children is being cared for by someone who is well known to them and feels part of their family. They wish for safe, inclusive care, allowing them to feel a sense of intergenerational belonging and continuity. They also want people to be able to recognise and accept them for who they are. The children desire carers who, as Eliza said, 'want to relate' to them, want to spend time with them, and have an affinity towards them (Mason, 2008).

Conversations about the children's own definitions should also include the possibility of different caring arrangements, and the caregivers' death, in the future. The children in kinship care arrangements think about these things, whether or not they are explicitly discussed (Burgess et al, 2010; Farmer et al, 2013). They have previously experienced a shift in care responsibilities within the family, and they, therefore, consider family as an active process that shifts and is in flux (Morgan, 2020).

Providing for the sharing of time, space, and narratives

The children used stories, routines, and rituals, such as shared mealtimes and family celebrations, to 'do' family (Spagnola and Fiese, 2007; Biehal, 2014; Lindsay et al, 2021). These included the children navigating separation/connection of those that mattered even if they were not physically present, such as those who were deceased. Sharing time, space, and narratives gave the children a shared sense of story, belonging, and affinity. It also assisted them to feel a sense of belonging in the intergenerational life cycle of the whole family. Focusing on family practices of sharing suggests that kinship can be maintained through everyday interactions (Cossar and Neil, 2013). It means dedicating time daily, although because time has power differentials inherent in it, how time is spent should be planned and negotiated.

A more critical understanding of time is required in child welfare. Time and temporality are often only fleetingly alluded to in child welfare literature on children's permanence. It is usually framed in terms of some children requiring more time to form attachments than those who are in their birth parents' care (Howe, 2011). Time is also usually constructed in childhood studies as linear rather than dynamic, wobbly, agentic, multi-perspectival and full of power relations (Murris, 2020).

For the children, doing family and doing home also involved different uses of space, whether shared spaces, private spaces, or spaces to be alone or with others. The most crucial prerequisite of home was that it was a safe place where the children felt they belonged and where they could be themselves. It mattered to the children that they had spaces like beds and memory shelves in their rooms and enough shared spaces to feel comforted while managing and enacting the connection/separation inherent in their lives.

Pets (Carr and Rockett, 2017) and siblings (Cossar and Neil, 2013; White and Hughes, 2017) were other ways the children could do kinship. Both often provided play, comfort, and somebody to care for them. Pets could not answer back and would listen without judgment. Sibling relationships were usually more precarious, so the children frequently had to work harder to negotiate them. Pets and siblings should, therefore, always be a central consideration in assessing and helping children navigate family life.

Life story work

Life story work requires its own attention. There is no single definition of life story work, nor how to do it (Hammond et al, 2020). In the UK, it is typically divided into Rose's model of therapeutic life story work, which requires specialist training, or Rees' (2017) interpretative model, which is more accessible for non-specialist practitioners and carers (Ricketts, 2023). Life story work can mitigate adverse consequences by assisting a child in understanding and integrating their past, present, and future (Coman et al, 2016). Most literature proposes that life story work is based on psychodynamic theories of attachment and loss and can aid a child's narrative identity and continuity of sense of self (Watson et al, 2020). Indeed, the children spoke about using narratives, photos, memory boxes, memory shelves, and presents, and storying other personal objects. This helped them navigate the in-between of connection/separation.

Nevertheless, the term life story work and psychodynamic explanations can only go so far. They do not necessarily wholly represent how these children in kinship care manage such activities specific to their kinship care family circumstances. Traditional life story work does not recognise that children perceive their specific kinship care family arrangement to be continually growing and in flux, not only with the relationships that can be seen but also with those that cannot be seen and may never be seen. Analysis of the children's insights suggests that children living in kinship care, and possibly all children, do not experience their care as discrete separation and loss. Their family life encompasses reconnections, whether through contact, stories, or even seemingly minor details that can have a significant impact, such as family resemblances (Ingham and Mikardo, 2022). Therefore, sociological concepts such as those of doing family can add to our understanding of the purpose of life story work.

Critical time studies can also be a helpful way of understanding permanence work and life story work practice. Life story work was traditionally seen as a time-limited task that culminates in a 'life story book' or later life letter. The life story book has many critics, including children (Watson et al, 2015). The children in this study demonstrated that time is not merely a linear construct of past, present, and future. Life story work is co-constructed daily, with children as active architects, reflecting and understanding their life course (Staples et al, 2023). Our minds are like a time machine, constantly 'travel hopping' (Murris and Kohan, 2021, p 583), where 'the past is never finished' (Barad, 2018, p 73). It is not enough to recognise chronological clock time; lived time, where different times bleed through one another, should be acknowledged (Barad, 2018). Life story work cannot be a one-off process or a chronological book that is completed, primarily by a social worker, and then put on a shelf. The past cannot be processed, completed, and put away. The past, absence/presence, and connection/separation are continuously negotiated, thought about, and navigated throughout our lives.

Traditional life story work also does not always appropriately consider a child's agency. The 'work' part of life story work sounds like an intervention that social workers perform on children (Hammond et al, 2020). It is now understood as letting the children lead the discussion, but more than this simplistic understanding of giving agency is needed. The children in the study spoke about already using various tools and methods to manage the connections/separations inherent in their lives without child welfare interventions. Therefore, doing work to children, even if child-led, can ignore the children's current managing strategies, and building on those strategies can also be the most effective start for further life story work. Children must be seen as agentic beings, active in life story work now and in the future (Ricketts, 2023). It would be even better if their current tools for engaging in life story work could be shaped by children so that they could continue to develop better ways to engage with the work in the future.

Lastly, the children did not use the term life story work once. This may be because the term is usually conflated with a social work intervention for children in state care or adoption and, as discussed in Chapter 9, the children did not want to be recognised as children in care.

Conclusion

Understanding that family and home can have multiple meanings requires professionals to invest in genuinely hearing children's perspectives. Social workers must acknowledge the children's definitions of family and home, how these are negotiated and lived, and what truly matters to them. This work is fundamentally relationship-based, demanding time, resources, and seemingly simple activities like walking or playing together. It is crucial to provide children with the space to have trusting yet precarious conversations about ambivalence and how they are managing the in-between spaces inherent in their family lives. More importantly, it is essential to understand that children already have these conversations and play out these tensions, whether internally or externally, daily. Rather than imposing our methods of assessment and intervention, we should join in alongside and support the children's current strategies for navigating the complexities of connection/separation. By embracing the children's perspectives and methods, we can foster a more inclusive and supportive environment that acknowledges their agency. This approach respects their experiences and empowers them to navigate their unique family dynamics with confidence and hope. The next chapter delves deeper into these relational spaces, focusing on permanence and the intricate balance of care, risk, and interdependence.

8

Valuing care and protection/ independence and risk

> Well, I think I should be safe outside with someone, and I think I should be safe always with someone. But, but I don't always need to be. Because sometimes I don't really need to be. But sometimes I do.
>
> Jordan, child research participant

This chapter delves deeper into family relationships for children living in kinship care. It explores what care, safety, and permanence mean to children living in kinship care. It focuses on the mechanism of care and protection/ independence and risk as shown in Figure 8.1.

When placed broadly into policy, practice, and legislation, the care and protection/independence and risk mechanism is like the continuing social work debates on care versus control and paternalism versus self-efficacy (Grimwood, 2015). It mirrors discussions regarding government and professional obligations, familialism, and whether many families living in kinship care should be left alone and unregulated.

Understood in the context of children's daily lives, the children's views illuminate that the care and protection/independence and risk mechanism is a core value from which children envisage their needs and aspirations for care. The children's insights reveal that care and risk are intricately connected rather than contradictory, as can sometimes be assumed. For example, while the United Nations Convention on the Rights of the Child states that children have the right to be protected from harm and provided for, it minimally mentions the right for children to take risks as they discover and employ their interdependence and agency (Fairhall and Woods, 2021).

This chapter highlights children's perspectives on care and parenting, emphasising the need to prioritise needs with an awareness of risk. This involves negotiation, collaboration, and balancing individual agency with collective responsibility through autonomous interdependence. The children's views show that this balance relies on negotiating boundaries and rules. Care and parenting are not unconditional acts that fit neatly into typologies. How care is enacted is as crucial as ensuring it is provided.

Figure 8.1: Care and protection/independence and risk – one of the three central mechanisms that emerged from how the children in the study managed family life and permanence

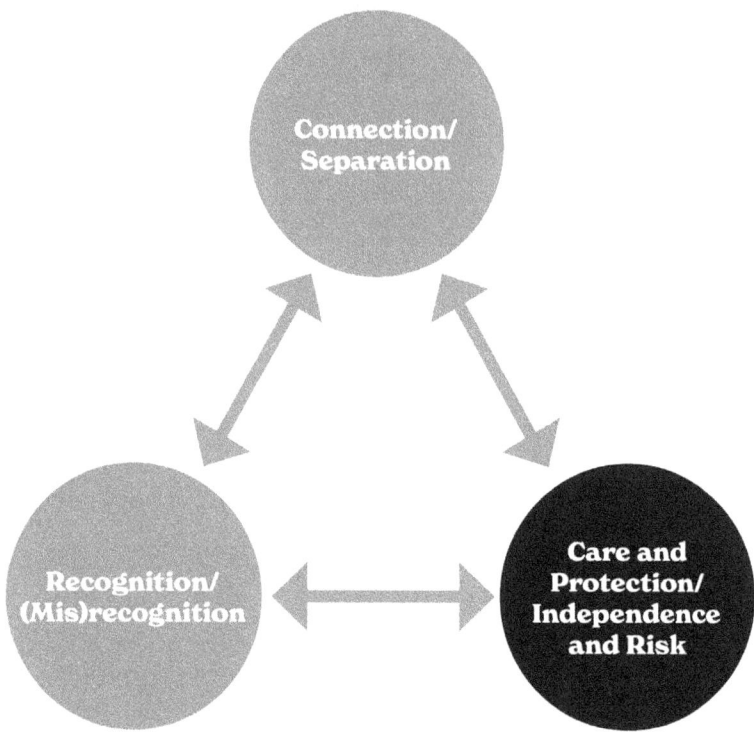

While various theories can apply to children's care experiences, the ethics of care offer a helpful framework to theorise and apply the care they desire. Specifically, mature care provides a unique lens to ensure that children in kinship care can thrive safely with a sense of permanence.

Care and risk

Care is attending to need

> Adults make money. And you got to get money to get food and to stay in your house and go to the shop when needed.
>
> Jordan

Maslow's (1954) theory of human motivation, which contributed to the development of the hierarchy of needs pyramid illustrated in Figure 8.2, is one of the most widely recognised psychological theories for conceptualising human needs (Bowen, 2021). Simplified, the model proposes that physiological needs such as food, water, air, shelter, and clothing must be met before other needs can be addressed.

The viewpoints of the children in the study corresponded to some degree with Maslow's often-assumed linear ladder of needs. When asked what mattered for their care, they valued carers who offered reassurance that their basic physiological needs would be met, and their development attended to. As Zack put it: 'Looking out for each other. Because my grandma looks out, well, my brother does as well, but my grandma gives me food every day, and she takes me to school every day. She picks me up from school every day. A good education or something like that.'

The children also explained that being cared for is about more than meeting their physiological requirements and ensuring access to quality social and learning opportunities. Like the other levels of Maslow's hierarchy, parenting also had to help build self-esteem and self-actualisation through social interactions. The children understood that parenting also had an emotional and relational aspect. Parenting was about patience and the ability to empathise (Meng et al, 2020).

Figure 8.2: Maslow's hierarchy of needs pyramid

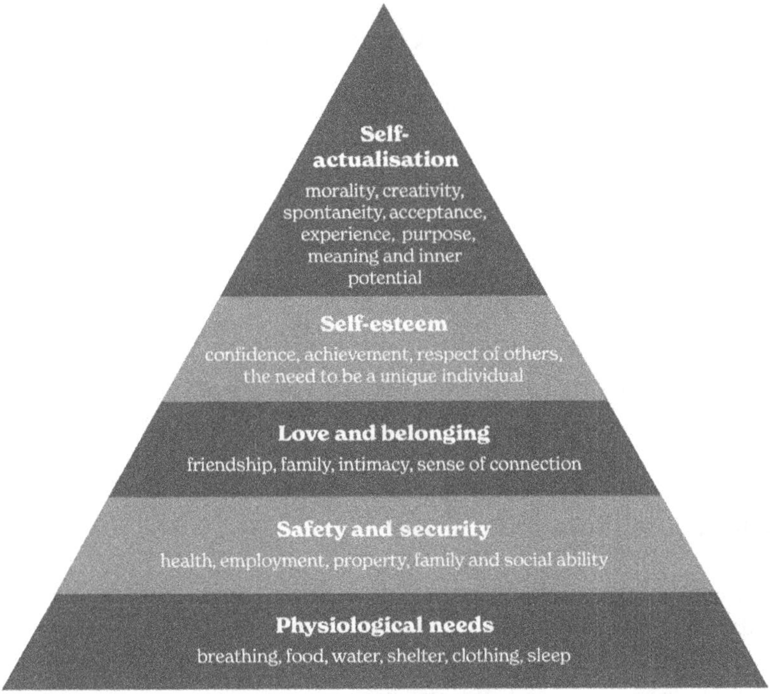

Self-actualisation
morality, creativity, spontaneity, acceptance, experience, purpose, meaning and inner potential

Self-esteem
confidence, achievement, respect of others, the need to be a unique individual

Love and belonging
friendship, family, intimacy, sense of connection

Safety and security
health, employment, property, family and social ability

Physiological needs
breathing, food, water, shelter, clothing, sleep

Paul:	What advice would you give to carers for children in a similar situation to you?
Danielle:	To be, to let that child have a good life with you and make them feel strong, and make sure they don't really cry about their parents.

As our conversations progressed, the children highlighted tensions between their needs. While providing basic needs and emotional support was essential, it required negotiation and was not as simple as climbing a hierarchical triangle or ladder to self-actualisation. The children noted that becoming more aware of their agency and voices could conflict with their desire to prioritise other needs.

Danielle:	Well, I have jacket potato with cheese and beans every day at school. Because I'm a fussy eater. No, but I'm trying new things like pasta what they do. And I think I'm going to be trying pizza as well.
Paul:	And why does it matter to try new things then?
Danielle:	For our own good. Because when you're older, you might be fussy, and you might just keep buying the same things when you're older, and then your kids might get bored of them.

The hierarchical framework of needs is not the linear set of building blocks that it is often perceived to be as. Instead, as Maslow initially intended, it is a complex, dynamic, and interrelated matrix of growth and personal development that shifts over a lifetime (Bowen, 2021). Danielle demonstrates how tensions between needs can cause dissonance and disequilibrium (Kaiser et al, 2012). This was reiterated by Zack, who also suggested that others with more experience would help you navigate through the seeming contradictions: 'Like, say I didn't want to do something, [my grandad] wouldn't make me do it, but he'd push me and push me and push me, and I'll end up enjoying it in the end.'

The children recognised that needs could conflict, which meant that they might often have to do things against their wishes. Being cared for frequently entails being challenged.

Adequate care is the prioritisation of need

Although being cared for entails being challenged, particularly when navigating conflicting needs, the children were often adept at knowing who was best placed to help them do this. The children in the study often had clear knowledge and first-hand experience of when carer priorities were not aligned with their needs. The children were familiar with what constitutes good care and what constitutes control, neglect, and endangerment, particularly regarding caregiving and parenting. The children understood that the care previously afforded to them by their birth parents did not provide them with safety or address their basic needs. Every child in the study felt let down by their birth parents. They mentioned work, violent partners, housing, drug misuse, or their birth parents' own emotional or mental health needs. Sydney said: 'And the reason why I don't live with my mum is because everyone is scared that she's going to see [M] again. Because [M] is the person who is really mean and does stuff and drinks.'

The children felt that their previous caregivers had chosen to place their own priorities ahead of theirs (Ward et al, 2014). This was why they were no longer in their care. Although it was acknowledged that adults have a responsibility to take care of both themselves and their children, the children believed that the adults' requirements should not, on the whole, take precedence over their own needs. Eliza said:

> I feel like if they do everything that they can to make things the best that they can. I'm not saying that they have to have, like, give all the kids everything that they need, everything that they want, but I just feel like if do their best all the time, or even if, even if they don't. Like, everybody has bad days. But I just feel like the good needs to outweigh the bad in every situation if you're trying to look after someone. When I feel like you should have the best intentions of the person that you trying to look after, rather than other things that you make like … so, basically, if you're a mother, your kids should prioritise over most things.

The children wanted to know that they would not be forgotten or neglected and that their carers would like to spend time with them. Zack said: '[Nan] doesn't, she doesn't ignore me. Like, when I lived with my mum, when I got home from school, I used to go about six hours straight on the Xbox. I never really used to see her that much and I was only five or six. So, yeah.'

Feeling safe

> Adults should be there for you and provide for you. But they're not here to, like, stop you from doing anything you want to do. And they just want you to be safe.
>
> Megan

The children were adamant that feeling protected from harm was essential to being cared for and having their needs attended to. From a psychological perspective, safety is the glue that holds our psychological selves together, even at the basic levels of Maslow's hierarchy of needs. It is more than a separate need. Instead, the issue of safety is an essential companion that enables the negotiation and interaction of all other needs (Bowen, 2021).

As highlighted in previous chapters, the complexities of safety and risk are rarely discussed in kinship care literature or policy (Hallett et al, 2021). Yet, throughout the study, all the children stressed the importance of feeling safe at home and with others. Feeling safe and the promise of future safety was complex. The children frequently switched their focus between the significance of being protected by others and the significance of being able to protect themselves. Harmony, for example, mentioned the need to take risks and enact her sense of agency.

Harmony:	To me, if people say to me, like, don't do that, I do it because you've just told me not to do it.
Paul:	But what if they're saying something to keep you safe?
Harmony:	No, because then I would tell myself not to do that, and then I listened to myself and looked out for myself [laughs]. Yeah, I trust myself more than anybody else, and also it's also important to learn yourself and make mistakes. It's just like everybody that I have trust in. I can't even trust my nan with anything because even if it's like your things that happened, she'll go and tell other people she doesn't even know.

The children repeated throughout every session that trust is a crucial value for any relationship, especially with people who give you advice and guidance (Cossar et al, 2016). Trust is not just about protecting physical safety; trust is vital for emotional safety, too. Erica said:

Erm, they are like another bit of my family where there I don't, like, feel safe with them. I don't trust them, and they've done lots of things wrong and blamed it on us – like called us liars and things like that. Grandma has never done that, and she would never do that.

Trust and safety needed to be felt and concretely measured. They needed to be evidenced and, to some extent, predictable.

Autonomous interdependence

Being dependent on carers and parents to meet their needs but wanting to feel independent was a continuous tension for the children. They frequently expressed a yearning to be independent while acknowledging their reliance on those around them for their wellbeing and safety. They also often desired responsibility but did not always welcome it when it was thrust upon them, such as having to help with pets or other household chores. Louise said: 'So I try to study, but then I've got house jobs as well. Yes. That's tough. And about here [points to a rewards chart]. And then because I've just done my SATs [standardised assessment tests], I get a one Chinese at Mario's.'

Psychologists would argue that this need for reliance yet non-reliance, for autonomy yet collective responsibility, is typical of any child, especially when they embark on adolescence (Van Petegem et al, 2012). For example, Erikson's psychosocial development theory stresses the negotiations of autonomy, particularly throughout childhood and adolescence (Maree, 2022). Also, humanist Rogers (1995) states that we learn to be free through our parents' care, compassion from our teachers, and being a good citizen to others.

However, psychological explanations of the tensions between dependence, independence, and autonomy, even humanist ones, often fall short, particularly for children living in kinship care arrangements. Additional tensions in their particular family lives cannot be adequately considered. The children have been let down by their birth parents and have experienced the precarious nature of care. Their kinship carers are often older and may be unable to provide continuous care throughout their childhoods (Wijedasa, 2015). The children also must deal with the psychological presence of birth parents in their lives who may have caused them trauma, even if they are not physically present. They want child welfare support but do not always welcome social work interference. In many ways, children in kinship care experience a heightened sense of the fluctuations between wanting themselves and their family to be independent yet being dependent on others for their safety and wellbeing. Louise said:

> My mum will always be part of my life, even if she's in the past. In a way, she's always going to be there whether I acknowledge it or not, whether I, well, I want her to be or not. Because my mum doesn't let me really see my sister unless it's with her, and I don't really want to see her.

Another way to help understand such ambivalences is to use philosophy to deconstruct the binary constructions of independence and dependence, similar to how connection and separation can be deconstructed. Hegel (2018) famously stated that we gain self-consciousness only through recognition from others. Sayer (2011) also alludes to this when he talks about humans being comparative and relational to provide us with a sense of ourselves.

Louise said: 'So I do karate. I'm almost a black belt. And we did an interclub Qatar competition, and I came third in my category of my medals up there. So that's very good.' Our vulnerability and dependence on others are not merely instrumental but also necessary for our very personhood. We need others to assess our performance through comparisons and assessments of our abilities. Additionally, we need others to keep us in check and ensure we are safely on the right path. This, in turn, enables us to become more independent. Erica said:

> The kitchen is where we sometimes you wash the dishes, help Grandma, and Grandma's going to, like [pause]. She's slowly teaching us how to cook – like we help … yes, because when we're older, we need to be taught how to cook, clean, wash, iron, and everything. I want to learn to iron, but Grandma says when we are a bit older because sometimes Grandma like kind of burns herself a bit.

Such insights reiterate Bhaskar's (1993, p 154) concept of autonomous interdependence. Carers, family, community, and society not only assist children in gaining intentional agency and a sense of self, but these, in turn, are necessary for the 'reproduction or transformation' of others around them. It is a two-way street with reciprocity – the constant struggle between our influence on society and society's influence on us. Autonomous interdependence is akin to Archer's (2003, 2012) conceptualisations of internal conversations, as discussed in Chapter 5 regarding critical realism. As a result of being given opportunities to enact their agency by others, children can subtly, or sometimes abruptly, shape their families', communities', and societies' identities and actions. Rainbow said: 'Look after the environment. You should help. It's important, you know. And you adults need to do it and not leave it up to us to sort out your mess. And Brexit.'

Rainbow shows that while adults may have more opportunities to exercise their agency, because of the power inequalities between children and adults, she was clearly able to assert her own agency in that moment and communicate that we are interdependent. She also felt that adults are not fulfilling their responsibilities to keep us all safe. She was highlighting the challenges we all have in navigating the mechanism of care and protection/independence and risk.

Rules and taking a firm hand

Navigating autonomous interdependence was challenging for the children and their families. One strategy for navigating the frequently emotive and confrontational terrain was through expectations and rules. Rules also allowed the children to have some predictability in feeling safe. After describing an event in her birth parents' care when she was scared because she heard monsters in her bedroom, Unicorn said: 'And that's what happened, and I've been writing signs all around my house everywhere. Because I need to put rules, rules in the house.'

All the children said that rules were needed. Purple said:

> To keep things in order ... because you don't want to be a danger to others, or you want to be able to keep everyone safe. And rules are a way of doing that ... rules should be something that is discussed with everyone that's in the place with rules, so then they can help come up with them in a way that it makes sense, and they can obey them.

The children inferred that rules, expectations, and contracts allowed social cohesion and broader wellbeing and safety. This was based on societal and intra-familial norms (Hardecker et al, 2017). However, not all rules were awarded the same value, and in many cases, their validity was contingent on those who made them. The children recognised that adults needed to take ultimate responsibility for their children's welfare. Louise said: '[Carers] should take a firm hand because sometimes, if you've been in that situation, you can come out of it being a bit feisty and unsettled and so need a firm hand to calm me down a bit.'

The children were clear that they preferred authoritative rather than authoritarian parenting. Authoritarian parenting characterises strict and rigid regulations, while authoritative parenting nurtures a more caring relationship where discipline is perceived as explanation and support rather than punishment (Baumrind, 1989). Consultation and talking were vital for setting appropriate boundaries, even when fraught power struggles and conflict occurred (Cho et al, 2020). Sydney said:

> Erm. The adults boss you around. They tell you what to do, and the kids get really annoyed. They go up to their rooms, slam the doors behind them, and starts being angry at them, and the parents, getting annoyed again, give them punishments and never listens. So yeah, that's what happens to me all the time. But then, at least it's my nana and grandad, and at least I know that it won't last forever, and we have to talk about it.

The children's insights showed how they valued interdependence and negotiations alongside the predictability of future care. They seek an understanding of, and trust in, the practice of caregiving, and this can involve conflict.

Care by social workers and child welfare practitioners

Most of the children felt that social workers did not provide them with consistent or adequate care. Many of them viewed social workers as authoritarian figures who followed procedures during times of family conflict. This often resulted in children associating social workers with, or even blaming them for, family problems.

Thomas: So, are you a social worker?
Paul: Yes. Well, kind of. I'm a social work researcher.
Thomas: [Smiles at his grandmother.] We don't like social workers. They just cause trouble.

This reticence and negative association with social work have also been found in research on parents' experiences of social work intervention (Baginsky, 2023). Wariness of social work intervention can also be born out of the shame of having state intervention in private family life. Different countries, cultures, and minoritised groups will also have different concerns about what they perceive as social work interference (Drew et al, 2023).

Many of the children in the study saw social workers and the state as often shirking their responsibilities. Eliza said:

> Yeah, we had social workers, and I had supervised contact at first. But after the first couple of years, that fizzled out and we were just left to our own devices. And there's no like guidebook on what you need to do and stuff, which is like parenting in the first place, but I just, yeah. I don't know. I just feel like there could be so much more being done, but there just isn't. Social workers don't really do what they say they're going to do.

The children also expressed concerns about the number of social workers in their lives, which they felt would often hinder their progress. Kimberley said:

> About social workers. We've had lots of social workers, and sometimes it's hard to tell social workers like the same thing. Like they ask you the same questions, and it's kind of annoying to tell them the same thing, like from the very beginning. Like you might forget things, and then you feel bad if you say the wrong thing, like, because it's a long time ago, and so it's kind of like the restarting. And you kind of live your life, and you kind of want to move on. And you kind of want to go forward in your life.

The heavy rotation of UK social workers has been a contentious issue for many years. Poor social work staff retention is known to have a detrimental impact on child and family outcomes (Turley et al, 2022). The Independent Review of Children's Social Care (MacAlister, 2022) highlighted this and suggested that a new national professional progression model would help keep social workers in front-line practice longer. This strategy is controversial and yet untested. No conclusive evidence for retention exists beyond the importance of supervision and mentoring (Turley et al, 2022).

Ethics of care

Values

We return now to a core theme of the book – the importance of values that underpin our actions and the importance of valuing things in our lives, particularly when tensions exist within them. As shown in Figure 5.2 (the values that mattered to the children), the children spoke about the values required for personal and professional relationships to be positive and for others to care well. The children weighed up not only what matters but what matters most. As also shown, these preferred moral orientations and values often seem at odds with one another. Nevertheless, further conversations with the children suggest that the need for such values to be displayed depended on who they talked about and the circumstances surrounding them. For example, the ways they expected social workers to care were very different to their expectations of family members. The children expected social workers to be there, listen to them, and help with their concerns, but not share their lives in the reciprocal and intimate ways close family members did. Rainbow said: 'It's like [social workers] would talk about their stuff, and stuff, so yeah. But I'm like, no, no, no. Just do what you say you're going to do and then leave us alone.' Highlighting the need for person- and situation-dependent expectations lends credibility to the notion that values are context-dependent mechanisms (Sayer, 2011).

Ethics of care versus ethics of justice

The ethics of care literature is a helpful way of conceptualising how different theories, values, and moral orientations intertwine, interact, and sometimes conflict regarding parenting and child welfare practice. When considered in the context of child welfare professions such as social work, the literature often debates the differences between the ethics of care and ethics of justice (Collins, 2018).

In summary, the ethics of care involve the values of mutual trust (Held, 2006) relational responsibility, responsiveness, attentiveness, and competence. It necessitates empathy, compassion, and a commitment to nurturing without causing suffering (Tronto, 1994). The ethics of care literature is grounded in ideas of autonomous interdependence, although it uses phrases such as relational ontology (Sevenhuijsen, 2000) and relational autonomy (Mackenzie and Stoljar, 2000).

Often seen in contrast to the ethics of care, the ethics of justice is frequently pitched as a starker and more rationalist alternative (Held, 2006). It focuses on the values of fairness, equality, consistency, and individual rights. It is more predictable and less risky. It is based on concepts of autonomy and the idea that everyone is different yet equal, also known as universality. The ethics of rights is the central consideration for judiciaries, regulations, policies, and rules.

As described in chapters 1–3, professionalism, modernisation, managerialism, regulation, legal processes, risk aversion, efficiency, and standards currently dominate child welfare practice and policy (Collins, 2018). They, therefore, also dominate the domains of children's services and permanence. This can be why there is often an overwhelming focus in research, policy, and practice on the ethics of justice, which considers legal orders and stability when contemplating permanence for children living in kinship care.

The children's insights do not undermine the need for the ethics of justice. They agreed that rights, regulations, and rules were vital for them. They emphasised that these helped parenting and child welfare practice to treat children's safeguarding and appropriate development with great importance. The children also wanted equal opportunities with other children to be brought up in a safe environment. They were concerned about the right of family members to maintain the connections/separations they desired. Furthermore, they wanted to ensure that social workers fulfilled their responsibilities, while also expressing a wish for practitioners to be more compassionate and understanding of their situations. Kimberley said: 'Our social workers didn't always do what they said they were going to do. I think that's bad. They also weren't very nice, except for one. [She] was good because she listened to us and made us feel safe.'

The children viewed both the ethics of rights and ethics of care as necessary, and this gives credence to Tronto's (1994) and Sevenghuijsen's (2000) conclusions that caring and rights are both vital and intertwined. Parenting, care, and social work practice should not be confined to considerations of rights and rules, although these are essential. They must also take account of human relationships and context. In terms of also upholding the ethics of rights, the ethics of care must be the primary consideration (M. Barnes, 2012). The ethics of care, how we do, must always come first, before what we do.

Mature care

The children never perceived care as one-directional or unconditional. Care was always reciprocal because, as echoed in some of the literature on children in care, they did not want to be seen as a burden (Hiller et al, 2020). Erica said:

> Erm like, we, instead of just saying to Grandma, 'Oh, we love you', and like we buy things for her, like, we sometimes make things for

her. And like, we've we're doing some knitting and where I'm knitting Grandma a shawl, and Kimberley is knitting Grandma a scarf. Erm, like when sometimes we help Grandma like with the bed, like putting the quilt and stuff and, like, hoovering up.

This reciprocity extended beyond their present family arrangement. The children also felt a responsibility to do well and repay the carers by caring for them when they get older. This demonstrates the wish for their flourishing to impact everyone's wellbeing. They endeavoured to gain a valued place within the whole family's life course, which would help them achieve a more permanent position within the family. Danielle said: 'Because when I'm older, I might not see my Nan and Grandad because they might be, they might be dying, and if they went to hospital, I'll always be there and do something nice for them.'

The concept of mature care is also based on the ethics of care literature and is helpful when considering kinship care. Mature care helps address the issues of rules, rights, protection, reciprocity, and their tension with values in the ethics of care literature, such as empathy. Pettersen (2012) furthered Gilligan's (1982) conceptions of mature care, challenging commonly held views of an ideal type of altruistic care.

Pettersen proposes that altruistic care is 'seen as a selfless, compassionate, and spontaneous act, the focus of which is to concentrate on the other's immediate needs' (2012, p 376). Selflessness is a characteristic commonly associated with how and why kinship carers should look after their children (Owusu-Bempah, 2010). Neither the children nor, according to the literature, the carers view their responsibilities in this way. The children inferred the need for interdependence and reciprocity in their relationships. As such, they would buy presents for carers or engage in other family members' activities, such as fishing with their grandad, despite the children finding the activities only, as Megan claimed, 'alright'. Mature care also involves the use of spaces, time, and an understanding of autonomous interdependence. Sydney said:

Well, what I do is, when I'm upset, I just talk to myself and go through what I wanted to do and then, yeah. And then I just, when someone's just shouted at me I start crying in my room and then just, ahh, and then I just leave the people who have just shouted at me for a few minutes, and then I just take the deep breaths, and then I just talked to them and do whatever, and then they'll just say to me sorry I shouted, and I'll say we're sorry and then we're fine.

This relational, reciprocal activity is the basis of mature care. It is not limitless or altruistic. The children also understood this as meaningful adherence to negotiated rules. They saw rules as signifiers that they were being cared for appropriately and kept safe. It allowed them a shared narrative and a sense of continuity, affinity, and permanence (Mason, 2008). Mature care also suggests sensitivity to the long-term physical and mental wellbeing of children from those who should be looking after them, including society. Harmony said:

> Well, I usually stay in the during the week and spend on the weekends 'cos I, because I usually never do anything because, like, my nan doesn't have enough money to do anything. And then, like, I see my brother as well, and then I try and meet up with my friends as much as I can but, like, sometimes I can't because I have no money. Well, that's not fair. It shouldn't like be like that just because of this is where I am.

Mature care is a valuable concept to apply to kinship care because theorising care as altruistic, unconditional, selfless, and unlimited avoids the ethical and political aspects of care (Pettersen, 2012). It can easily allow placing all accountability back on the families, who should take care responsibilities without kudos or payment. It echoes familialism. However, as also highlighted in the next chapter, the children were clear that it was unfair that their carers were often expected to care for them without acknowledgement or any extra practical, emotional, or financial assistance from the state or child welfare services.

Permanence

> I think it's the fact that you know you can go, and you're not going to be, like, there's no pressure in your family home. There's no like tension. Well, obviously, there is sometimes, but there's no like … you can always go there and it's just kind of like you can relax and be yourself, and like there's no stress or anything. So that makes a home.
>
> Eliza

This section of this chapter uses the concept of mature care to navigate between the ethics of care and justice, and applies the concept to child permanence. The discussions with children in the study support the current dominant way of thinking about permanence in fostering and adoption literature, policy, and practice. This, as discussed in Chapter 3, is that a sense of permanence is 'a sense of security, continuity, commitment and identity' (DfE, 2010, p 12). This was echoed but also supplemented through the children's discussions of physical stability, legal stability, and emotional permanence.

Can physical stability ensure permanence?

As part of the study, I asked the children to devise suitable family mottos as part of their 'what matters' valuations. This helped them value what they felt mattered most regarding their home and family life.

Paul: So, in terms of your family, then, if you could make up a motto for them, what, what do you think it would be?

Lucy: Erm, probably something like family always sticks together. Yeah, something like that.

They also discussed what matters to make a home a home. Zach said:

> Something that you live in. It doesn't have to be a house or a flat. It can even be like the homeless people, so they live in the streets, or something they could, that could be their home, kind of. So, it's anywhere away like, er like, um like, you feel settled. Yeah, so, like every, not everywhere, but somewhere where you stay most times or yeah.

A few of the children, such as Thomas and Jordan, had shared care arrangements. They determined that having multiple residences for some children was manageable and even desired so long as they were assisted in navigating their ambivalent family relationships. Jordan said: 'Well, I don't mind because as long as I have a bed. We do different things in different places coz there are different people around here. And I don't have [the main carer's birth children] here, which can be good but can also be bad.'

In addition to receiving care from her grandparents over the holidays, Sydney frequently spent extended periods with family members living in other regions of the country. She also felt this had both good and bad repercussions: 'Actually, well sometimes, like when I'm at my dad's house, I can't sleep because it's somewhere different, but I'm used to sleeping here because I go here like pretty much every holiday.' However, she also liked having various people around her, as she felt that having the same adults and other children around could get boring, especially for preverbal children:

> That's home because that's the usual place that I go to, and I normally live with my nan and grandad. Because I go to see other people I would call my family in the holidays for half the year. Because, yeah, I love seeing them, but I felt a bit bored because every single time people keep talking, I get really sad and go to my room. And erm, well, it's a good job that we have children that can talk because then you can play with them. Children that can't talk, it's really boring. You can't play with them.

Sydney's reflections suggest that stability in one place was not necessarily a prerequisite for a sense of permanence, wellbeing, and happiness. Harmony's experiences (described next) also powerfully illustrate how stability in one place does not necessarily equate to emotional stability. Furthermore, her account demonstrates that safety is fundamental to addressing children's needs, maintaining relationships, and fostering a feeling of permanence. Safety and risk should always be considered. As previously recognised, safety is the bedrock required to meet all other needs.

In our second meeting, Harmony considered moving in with her father. This type of experience must never be forgotten when discussing kinship care or permanence:

Harmony: Erm, so me and [Nan] got into an argument, I can't really remember because this was like three years ago. Erm, but it was about, I don't know what it was about, something because she will be like, 'Oh, it's about the Wi-Fi', but it's not just about the Wi-Fi, because I used to, like, always want the Wi-Fi on and stuff, and then she just screamed at me even more about that because I was screaming at her about, like, 'Can you please turn the Wi-Fi on?' and stuff. Erm, and then what would happen was like after I will tell her to turn the Wi-Fi on, you will get even more escalated, and then she'd say stuff about like, 'Oh, it's [Ph's – brother's] fault. No, it's your fault that [Ph] got adopted. She would say stuff like that. And that would annoy me a lot. So usually, me and her would actually start fighting, fighting like, erm, like I would pull her hair, she would pull my hair. And then I'd like push her, and then she push me, and then it would escalate even more. And then erm, well, it would just get to a point where I would, like, give up. And then, and then she went to go and hit me once when I was in my room, and then she hit my base of the thumb like that. And then she broke it.
Paul: Ow. That must have hurt.
Harmony: Because I have had opportunity to go with my dad and my mum, well mainly my dad because I don't want to live with my mum. Erm, but yeah.
Paul: And why didn't you?
Harmony: Erm, I don't know [laughs]. I honestly don't know. Like, she hasn't, like, made me stay here or anything, it's just that, like, I just I don't know [pause]. I just don't know why I want to stay here.

Harmony was unavailable for the final session of the study. She had gone to live with her father. While Harmony's grandmother was surprised by this, I felt it was foreseeable considering Harmony's previously voiced concerns. Harmony was older, thought about what it would mean to be more independent and have autonomy, and relayed that she did not feel comfortable remaining with her nan beyond 16 years. Stability of care for Harmony, Sydney, Thomas, and Jordan included something broader than being in the care of one or two carers or living in a single house until adulthood. They were not confined to the traditional fostering and adoption notions of home or substitute care often portrayed in child welfare research, policy, and practice. Moreover, those confines could have been detrimental to their wellbeing if forced on them. The ethics of rights would have superseded the ethics of care.

Can legal stability ensure permanence?

Some children cared deeply about their legal status with their carers, and some less so. Some did not even know what their legal status was. Thomas, for example, was dismissive of the question.

Paul: So, is your nan your special guardian, or has she adopted you or fostered you?

Thomas: Are you being silly? I don't know. You know, she's my nan, and she looks after me and does things.

By contrast, Rainbow emphasised that being adopted was as crucial, as it signified for her that her kinship carers were her new parents. Adoption allowed her to feel more claimed. Rainbow said:

I don't know why it's special [to be adopted]. You know the didgeridoo? We didn't own it from the very start. We got it and kept it. Because I feel like the didgeridoo. So, Mum and Dad adopted me, and now it means they're going to keep me forever and keep me safe. I belong here and won't be going back.

Erica and Kimberley felt that their legal order, a child arrangement order, did not match their wish to feel safe and cared for by their grandma. Indeed, the order seemed to work against their wishes, their need to feel safe, and even their wellbeing, particularly in terms of contact with their birth parents. Erica said:

Well, we had to go and see Dad, erm, but we went with our social worker to his house, and, erm, apparently it went well. But it didn't, and I wet myself then, and I was like really scared, and we didn't want to go. And then the social worker said that it was a good visit with him and that we were good to see him on Sunday, and we really didn't want to. And he came round on Sunday, and we were crying, and I was sick, and Grandma said, 'come on, you have to go because [the social worker] said'. And we were screaming. And it feels like they're just forcing us to see them when we don't want to.

Legal standing and legal orders can provide some children with a degree of security from which a sense of permanence can be established. Time spent with children and physical stability can also play a part. However, it is vital to think beyond legal permanence and physical stability to find the right match for children's needs (Skivenes and Thoburn, 2016). The children stated that legal orders should match their needs and wishes and assist them in negotiating and safely sustaining the many kin and non-kin relationships in their lives. Fundamentally, the ethics of care should be the primary objective, incorporated into and reinforced by the ethics of justice, which can be implemented through law. Again, the ethics of justice should never come first.

At times, some of the children felt this was forgotten. For example, sisters Kimberley and Erika wished their grandmother had more control over their lives. They viewed their grandmother as more likely to prioritise their needs and keep them safe. Nevertheless, their grandmother insisted that they go to the contact with their parents so as to obey legal stipulations, even when they were vomiting and wetting themselves, making them doubt the safety that she could offer them. Legal permanence again worked against the children's sense of permanence in this instance. Family arrangements must not be led primarily by legal processes unless synchronised with the children's emotional needs. Unfortunately, research suggests that in practice, intervention and support for families are often led by legal timescales or mandates from legal orders (Yuill and Mueller-Hirth, 2019).

Emotional stability

In keeping with the literature on children in care (Boddy, 2017), the most crucial goal for the children was to achieve emotional stability. However, this is a broader understanding of permanence than either substitute parenting or ensuring families maintain a presence. As noted in the previous chapter, children think about their continued care, the presence of those around them, and the potential absence of those who matter. Permanence is not only about the assured presence of somebody; it is also marked by their changeable presence/absence. This is understandable considering their past experiences of being removed from one part of a family unit and being placed in another (Farmer et al, 2013). As such, a broader sense of family also considers who could be next to care for them and how emotional stability can be sustained. Lucy said:

> And yeah, Grandma said if she drops down dead the next day, then we have to go and live with Uncle M. and Auntie J., and her sister. We have to move all the way to where they are, and so then I'll have to, like, go to a different school when I'm, like, literally in my second term at secondary school. I don't know. I think that would be OK, but it'll be hard.

Note that Lucy is explicitly planning for permanency. Also, she demonstrates that permanence for children living in kinship care is not just about reliance on one or two caregivers. It is not about permanent substitute care with particular carers throughout their childhood. The children proposed that permanence, like family, is an ever-evolving fluid construct which they are active in shaping. It is also contained by their own particular constructs of family, fixed genetic relations, different roles, and desire to remain within their ever-growing family. Jordan said: '[Shows picture.] This is, that's Nan's car. That's Nan, that's me, that's Thomas. We're just. I'm looking after Thomas, and Nan's looking after me and Thomas. There are other people not in the picture. You know, there are other people that will look after us.'

The children desired a sense of permanence to happen across the family. This was not dependent on legal ties or whether family members were living with them at the time. Instead, it depended on the feeling that someone would always be there for them. Louise said: 'Erm, I see family as people who will drop what they're doing for you, like on the other end of the phone or, and [pause]. I think the kind of family motto would be like: if someone calls, drop what you're doing.' The commitment is not unconditional. Emotional permanence includes providing a reciprocal sense of belonging, affiliation, and safety. Feeling a sense of permanence is about mature care.

Enacting permanence through sibling relationships

As noted in the last chapter, the children often viewed sibling relationships as beneficial because they felt they had a shared experience that predated their current family care arrangement. Lucy reiterated the point that siblings are more likely to be with you throughout your life, but she also noted that they share any inheritance should the kinship carers die: 'because when Grandma and Grandad died, they said that we can have half of the house each, and we'd still live in it and look after each other.' Such thinking again demonstrates how the children in kinship care are frequently permanency planning and envisioning continuity in their lives. It shows that sibling relationships, even though they may present as turbulent relationships, can be a way to assure some permanence and wellbeing throughout the life course.

Enacting permanence through relationships with pets

As described in the previous chapter, pets were considered part of the family. Pets were also often described as being like a sibling or another child. Pets were usually introduced not only by name but also by how long they had been with the family. The children would also often describe how frightened the animals were when they came to live with them. Lucy said:

> They were quite scared, and they were really small, because it's a new habitat for them and because, I can't remember where Grandma and Grandad got them from, but I don't know. But Grandma bought them toys and everything, and we played with them. And they're much better now. Well, not [cat's name], but he lets you stroke him. But he's more of an outdoor cat.

In this sense, the children often found similarities to pets and their experiences as part of a new family arrangement (Irvine and Cilia, 2017). The animals were cared for mainly by the parent figures in the household, and even though they may have needed a period of readjustment, they were accepted as part of the family. Pets were another way for the children to conceptualise and compare their own sense of permanence. It allowed them to predict their care experience and envisage how their connections may endure and how they will likely achieve a sense of permanence.

Enacting permanence by feeling safe and supported in the neighbourhood

Ensuring children feel safe was not seen as just the responsibility of individuals. The children said it was essential to feel safe in their neighbourhood so that they could feel safe in their family lives. Harmony said: 'I want to feel comfortable to come outside and feel safe to come outside because that's one thing I don't feel out here. I think when I'm out and about, I'm surrounded by strangers. Strangers tend to scare me, even though some strangers are friends you haven't met yet.'

The children did not just want to feel safe in their surrounding community; they wanted to feel supported and cared for by it. Megan said: 'That there's a lot of people that, like, look out for you. Like next door. And they, like, support everyone. And across the road. They will support everyone then, like, as a family on just our street, and that we're, like, all just together.'

The children often spoke about a sense of belonging and affiliation that did not solely depend on their genetic, extended, or chosen family members. They also needed to feel connected with others outside their family constellation. This was not dependent on whether someone was the only child in the household or if there was a single kinship carer. This connection was equally important for Megan, who lived with her nan, grandad, and three siblings, as it was for Rainbow, who was the only child being raised by her adoptive mum and dad.

Enacting permanence by feeling safe at school and when engaging in hobbies

The children found that hobbies outside the family home helped them navigate a sense of permanence. Activities at schools and clubs allowed for a sense of achievement, as previously discussed, and time away from the family home. Zac said:

> The good things about hobbies is that it's a fun thing in that you can interact with others and make new friends and do whatever. Well, not whatever. You make friends, have fun, feel part of stuff and learn something new. I think because it, like, calms you and you don't really focus on like problems. You just focus on, like, what you're doing in the moment.

It is important to note that these spaces also had the confines of rules, structure and routine. The children still had to feel safe. Even so, sports and hobbies allowed socialisation away from the family home with like-minded individuals and helped the children form their identity and helped them feel they belonged.

Insights for practice

Children's struggles through autonomous interdependence often cause internal and external struggles, particularly regarding the continuum of care and risk (Arce, 2018). As Louise stated, the children in kinship care frequently challenged boundaries and sometimes needed a 'firm hand', because managing risk and ensuring safety underpin all other needs. However, how conflict was approached signified to the children whether or not they were receiving care that prioritised their needs and had regard for their autonomous interdependence and safety. Depending on the response from the carers and professionals, negotiation showed recognition and respect for their agency and personal circumstances. Instead of feeling like a burden, the children were engaged in mature care, which helped define the rules, needs, and values that mattered to the family and society. This also allowed them to envisage a continuity of care. Therefore, carers, practitioners, policy makers, and courts must allow a dialogical space for flexibility and negotiation with children to adapt boundaries when deemed fair and practicable. The principles of the ethics of care must guide them. These are mutual trust, relational responsibility, responsiveness, attentiveness, and competence. Work must also be supported but not primarily guided by the ethics of rights. This is particularly important because the desire for permanence made the children work exceptionally hard to make family life work. Louise said: 'Sometimes when I'm in bed, I think of all my family and try and cut them out. But I can't because it's way too big.'

This dialogical way of perceiving relations to each other also helps address the challenges posed by the simplistic notions of agency, participation, and empowerment that often dominate child welfare discourse. With the insight of autonomous interdependence, agency no longer merely becomes synonymous with a child showing independence, autonomy, or simply being allowed to provide their views. A child speaking up at a meeting full of adults may not necessarily have any effect and might even negatively influence future relationships. Empowerment, as theorised through autonomous interdependence, can be better conceptualised as a collective struggle over time in which the responsibility for meeting needs and ensuring safety is shared. This also better acknowledges that child participation relies on available resources. It is relational and becomes something to be pursued and revisited throughout one's life rather than being confined to the present moment. Effective participation is part of mature care.

The concepts of autonomous interdependence and mature care also have particular relevance for kinship care, where wishes for complete family autonomy are at odds with the need for state intervention and support. Reframing state intervention as an ongoing relationship shifts the focus from whether kinship carers should be supported by taxpayers and the seemingly intrusive social workers, who the children felt did not fulfil their duties. It is no longer a question of whether the state should support these families, as all families are supported and support others to some extent, but rather to what degree support should continue and how.

More explicitly, regarding permanence, the children described that maintaining permanence over their life course mattered more than staying with specific carers or in particular places of residence if their safety and needs could no longer be prioritised. Such framing recognises multiple families and belongings in the children's family lives, which are in flux by their very nature (Rustin, 1994). Emotional permanence and mature care should be envisaged as a responsibility across the family network – not just as a string of substitute care, but as care from all family members, which changes and adapts according to needs, ages, development, and circumstances. The children will benefit from access to a range of services throughout childhood and beyond, irrespective of their legal status and caring arrangements. Overall, the ethics of care must be the ultimate goal, integrated into and supported by the ethics of justice – not the other way around.

Children used objects, memories, people, siblings, pets, and time as tools and transitional objects daily to help bridge the spaces in the care and protection/independence and risk mechanism and to manage their sense of permanence. This echoes the implications from the previous chapter. It is essential not only to provide space for the talk to children about their lives and future but also to ground specific work in the tools and strategies they are using. These should be the starting points for any support. There must be an acknowledgement of how children mobilise permanence and are active in this challenging work.

This type of shared compassionate care and working towards permeance depends on working with the family as a whole in a systemic and timely, rather than time-driven, way. Potential carers must be identified as a priority so that work on family relationships can start as soon as possible. They must be given appropriate time to engage in the challenging and emotional work. Furthermore, everybody in the family needs to be consulted, including the children. Permanence happens across the family. All must agree on rules and responsibilities, which, if necessary, should be monitored or even regulated. Feeling a sense of permanence also involves a reciprocal, mature, caring arrangement supported by the family's communities, social work, other agencies, and the state. Therefore, any arrangement requires a dialogical participatory process. Family group conferences are good examples of such approaches. They can obtain solutions from the whole family while ensuring that family roles and responsibilities are made clear alongside an agreed commitment from social workers (Edwards and Parkinson, 2018).

Conclusion

The children in the study showed remarkable insight into their safety, interdependence, and care. They understood the delicate balance between being safely cared for and having the freedom to grow and learn from their experiences. They recognised their dependency on others and that their carers should prioritise their needs. This underscores the importance of acknowledging risk, autonomous interdependence, and mature care, moving beyond the overuse of traditional psychosocial theories to provide a more nuanced framework for support and parenting. By also centring the ethics of care within the ethics of rights, we can guide meaningful practices that transcend mere stability and legal permanence. The children also demonstrated they were not passive recipients of care. Instead, they were active architects of their own permanence, striving to make care and family work despite the challenges.

The next chapter further explores the need for broader recognition of the children's voice(s), their family lives, and the state's function in kinship care. Accurate recognition of children's family dynamics and their role in shaping the meaning of family and permanence is crucial for providing appropriate support. This recognition can be empowered through compassionate understanding and collective responsibility.

9

Valuing recognition/(mis)recognition

Paul: If you could choose another motto for your whole family, what kind of motto would it be?

Danielle: Love. Love yourself, love your world and not only your family.

Previous chapters have highlighted the importance of managing relationships with others. This chapter builds on this and demonstrates the interconnectedness of children's family life, kinship care, child welfare, community, and the state. The chapter emphasises collective responsibility and explores the mechanism of recognition/(mis)recognition. Recognition/(mis)recognition is the value of being yourself and being valued for yourself, as illustrated in Figure 9.1.

Recognition occurs in relational spaces and involves acknowledging others and coming to be acknowledged by others. For the children in the study, recognition/(mis)recognition was often aligned to their status as a child and family in kinship care, ensuring social justice and protection of their rights. The term (mis)recognition is used here instead of misrecognition to re-emphasise that separate distinctions are not always helpful or appropriate. Even recognition can involve elements of (mis)recognition. For instance, children in kinship care may not always want to be recognised as such.

This chapter briefly explains recognition theories and then explores the three spheres of primary relationships, law and society, and community, and their impact on children living in kinship care. The children's insights demonstrated how they wish to be acknowledged as both children and not-yet-adults, the importance of listening to children and making them feel valued, and the dynamic ways in which they influence and are influenced by society and culture. The chapter demonstrates the implications of children's struggles for recognition for further research as well as policy and practice. Understanding these complexities, alongside their interactions with the other mechanisms, is vital for researchers, policy makers, and child welfare professionals to promote personal wellbeing and social justice.

Recognition theories

Child welfare workers, researchers, and policy makers can benefit from the ethics, politics, and values that form the foundation of recognition theories.

Figure 9.1: Recognition/(mis)recognition – one of the three central mechanisms that emerged from how the children in the study managed family life and permanence

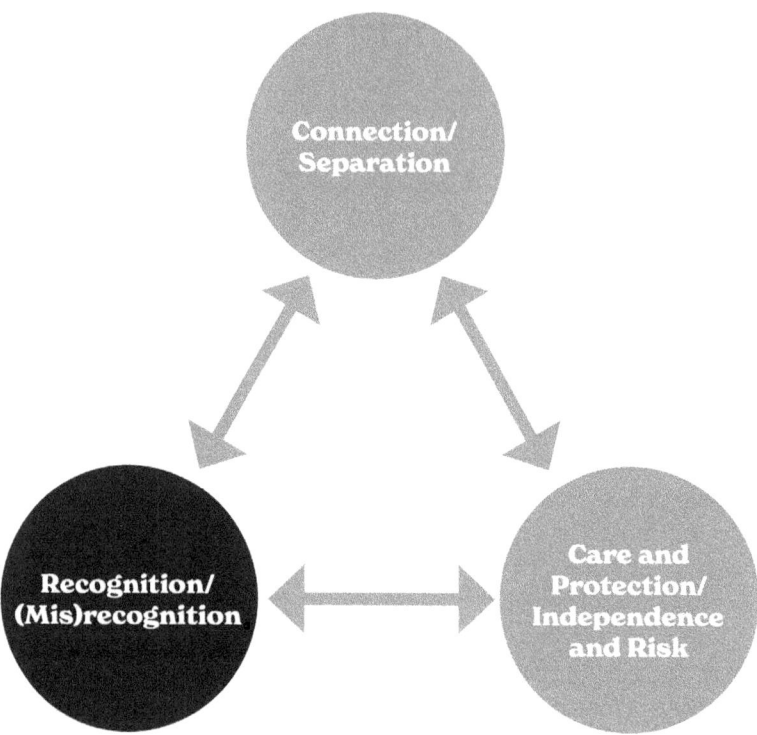

Theories of recognition were initially developed by Axel Honneth (1996), Charles Taylor (1994), and Nancy Fraser (2003). While recognition theories are not yet widely used in social work practice or research, influential radical social work scholars, including Garett (2010), Web (2010), and Houston (2016b), advocate for their value. Mitchell (2022) also applies recognition theory to develop theoretical frameworks for supporting children and young people involved in child welfare services.

Appropriate recognition allows self-respect, self-confidence, and self-esteem to flourish. This aligns with social work values and the task of social work to instigate change for individuals. Recognition theories can also tackle the political responsibility of child welfare work and participation. Recognition theories can enable true empowerment by ensuring those we work with become engaged with making societal change by being heard and enacting their agency to enhance their lives and the social situations of others. In this way, theories of recognition help bring together the other themes and theories in this book. They assist in conceptualising the ongoing process of nurturing participation, permanence, and family, while highlighting the importance of interdependence and collaborative caring relationships for both the personal and political dimensions of social life.

Spheres of recognition

Honneth (1996) describes three spheres of interaction that require constant negotiations, also known as struggles for recognition. These struggles are due to the power relationships inherent in any interaction. Ongoing struggles for power and recognition are experienced profoundly by children, who are often viewed as merely immature, incompetent, and vulnerable (Fitzgerald et al, 2009). It is even more applicable for children in family relationships where some adults are told they are not good enough parents.

Honneth's recognition theory builds on Hegel's (2018) ideas of interconnectedness and a Kantian focus on values and ethics. It suggests that human relationships thrive through connections, reciprocity, and a shared understanding of everyone's collective values (Houston, 2016b). Honneth predominantly focuses on the psychological and psychosocial aspects of recognition. Honneth's recognition theory reduces the layers of Bronfenbrenner's (1979) ecological theory of child development into three spheres while continuing to highlight the importance of agency, empowerment, and social justice. These spheres are:

- Love: This sphere involves intimate relationships, such as those with family and close friends. Recognition in this sphere is crucial for developing self-confidence.
- Rights: This sphere relates to legal recognition and acknowledging individuals as autonomous agents with rights. It is essential for self-respect.
- Solidarity: This sphere involves social regard and the recognition of individuals' contributions to their communities and society, which is vital for self-esteem.

The first sphere of interaction for recognition
Love, respect, and regard in primary relationships

The first sphere of recognition – love, emotional affection, and primary relationships of positive regard – is primarily rooted within the family and is derived from Winnicott's object relations theory (Bainbridge, 2015). Positive interactions within this sphere promote self-confidence.

Paul: What does home mean to you?
Louise: A place to be yourself.

While the desire for children to be themselves seems straightforward, the complexities of primary relationships mean that learning about and being oneself involves challenges. Recognition and respect within these primary relationships can lead to conflict and the disclosure of potentially upsetting information, especially for children living in kinship care. However, the children noted that, over time, most challenges could be weathered depending on the quality and perceived durability of the relationships. Eliza said:

> If we do have an argument, we're kind of over it by the next time anyway so it's, it's. I know, I know I'm never going to have an argument, and then it's going to carry on for ages, and it's just going to escalate. So, there is sometimes tension in the house, but I feel like that happens in every house. But for us, we just kind of move away from it quite quickly and know that we still love each other, so it's not really an issue.

The children discussed the need to trust that conflict and any challenging information provided is for their best interests at the right time, in the right place, and with people who have caring relationships. Erica said: 'Like, we respect each other and love each other, and just feel safe together, and help each other in life.' This reiterates the emphasis on how, for the children, safety, permanence, and relationships are done and negotiated with those who mattered around them. For relationships to be meaningful and positive they should entail trust, empathy, compassion, and commitment, as outlined in the ethics of care.

The influence of gender roles

The influence of cultural expectations illustrates how different spheres can interact and, perhaps surprisingly, affect the first sphere of close relations. For example, the children involved in the study wanted to discuss the significance of clothing, shopping, make-up, and, as Rainbow mentioned, 'looking pretty'. There were gender differences regarding the importance of these aspects. For example, some of the girls used make-up to try to resolve their insecurities.

Paul: Why do you like make-up?
Harmony: It's just something because I, erm, don't have very self-confidence in myself, and I suppose it's like something that all girls use, particularly, like, if you want to be with a boy. Well, not all girls.

This level of performativity gives some credence to Butler's (2006) gender ideology that sees gender as primarily created through behaviour. It also means that the gendered patriarchal environment in which the children are positioned affects how they are viewed, as well as shaping the forming of their identity and close personal relationships.

Another example involves the two siblings from a household where the carers held stereotypically gender-defined perceptions about them. Jake stated that his family often viewed his behaviour as naughty. In contrast, his sister Ellie sensed that her behaviour was generally regarded as favourable. Ellie was recognised for her academic achievements, while Jake was seen as destructive, boisterous, and, at times, violent and overactive. Ellie's positive reputation persisted despite her occasional bluntness and unkindness towards her brother. She said: 'And so, yesterday, if you did not notice, well not yesterday, but the day before that, my brother drawed on the bed. That's a very bad drawing. I think my brother would say it's good for him.'

Gender differences have been highlighted in foster care studies (for example, Heslop, 2019). These differences are associated with how children relate to carers and others, as well as the stereotypical roles they often adopt. Gender inequities also extend into the parental roles of caring for children. Only one of the families in the study had a male primary carer, reflecting the demographics in the UK, where most kinship carers are women (Delap and Mann, 2019).

The presence of gender and care politics highlights that children are reflections not only of their immediate environment but also of their cultural, political, and sociological ones, such as a patriarchal society. Cultural norms are then often reflected in legal processes and orders. For example, women are more likely to be perceived as the primary carers for special guardianship orders even if both male and female carers apply (Harwin, Simmonds et al, 2019). Girls are also more likely to be in kinship care arrangements than boys (Schoenwold et al, 2022). Any understanding of children's family lives and a sense of permanence and kinship care must have a critical understanding of the impact of gender on the personal, societal, community, and legal spheres of recognition.

The influence of consumer capitalism

The children showed how they reflected not only the patriarchy embedded in society but also consumer capitalism, an economic and social system where consumer demand is deliberately influenced and manipulated on a large scale through mass-marketing techniques, primarily to benefit sellers (Martens, 2018).

Many children in the study described the cost of certain items and whether these were the current trend. These appeared to reflect their self-worth. Sydney said: 'That's one of my Smiggle pencils. They are scented, and they're really nice, and I've got lots of them. Some of my friends are quite jealous, actually.'

Shopping as an activity also helped the children sustain social bonds with their family members, friends, and the community. Kimberley said:

> And this is, erm, a picture of TK Maxx, and this is one of the managers there and, erm, he's nice, and he just chats to us sometimes about, erm, things that are fun … and you can just wander around the shop, and I feel safe there because sometimes Grandma let's Erika and I just go there. Not together but, but to wander around the shop together without Grandma a bit. So, I think Grandma knows that will be safe inside the shop.

Shopping and using space outside the family home allowed the children to feel a level of independence and connection with society and their communities while also being monitored to some extent by their carers and other trusted adults. Through shopping, the children were receiving acknowledgement in all spheres of recognition. Shopping allowed the children to buy gifts for others, to return the care they had received. Consumerism led the children to value presents, objects, and experiences as indicators of care, love, and connection. It also allowed them to participate in the consumerist world (Compeau et al, 2016). Buying valuable objects and experiences helped the children feel a sense of affiliation, investment, permanence, and reciprocal mature care across the family.

The second sphere of interaction for recognition

Laws and the judiciary

The second sphere concerns rights, which can be upheld through legal rights and moral respect between actors. Honneth (1996) proposes that protecting rights results in self-esteem. Recognition of rights also means that the children, in return, respect the rules and laws of society. Law, institutions, and society should recognise the rights of children as dutiful, interdependently autonomous legal subjects. Zac said: 'It's good to have laws because if we don't, everyone would be dead. If murder was not law, there'd be a lot more deaths and stabbings and things like that. Everything would be a lot more worse.'

Regarding their own care, most children recognised the value of the courts. Despite their ambivalent relationships with their birth parents, they understood and often reluctantly agreed with court decisions. Ellie said:

> I wish I could live with my mummy because [pause] I don't [pause]. Well, she does go to court because my mummy, when she just had

Jake, she was very ill, and we went [pause]. So, they went to court, and then the court people decided it was better here with Grandma. And I think that was the right thing.

However, some children, like Kimberley and Erika, agreed with some but not all court decisions, mainly because they felt their views were not considered. Kimberley said:

> Erm, like if we were taken away and had to go to foster care and like we got separated, I would, I would have been like devastated and really sad. So, we agree with that. And [not] contact. Well, we feel safe there because there's contact supervisors. But also, when we go on visits, we don't really like having visits with them. I'd rather never see [our mum and dad] ever again. But the courts decided. I'd like to, we'd like to be able to be listened to by [the courts] more.

Feeling heard

The children were emphatic that being heard was the primary way to ensure they were recognised for who they were and their rights were upheld. However, they also realised that as children, they were less likely to be listened to. This lack of attentive listening to children by adults often bemused and frustrated them.

Paul: But people may say that adults have more experience and are more clever, and so that's why you should listen to adults more.

Zac: Yeah, well, maybe they are, but children should still have a chance as well, as we're not just dumb brats. And if adults have more experience, then why are most adults stabbing each other and causing all this war? And kids aren't doing anything.

All the children highlighted the need to be heard by adults but also understood that perspective limits everybody. As our discussions progressed, it became apparent that the children valued a dialogical approach involving negotiations in intergenerational spaces. Often, this process was more important to them than finding solutions. Kimberley said:

> I would say that we do know things, but sometimes we don't really understand, like, things that are happening in life. Like with our mum and dad, we don't know everything. But things that we do know and that we have experienced, like, we had gone and seen them, they should listen to us. But they should listen to them as well. I think they

should listen to both of the sides of what they have to say because I don't think that all of the time that adults are listening to children, and I think they don't listen about their feelings, how they're acting, and not all of the time adults are listening to them. Like you listen to me, Grandma listens to me. But like the social workers, they don't really listen to us.

As highlighted in Chapter 3, participation literature often expresses concerns that participation may become tokenistic and exploitative, especially when seen as an isolated, individual task rather than an ongoing dialogical political activity. The children reiterated this concern. Purple said:

Adults should also listen to children. Because adults can sometimes ignore the children even if they've listened to them. Because we've listened to them, and so it's rude that they don't listen to us and ignore what we've said. It just makes us feel bad, like nothing, like not worth it. Like nothing.

Purple demonstrated that a lack of respect for their views impacts their self-respect (Honneth, 1996). She reiterated Kimberley's insights that indicated participation must be a collaborative dialogical process.

Returning to theory, embracing collaborative dialogical participation alongside recognition theory can help incorporate Fraser's (2003) contributions to theories of recognition. She shifts away from Honneth's (1996) more identity-focused model, arguing that his approach relies too much on 'psychologisation'. Fraser proposes that social justice also requires recognising cultural differences and economic redistribution. It takes a broader approach and takes individual responsibility away from just the families or professionals. It is not enough for families and children to be given a tokenistic opportunity to participate; they must feel well-placed and able to do it and be provided with appropriate spaces. It is not enough to listen; the children want to be heard. The ethics of rights must be addressed alongside the ethics of care. Children must be heard with compassion and respect from all spheres, including society and the state.

However, Garrett (2010) argues that many recognition theories, including Fraser's, often overlook or underplay the role of the state and the multifaceted nature of oppression. Therefore, adopting a theoretical framework that critically examines and challenges state power structures is crucial. This critical awareness is particularly relevant for kinship care, which straddles the line between private family concerns and state responsibilities. This is why critical realism served as a valuable under-labourer for the child participation research with children in kinship care. It is a critical theory. Critical realism produces a deeper understanding of the historical, political,

The difference between children and adults

How society values children's views depend on societal perspectives regarding whether children should be considered capable beings in their own right or not-yet-fully-formed adults who are incompetent and vulnerable. Society frequently perceives children as not quite fully developed, or even lacking moral awareness, and this was reflected in the children's view of parenting responsibilities. Sydney said: '[Nan and Grandad] want me to grow up to be a good person.'

The previous chapter on permanence and care also emphasises the importance of nurturing children's aspirations and growth through parental guidance. It highlights that children value guidance and self-development. Nonetheless, there remains ambiguity about whether 'becoming' and 'being' are distinct concepts or if these objectives are exclusive to childhood rather than applicable throughout the life course. For instance, it was noted that children often expressed a need to pursue education to secure a good life in their adult years. They articulated that part of parenting involves considering children's future prospects. Zack said: 'Because Grandma cares for me, and she wants me to grow up and have a good life. So, a good education is quite important. So, she kind of thinks in the future. Not just in the present, not the past, but in the future.'

Nevertheless, within five minutes of our discussion, Zack demonstrated that being in the moment was also essential and that learning and socialising for future gains are not everything.

Paul: Why did you take a picture of your bike?
Zack: Because I got it when my birthday was in September. So, last time you saw me, I was ten. So, I took it because I think it's important, I think it's important to me because, I erm, think it's important to know how to ride a bike and it's like my idea of fun, and like you have to have at least a little bit of fun when you're a child.

It was intriguing that Zack and the other children frequently connected riding a bike with childhood. However, in further discussion, they would struggle to differentiate what it meant to be a child or an adult, sometimes navigating between the two within just a few sentences. Jordan said: 'Because adults are children, but just with another number and a bit older, so they're different. But they're still children, and children are just younger versions of adults.'

Overall, the children spoke about this need to both be and become. The developmental, the social, and the positioning by others were also interwoven. Being and becoming were not separate for the children; both were important and intertwined (Uprichard, 2008). Louise said:

> There isn't much difference between children and adults. In a way, we're all children, but just some are more independent and smarter. Sometimes adults are more smarter than kids about some things, but kids can outsmart them. Like it's just an age, it doesn't mean anything. You can have more experience, but some choose not to learn, and then some do. And then some chose to keep those experiences to themselves. And then some will choose to use it to teach others how to carry on with life and be themselves.

The children often navigated the in-between spaces of childhood and adulthood through philosophical thinking about the world. They would contemplate what is real, what are the impacts of experience, and how we learn. This imitates critical realist thought. The children often steered away from labelling others based solely on their descriptive attributes, such as age. However, at other times, they would determine that specific characteristics, such as age, mean certain groups need specific roles and protections.

The recognition of kinship care by governments, law, and society

Navigating through what is (ontology) and how we know (epistemology) also applied to their thoughts on how society recognised/(mis)recognised kinship care. Most acknowledged that kinship care is a specific scenario that requires specific recognition, knowledge, and support. Eliza said:

> It still annoys me really today because nobody really understands or seems to want to understand. Like we never see on the news about like anything to do with kinship care or anything. And then so much goes wrong with it. Like the money in the benefits is just like one of the biggest things. I just think, like, it's so unfair to see someone like adopted or fostering. They get so much more support with like money, also, with like social services in my opinion. And you can't expect then these kids to have the same opportunities. It is left down to the child themselves, which is why I think some people are like, 'Wow, how do you deal with it?' Like, because we don't like have anybody else to like help us deal with it, or like any funds to help us get away to deal with it.

The children also suggested that support should not just be shaped according to a homogenised view of kinship care, but should be centred on specific circumstances. Harmony said:

Yeah, like it doesn't need to be like labels. Like, there is no authority. It just needs to be, I think, it needs to be a facility that is available to people if and when they need it, rather than something that's been put in place by someone else, which is just like ... it doesn't even need to be formal or anything like that. It just needs to be there, I think, for however you need it.

All the children were clear that kinship care needs better support. They also emphasised that this support should focus on specific needs. This is not exactly a radical approach. However, as discussed in Chapter 2, arguments are often swayed by political discourse, tussles around responsibility, labelling, and risk avoidance, which can overlook the fundamental value of kinship care support. Beter support could mean that each child receives the support and protection they need, tailored to their specific requirements, rather than to the labels they acquire.

The political child

The children were passionate about having their opinions heard on broader political issues. They frequently voiced their concerns about topics like the climate emergency. Rainbow, who was six, shared her thoughts on Brexit with me. Zack talked about homelessness, and Danielle also contributed her perspective on structural racism:

Because homeless people don't really get family. They just live on the streets, and when I'm older, I want the homeless to come off the streets and get in houses theirselves. And then people help them, which is what I will do. And then if it's Black people, Black people don't really, erm, get paid as much, and they just live on the streets with no money, and they could die.

Megan wanted to clarify that adults seemingly have more choices in life. Yet, she felt children should also be given choices about major political decisions more likely to affect their lives. She said:

I think the children and adults, they both get like their choice, obviously, because it's a free country and you are allowed to do what you want to do, but I think adults are given more of a choice. Like with the whole Brexit thing. All adults were given a choice, whereas I think maybe the children should have been able to choose because it's our lives more than it's going to affect them and some other people.

This supports research on children as political actors and the diverse ways they engage with politics in their daily lives. It emphasises that even at a young age, children demonstrate political knowledge and a desire to participate in creating a fairer society (van Deth et al, 2011; Moran-Ellis et al, 2014).

The third sphere of interaction for recognition
School and extra-curricular learning

The third sphere of recognition proposes the need for solidarity to provide self-esteem, resilience, and a sense of permanence through acknowledging children's contributions to their communities. This echoes the findings in the last two chapters that a child's sense of family, safety, and permanence is not just confined to family relationships but also requires community involvement.

As Zack suggested, school was vital for all the children in terms of learning for the future to get a 'good life'. When I met with the children, all were keen to show their learning and display their achievements through framed certificates, medals and pictures. Kimberley said:

> Erm, I love playing my flute because I love music, and it makes me happy. And last year, erm, we went to this church by our school, and I played in front of like the whole school, and I like really enjoyed myself and everyone said I was actually quite good.

This reinforces the idea that humans are comparative beings (Sayer, 2011) – we must assess our progress through recognition and comparison with others. Therefore, the children were keen to display their achievements also as a comparison to raise their self-esteem.

Frenemies

Reiterating most literature and research, being at school and in clubs undoubtedly serves a sociocultural function, helping children's development and allowing them to be valued by others (Jessiman et al, 2022).

Megan:	Yeah, I like, like being at school and just being away from [laughs] the others. Because sometimes I think that we spend too much time around each other. I get to see my friends and [pause].
Paul:	Do you have a group of close friends and stuff? What makes a good friend?
Megan:	I prefer to just keep it like close and not like have loads of different friends because I think it's quite hard to like be there for every single one of those people. Because, like everyone's going to have issues, like whether it's home or

friend issues, or anything. So, you don't really want to like feel like you're letting like people down.

Navigating social relationships can be challenging, particularly when the children feel they have what could be perceived as unusual and not-as-good family circumstances.

Paul:	Do others at school know about you not living with your birth mum and dad?
Rainbow:	They do. They just make fun of me for it.
Paul:	Oh, do they? What, your friends?
Rainbow:	No, my enemies. She's called [redacted]. She is very unpleasant. She treats me like muck off a shoe, trying to wipe me out.

Winnicott's (1960) psychoanalytical theory on the true and false self can be applied here. The children's experience of feeling alive and spontaneous, their true selves, was eroded by others who made them feel dead inside, like a shadow of who they should be, their false selves. To guard themselves against the intrusion of others' views, the children tended to restrict sharing details of their past and their kinship care living situation to a few close friends and those who needed to know. Lucy said:

> I tell some people. Like, I feel like I have to ask whether the people think, like what they think about it, kind of thing before I tell them. Like when you meet and you kind of like judge their reactions a bit. It's just, I don't, like, want people to ask me stupid questions about it, and I can just, like, kind of judge if they will.

This partitioning was a way of protecting their feelings from others stigmatising them (Smart, 2011). It was also a way of compartmentalising their lives and protecting their identity (Farmer et al, 2013).

Being different or normal

The children acknowledged that norms exist and can determine how people are perceived. Yet, for them, normality included an ideal. The perspective that normal is good and not normal is deviant was so compelling that they believed being cared for in a traditional family set-up could address many of their concerns. They assumed that others who were not in similar situations would not have the same difficulties in their lives. The children imagined that other children would not have challenges concerning their primary attachments, loss, stigmatisation, or permanence. A sense of normality was synonymous with not being different and life going well (Madigan et al, 2013). Danielle said: 'Some people pick their children up, and I just look at them, and I just have to walk with my sister and my grandad. And when I see other people with their mum and dad, they have a big laugh, and it makes me feel upset.'

The children's attempts to have their lives recognised as normal were further highlighted by all of them using the word 'like' when describing their family relationships. Zack said: 'Because she's looked after me for five years now, and she's technically like my mum and I, erm, and yes, so … like, she's like a mother. Like she treats me like her son. She, she cares for me like a son.'

Research suggests that a sense of normality is one of the benefits of kinship care and remaining within the family (Burgess et al, 2010). However, children's idealised views of normal family life are problematic. Protection from loss is impossible in anyone's life, and concerns about relationships are inevitable. Additionally, stigmatisation can occur for various reasons. While promoting kinship care for its potential to increase a sense of normality may seem prudent, it can unintentionally highlight and perpetuate differences and stigma. This can make children living in kinship care or other arrangements where they are not living with birth parents feel their lives are lacking.

These problems with navigating recognition/(mis)recognition of kinship care and family cause cognitive dissonance for children living in kinship care. One of the most emotive, possibly intrusive, questions asked in the study was whether the children viewed themselves as different. Harmony said:

> I don't think [pause] I don't like being called different. I don't like, I don't like being called different because I know I'm different and stuff, but I like different to be a nice …. Yeah, I know I'm like different because this doesn't happen every [pause]. This, like, doesn't happen. Well, it might. It might happen to other people. But I don't know. It doesn't happen to many people. Yeah, like, I'm not trying to be dramatically different. Like I'm not dramatically different.

And Zack's very forthright response was:

> I don't mind living with my grandma because the only thing that's really different is that I live with my grandma. I do what ordinary ten-year olds do, like play sports. I go to school. So, I'm technically a normal ten-year-old. But some people might not think that, but that's my opinion. So.

Groups exclusively for children living in kinship care

Another relevant example of the tension between being perceived as normal or different emerged when the children discussed the value of kinship carer groups. Most children felt these groups primarily benefited their carers. A few acknowledged that they also found value in them. For some, the groups were appreciated because they provided an environment where the children were not treated differently and were listened to without prejudice. Eliza said:

> Yeah, like it's nice that we're all there in the same, like, position. Like, nobody's better than, well, not better than anyone else, but nobody's, like, different from anyone else … I don't need to announce it there or speak about it there because everyone just kind of knows anyway. And it's nice just because it's like, well, other kids are doing it so … and you, if you want to talk to them about it, you feel better when you're speaking to them about, erm, all of it, all of the things and, erm, the advice helps a lot.

In contrast, some of the children felt that although there were benefits, they did not necessarily want to see themselves as part of a group specifically for children living in kinship care. Kimberley said:

> Erm, it's fun to, like, erm, talk to other children as well and, erm well, like, the carers. They, erm, help, and we see their children as well. So, erm, I don't know. I don't always want to go because, erm, sometimes I don't want to be with them. I just want to forget sometimes.

Feeling listened to by schools and other child welfare professionals

The children desired to feel respected by those within their communities. In line with Honneth's (1996) third sphere of recognition, this helped their self-esteem. Recognition by communities was particularly necessary because it was also often helpful to have somewhere outside the family home where they felt listened to. Rainbow said:

> The hub is just like where you can just like calm yourself down, and this is basically private, where you can just go and [blows out through mouth] just calm down … because sometimes, when I'm panicking, I can always go there. Mrs. J., yeah, she helps me do a lot of things and we always have like a little session. We talk about our feelings.

Rainbow proposed that there is merit in those outside the family constellation who can listen. This is because others are less likely to act unless necessary. However, the children's feelings could still be acknowledged and recognised. The children were also not as anxious about hurting the feelings of those they were talking to. Repercussions and conflict were less likely (Geldard et al, 2017). The children understood the need for consultation, generational perspectives, mutual responsibility, and dialogue (Abebe, 2019). They wished for a dialogical approach with some in their communities where they could express their inner voice(s) and ambivalence without repercussions.

This dialogical approach was vital for the children, especially if they had social work intervention in their family life. Particularly for some issues, like contact, the children were clear that they could also offer valuable solutions, and their views had not only intrinsic value (out of concern for wellbeing) but instrumental value (in terms of service outcome). Erica said:

> Once a social worker came. He said, 'Have you ever thought about, like, other ways of seeing your mum and dad or anything, or having visits or contacts?' And we said, 'What about writing a letter or like writing an email or something?' And then he was like, 'Oh my gosh, I'd never thought of that before. Like, that's a really good idea.'

Cultural affiliations and religion

Lucy was eager to share her Traveller heritage with me. Kimberley and Erika emphasised the significance of understanding their cultural background in Singapore. They also expressed a desire to learn how to cook traditional dishes. Additionally, they recognised that cultural and ethnic differences, including skin colour, can influence their lives and feelings. Kimberley said: 'Erm, the last contact with our mum was, was saying, like 'Oh, you're really dark' and 'I like Black people'. And it was a bit strange because we didn't feel like right.'

Religion, spirituality, and places of worship played a crucial role in shaping many of the children's identities. This aspect is often overlooked in kinship care literature. However, these elements provided significant support to many children, aiding them and their families in socialising, finding support, and guiding their inner conversations and thoughts about the world. Danielle said:

> Church matters because we get [pause] because me and [Purple] go out with these adults, and then we learn about more stuff. And we also do fun activities. Because God, because God's real, and also God could be in your heart. And if you feel sad, you can just pray. But if you're at school, some people might laugh at you if you go to church.

The cases of Kimberley, Erika, and Danielle illustrate that engaging with family culture, ethnicity, and religion is crucial for addressing everyday concerns and forming a sense of identity and belonging (Owusu-Bempah, 2010). They also highlight that (mis)recognition can lead to unhappiness. Therefore, social work tasks, including permanence planning, must recognise the individual identities important to the child and how society and others perceive them. This is especially relevant given the disparities minoritised children face in kinship care in the UK (Schoenwold et al, 2022).

Slime and the interaction of all the spheres of recognition

Slime is an excellent example of how Honneth's (1996) three spheres of recognition regarding primary relationships, society and law, and community interact. The study was undertaken between 2017 and 2020, when slime was a social and cultural phenomenon. In the sessions, the children often spoke about slime parties, slime poking videos, slime stations, and the process of making slime. Nevertheless, towards the end of the fieldwork, its importance had diminished for the children. Harmony said:

> And then this is a slime area where because I used to, like when I was in year six or seven, I used to love making slime. We plan things, and I had slime parties. And I used to sell it to people as well, which was like me having my own business.

It took some time for me to understand children's obsession with slime. There is minimal research on it. Most research frames it around autonomous sensory meridian responses acquired from touching it or watching others touch it (Harper, 2020). Some describe it as a 'tactile manipulative' aligned with science education (Levingston et al, 2019).

After reflection and many slime conversations with the children, we realised that slime was not just a developmental tool, a social interaction, or a way to receive pleasant physiological responses. As adults, we were not meant to understand it. This was one of its primary purposes. Slime helped the children hold onto their child status while having fun, exploring, socialising, and even making money within their communities. It was challenging for me to understand slime because the children were actively ensuring that I did not fully understand. They were developing their own popular culture and excluding adults from being members of their communities (Horton, 2010). Sydney said:

> Some people might ask why do you have slime, and it's none of your business. You have alcohol, why can't we … we don't understand you. We don't understand about alcohol. Grown-ups do, but they don't understand about slime. So, we don't need to bother about them. They don't need to bother about us. We just have it.

The children were active in defining the spheres of recognition rather than passively being positioned within them.

The implications of recognition/(mis)recognition on child welfare research, policy, and practice

This section highlights the implications of recognition/(mis) recognition mechanism, but it also draws together the other two mechanisms – connection/separation and care and protection/independence and risk – to recommend research, policy, and practice directions.

Recognition that kinship care relies on communities

The predominant focus of kinship care research and literature has been on the responsibilities of individual carers, birth parents, and social workers in promoting a child's welfare and sense of permanence (Brown et al, 2019). However, children's insights emphasised the community's role in providing wellbeing, belonging, and continuity, supporting Honneth's (1996) call for community recognition. The children also gained achievement, self-confidence, and self-esteem through activities outside the family, such as school, hobbies, and clubs. These activities offered time away from family tensions, allowing them to navigate their complex circumstances and form meaningful connections. This time fostered shared narratives, routines, and a sense of agency, contributing to their sense of permanence. Recognising the community's influence on family life and permanence broadened the concept of family to include friends, teachers, and activity leaders.

Events and groups exclusively for children in kinship care offered a space where they could feel normal and not focus on feeling different. These events helped them to be seen as children in diverse family set-ups rather than just kinship care. However, the tension of being seen as normal because they were different often caused a struggle for recognition, with the children navigating the tension of being both unique and ordinary. This cognitive dissonance could be exhausting, leading some children to avoid these groups. For others, these events provided a chance to discuss concerns and understand that their feelings were due to their circumstances, not personal flaws. More research is needed, but the children in the study suggested attendance should be a choice, not mandatory. Such events and groups should also not replace other essential recognition by the law and the state through financial and practical assistance. All spheres must be attended to.

Children stressed the importance of talking to people outside their immediate family and care professionals. They valued social workers who listened and acted on their views but also cherished those who listened without taking action. Close friends and pastoral teachers provided non-judgmental support and reliability. This underscores the need for accessible talking therapies, independent visitors, and ensuring children have trusted, empathetic friends beyond their family and professional networks.

Recognition that kinship care relies on upholding rights and social equity

The children's views reiterate the importance of Honneth's (1996) second sphere of recognition, which involves upholding children's rights through legal and moral respect, especially in kinship care. Despite being the most common form of care when children cannot stay with their birth parents, kinship care is often underfunded and overlooked, receiving minimal training, resources, and support (Kiraly, 2015). Consequently, kinship care can be easily overlooked and exploited as merely a private family arrangement to save costs (McCartan et al, 2018).

The children desired recognition of their specific relationships with their family and community, their approach to permanence, and their legal and symbolic rights. However, as proposed by Fraser (2003), none of these can be achieved without adequate resources. Financial support for essential activities, even simple ones like shopping for cultural trends, is crucial and cannot be an afterthought or considered a luxury. The children stressed the importance of money, noting that the lack of funds often caused concern for their carers, impacting the first sphere of recognition. Harmony said: 'Like, my nan worries about money and doesn't have enough money to do anything.'

Lack of funds and resources can make children in kinship care feel like a burden. They seek reciprocal, mature care from the state and those who matter in their lives. Societal marginalisation, especially due to racialisation, significantly impacts their wellbeing. Many children in kinship care come from ethnic and racially minoritised families, facing additional challenges due to a lack of bespoke resources like financial assistance, educational support, and mental health services.

These disparities highlight the need for inclusive policies and support systems to ensure all children in kinship care receive the necessary resources and opportunities. Recognising both their specific situations and the broader effects of social policy, marginalisation, and inequalities is crucial. Policy makers, practitioners, and researchers must listen to lived experiences and correlate them with macro data for meaningful resource distribution (Fraser, 2003). To avoid essentialist determinism, macro data should be combined with individual cases and localised data. For example, kinship care policy and practice documents and reviews must consider the impact of austerity policies to provide appropriate support (McCartan et al, 2018). A mixed methods approach is essential, yet many local authorities have not used local data on demographic characteristics and needs to inform their family and friends policies (Mercer et al, 2015).

Finch's (2007) concept of family 'display' is another helpful theory for advocating practical and financial support for kinship carers. Children in the study emphasised that they deserved the same opportunities to demonstrate how their family members 'do' family, just like families not in kinship care arrangements. If they were not able to display their family life as acceptable family life, this could lead to vilification by others. This need to 'display' family is universal (Dermott and Seymour, 2011). This displaying of 'practical kinship' (Bourdieu, 1977) includes family holidays, day trips, school trips, homework help, household chores, buying presents, using social media, and family mealtimes. Families need time, resources, and capabilities to engage in them. Again, they should not be perceived as luxuries.

Children also highlighted the need for time and space to manage separation/connection, which should be supported by their community, professionals, and the state. Opportunities depend on having enough time with others, financial means, and safe real and virtual spaces.

Recognition of how children view their family arrangement

Recognition is a vital human need (Taylor, 1994), especially for children in kinship care, who are living in set-ups which others often perceive as unusual or somehow worse than being brought up by birth parents. These children seek recognition and support tailored to their unique circumstances. They want their family lives to be seen as normal, though not necessarily typical, and they emphasise celebrating diversity rather than differences within family structures. Kinship care should be viewed as child-rearing by relatives, not just a state-dependent service like fostering or adoption (Skoglund and Thørnblad, 2017).

However, from a critical realist, both/and, non-monological perspective, kinship care cannot just be viewed in one way. It also exists independently of our perceptions and is interconnected with familialism, social services, welfare, and judicial systems. Reality should not be conflated with our knowledge of reality (Bhaskar, 2008b). Safety and the right to be protected from harm and suffering were essential to these children who experienced fractured family relationships and often have experienced abuse and neglect. They were also aware of the impact of isolation, poverty, and lack of appropriate resources. The children spoke about the risks inherent in their kinship care arrangements. Therefore, the in-between relational spaces should be acknowledged and navigated. Kinship care can be a favourable permanence option for children, but they felt it was also inherently risky, which required appropriate support, scrutiny, and, possibly, monitoring. Kinship care is a family practice that at times requires being part of child welfare and social work services.

Viewing kinship care in this both/and way and as something unique that reflects the children's experiences requires a cultural shift. It means not adopting assessment and legal procedures from fostering or adoption, or comparing allowances between foster carers and kinship carers. It means not pushing the narrative that kinship care is an alternative placement with better outcomes and lower risk, and that it will save local authorities time and money. First, there is not enough robust evidence to support this. Second, such (mis)recognition perpetuates endless binary debates and relativism.

Kinship care should not be seen as a solution to keep children out of state care, but as a unique family set-up needing specific support. It would be better for policy makers to perceive kinship care as delivering family support rather than an alternative child placement service. Considering kinship care as a heterogenous family set-up in its own right also questions how the experiences and knowledge in Fostering or Adoption Panels can relate to the specifics of kinship care arrangements. It also asks why most support in the UK comes from the Adoption and Special Guardian Support Fund rather than a kinship care support fund, and why most resources depend on a child's legal care status.

For research, navigating the middle ground between kinship care as a private family matter and a service requires moving away from including kinship care in broader studies of looked-after children, for two main reasons:

- Perpetuating the effectiveness debate: The debate on whether kinship care is better or worse than other placements often focuses on 'what works' outcomes and economic costs, overlooking the complex relational spaces in kinship care. This could lead to exploiting kinship care as a low-cost solution with minimal support.
- Representation issue: In the UK, formal kinship care represents only 5 per cent of all kinship care arrangements (Selwyn and Nandy, 2014), leaving 95 per cent unrepresented in studies of looked-after children. This creates a significant data gap, as children in kinship care have different demographics and relationships. Comparative studies can obscure the unique needs of these families and overlook subgroups with similar characteristics.

In child welfare practice, avoiding terms like 'placement', 'contact', 'life story work', or 'out-of-home care' can shift the discourse, encouraging empathy and reducing bureaucracy. Using clinical and less emotionally charged language might simplify the process for professionals to maintain a professional distance from these highly emotional, ambivalent, and complex situations. Nevertheless, practitioners should use language that reflects how children describe their lives, demonstrating recognition and sensitivity.

Recognition of the merits of child participation

Recognising the multiple meanings of family forms, kinship care, permanence, and home requires professionals to spend time understanding children's perspectives. Child welfare practitioners must learn what family and home mean to these children, how their family is negotiated and lived, and what matters to them.

There are many effective tools for practitioners to communicate with children (Lefevre, 2018) – for example, using Kitbag, photo-voice, walking tours, role-play, drawing, and simply listening. In the initial study, with just three sessions each, children provided rich insights into their lives, discussing their ambivalence, inner conversations, and how they make do and get by. Many of the children told me that they had not had the opportunities to talk through their feelings, but instead, they had been shut down and told to forget about the past. This is not about the necessity for many children to have clinical therapeutic intervention, which is unlikely to be resourced for all children who need it. Instead, it is about providing space in the everyday for dialogical conversations.

The children preferred relationship-based professional interactions (Ruch et al, 2010), suggesting that in line with the ethics of care, they should be undertaken with sensitivity, empathy, compassion, competence, responsiveness, and trust. Nevertheless, the children also wanted to be safe and often became frustrated when things were not done. Erika said: 'Things can take too long ... [social workers] don't listen to us. They don't always do what they say.'

Regulation, administration, boundaries, and paperwork are necessary. Children's right to safety and wellbeing in their family lives must be recognised and attended to, but not at the expense of positive relationships. These measures should support relationships, which must come first (Munro, 2011). Once again, the ethics of rights must not supersede the ethics of care.

The participation and inclusion of children are also not the responsibility of individual child welfare workers. Sociological understandings of recognition (for example, Fraser, 2003) suggest resources must support professionals in child welfare. For example, managers should ensure that social workers' compassionate time must include, but take priority over, 'paperwork time' (Yuill and Mueller-Hirth, 2019). Resources need to also be available for the families and the children. Discussing wishes and feelings can harm relationships, especially for children such as Erika and Kimberley, who did not want face-to-face meetings with their birth parents. The whole family, not just the carers and the children, will often require assistance.

A key concern for children's participation is the responsibility of professionals and carers to protect children from upsetting information. This protectionism, seen in kinship care and child welfare work, echoes the view of children as vulnerable, which is disputed by the new sociology of childhood ideology. Children in this study persistently thought about matters affecting their lives, contemplating their identity, influence, and position. They contemplated who they are in relation to those around them, how much influence they have, and why they are in the position they are in.

These 'internal conversations' do not diminish without discussion (Archer, 2012). If insufficient information is provided, children often fill in their life stories with piecemeal memories, half-truths, or untruths. Like many of us do, they imagine the worst-case scenarios (Staines and Selwyn, 2020).

Professionals and family members must be mindful of the individual child's circumstances. There must be a trauma-informed approach (Hickle, 2020). Again, the ethics of rights, including the right to participate and be informed, must not take precedence over the ethics of care. Discussions must be done in a timely, not time-driven, and sensitive way by a knowledgeable and competent person. It should be done with a personal or professional person who the children trust and who understands and recognises the child's particular situation. Furthermore, this relational, dialogical way of 'doing' participation, of being given agency rather than autonomy, must not be considered a one-off process, but regarded from a life course perspective.

The children wished not only to be consulted but also to help collaborate on all discussions that involved their lives. This is their right according to legislation, but also children should be seen as valuable resources for social workers. They can provide feasible solutions because they have been thinking about their needs throughout their lives and have many everyday experiences of how their families function. Their views should, therefore, be prominent in risk assessments, child permanence reports, and viability assessments. They should be at the beginning of reports and conversations about a child's wellbeing, not in a small box at the end.

Conclusion

Analysis of the children's views demonstrates that maintaining their lives and a sense of permanence involves their ongoing complex, challenging, changing, and ambivalent thoughts and processes. The children wish for better recognition of this by their families, carers, communities, and social work practitioners. Recognising that children and their families are navigating the relational spaces inherent in their family lives should also extend to legislation and policy because context matters in activating and deactivating their strategies and mechanisms.

The children have also been keen to display that recognition should not just extend to their challenges, deficits, and troubles. Recognition must also extend to how they make do and get by. It is not just about ensuring that there is less (mis)recognition of kinship care family practices – for example, by not using placement phrases or not integrating kinship care with fostering and adoption thinking and processes. The children also wish for better recognition of how they navigate and work with the tensions in their lives – for example, by using objects, photos, spaces, and time.

The most important finding from the children's insights is that relationships are the building blocks for these children's lives – relationships with their families, professionals, local communities, and broader society. The children desire relationships built on trust, reciprocity, compassion, and respect. They want these to be safe, positive, and enduring. The children identified which relationships were essential to them and which needed managing differently. Therefore, presumptive adult-centric notions of family, support, and kinship care can only go so far in reflecting the realities of the children's lives. The children see their care as an interdependent collective endeavour that celebrates diversity rather than difference, and this can only be achieved by including them in the debates around their family lives and kinship care arrangements.

10

Navigating relational spaces

> We're not like stupid. We know what's going on. Like, we're probably in the best situation to deal with it. Yet, there is like a lot of shock and surprise when children come out with certain things and ways to deal with things. And people are like, 'well, I don't know how you know that'. And I think it's just very underestimating.
>
> Eliza, child research participant

This book promotes children's voices to challenge and redefine deeply rooted assumptions about kinship care, permanence, child participation, and family life. Traditional child welfare policies often impose monological perspectives on the complex interactions between kinship care, fractured family dynamics, social inequality, and state support. A new 'what matters' approach to listening to children embraces the dialogical, navigating the ambivalences and relational spaces in between.

This approach emerged from a study which explored what matters to 19 children living in kinship care arrangements. The PhD research was the first to focus exclusively on children's perspectives to understand the meaning of family life and permanence in kinship care in England. Prioritising children's accounts of family, care, and childhood disrupts dominant adult-centric narratives in child welfare debates, which often overemphasise the professionalisation of kinship care as a process-driven placement or placement-adjacent service. The children's perspectives also contest simplistic notions of family life as merely a socially constructed, subjective private matter that transfers to policy by overly relying on increasingly impoverished family and community resources to support children who have experienced trauma.

Listening to children living in kinship care also reinvigorates debates on permanence, highlighting how kinship care challenges traditional concepts of both substitute psychological parenting and family preservation approaches. The children's experiences reveal the fluidity within their family structures, which must be balanced with the more static responsibilities and roles essential to prioritising their needs. Analysis of the insights from the children in the study demonstrates how they navigate and manage relationships marked by absence and presence, mature care, autonomous interdependence, struggles for recognition and a sense of permanence within, across, and sometimes beyond traditional family networks.

The children's accounts suggest that child welfare policy and support should centre less on the authoritative procedural approaches initially designed for fostering and adoption. While procedural approaches and scrutiny are essential regarding a child's right to safety, there must be more focus on the more cooperative practices that include the child's voice(s) and recognise the specifics of the children's family arrangements. Such recognition can help manage the challenges of kinship care, providing meaningful support where multiple family relationships endure and grow but are also in flux, promoting a lifelong perspective.

The need to establish valid ethical and meaningful methods to engage and elicit insights from children has also challenged dominant methodologies in childhood studies and child welfare research. Reductionist accounts of agency, often derived from overly celebratory and fetishised sociocultural narratives of childhood and participation, fail to capture and understand children's lived experiences adequately. Similarly, child welfare's over-reliance on conventional, descriptive, and supposedly apolitical 'what works' models fall short. Instead, employing diverse, needs-aware, participant-led, creative methods, understandings, and hypotheses through critical realist thinking, dialogical participation, and sharing theoretical explanations nurtures more reflexive and collaborative dialogue. This approach brings forth inner conversations, enabling children to value their lives, discover what matters to them, and highlight what should matter to us. This critical realist 'what matters' participatory approach can enhance child welfare research, policy, and practice by providing more ethical and meaningful access to children's views.

In this final chapter, I summarise and reflect on the main implications of listening to children. I illustrate how children's insights foster dialectical thinking and the navigation of relational spaces. This applies to everyday activities like trampolining and emphasises the importance of authentically listening to children to support their current coping strategies. I also stress the importance of employing a variety of theories to collectively understand family life. The sensitive topic of contact is then addressed, and, crucially, I acknowledge the value of children's voices and the importance of recognising permanence and kinship care family life for what they truly are. I conclude by underscoring the importance of reflexivity and share my gratitude for the children involved in the study.

Dialectical thinking

Critical realist Roy Bhaskar (1993) extends one of Marx's sociological concepts by advocating a shift from binary monological to dialectical thinking. Dialectical thinking is similar to dialogical thinking, although it aims for a higher level of understanding that could lead to reconciling seemingly contradictory ideas. Unlike analytical thinking, which separates distinctions and connections, dialectical thinking considers them together. It is 'the art of thinking the coincidence of distinctions and connections' (Bhaskar, 1993, p 190).

This book is grounded in dialectical thinking. It had to be. The children in this study exemplify why dialectical thinking is crucial for understanding their lives and kinship care. They challenge simplistic either/or views of their family lives, navigating the ambivalence of in-between relational spaces that simplistic binaries fail to capture. Sociologists refer to these binaries as 'dualisms' (Craib, 2000). These dualisms are prevalent because, as discussed in the first few chapters, kinship care, permanence, legislation, child welfare, childhood, participation, and research often rely on discrete either/or binaries. For example, kinship care is typically seen as either a private family arrangement or a placement. Permanence is generally viewed as either remaining with birth parents or substituting them. Permanence is also usually measured in terms of stability and legal permanence or through the child's feelings. Child participation is perceived as either tokenistic or empowering, and research is often viewed as either predominantly empirical or interpretivist.

Bhaskar (2008) suggests that such dualisms arise because individuals often focus solely on the differences between things. Overly focusing on differences leads to rigid classifications and groupings, such as species, age, 'placement' types, legal statuses, and other concepts. Such categorisation assigns objects and people into fixed groups and separates them according to their function. Child versus adult, reason versus emotion, mind versus body, kinship versus non-kinship, private versus public, and permanence versus impermanence are among the countless resulting separations that dominate child welfare thinking (Kjørstad and Solem, 2017). Notions such as doing family, mature care, and autonomous interdependency connect these dichotomies and address such paradoxes head-on. Dialectical thinking traverses the continuum between rights and care, absence and presence, recognition and (mis)recognition, independence and dependence, adulthood and childhood, vulnerability and ability, psychological and sociological, philosophical and pragmatic, and theory and practice.

Importantly, transformation at any level can only occur through the dialectical process (Simpson and Price, 2007). For example, it is not enough to consider the child before their kinship care arrangement as a different child from the one in their new family arrangement. There are undoubtedly continuities as well as differences. Like all of us, the children are their past, present, and becoming selves, time hopping in continuously changing patterns. Their needs must be addressed holistically, collaboratively, therapeutically, and across the intergenerational life course. As it has been suggested, 'the beginning of wisdom is the discovery that there exist contradictions of permanent tension with which it is necessary to live, and this is above all not necessary to resolve' (Gorz, 1982, cited in Cree, 2000).

Overall, the children in the study demonstrated a natural ability to think dialectically, navigating the complexities and nuances of their experiences. The challenge for practitioners, policy makers, researchers, and academics is to adopt a similar approach. They must engage with these relational spaces and embrace the inherent ambivalences rather than constantly seeking to resolve or fix them.

The mechanisms that matter to children living in kinship care

The children in this study navigated the in-between relational spaces daily, testing them out and using various tools, approaches, and relationships to help them achieve a flourishing and safe life. They relied on specific strategies aligned with their core values to manage their lives effectively. The PhD research identified these strategies through thematic analysis and a retroductive process using a new 'what matters' approach that combines critical realism and dialogical participation. Theoretical explanations emerged from and with the children's own valuations of their family lives. Discussing what matters demonstrated how the children manage the mechanisms of 'connection/separation', 'care and protection/independence and risk', and 'recognition/(mis)recognition' (shown in Figure 5.3), especially regarding kinship care and the meaning of permanence.

These mechanisms are not static and need to be constantly negotiated. They often intertwine and affect each other, sometimes causing tensions between them. Each mechanism also has its own tensions within it. Examples are the children's need for, yet ambivalence towards, personal relationships. Also, the children desired to feel connected to their carers and birth parents, even though, at times, they did not want to have their presence felt. They mostly welcomed their sibling relationships, even though they could sometimes be challenging. They wished to conform to societal constructs of family, yet they embraced them as non-static, diverse, and ever-growing. They wanted to be listened to about their lives and to take risks, but felt they needed to be protected from responsibility and harm. They wanted to be normal children of their generation, yet they recognised their specific needs and circumstances. They were able, yet vulnerable. They were independent, yet dependent. The children wanted a sense of permanence even though they knew from past experiences that nothing can be guaranteed. Moreover, the children wished for social work to help them and their families, yet they did not want to be seen as kinship care children and did not want further interference. The nuanced depth with which children think about and manage their lives, often embodying conflicting values, lends support to the principle in the sociology of childhood that children are experts in their own lives (for example, Smart, 2011).

Enacting the mechanisms and navigating relational spaces
Use everyday objects and events: trampolines

Navigating these tensions can be challenging for child welfare practices focused on definitive procedural mandates and legal distinctions. However, an important insight from listening to children is how they creatively use space, time, and resources to explore challenges and find respite from the inherent contradictions of their world. Legal frameworks, policies, and procedures should align with what children value as necessary and what they are currently doing, focusing on effective 'real' mechanisms rather than merely descriptive 'actual' and 'empirical' interventions. A prime example of this is the use of trampolines. As Ellie explained: 'Because when we're [on the trampoline], we can do what we like. Watch.'

Except for one, every family in the study had trampolines in their garden. This demonstrates how, in their everyday lives, children often tested and enacted the mechanisms essential to making their family life work. For example, it shows how they navigated the tensions between safety, trust, independence, and risk (Zinn, 2020). Trampolines were not merely places where children could increase physical activity and relieve stress by combining the link between mind and body (Schöffl et al, 2021). The children also inferred trampolines were boundaried places of play. They all had nets around them. They could do almost as they chose, with some rules and literal boundaries to keep them safe.

On the trampolines, children navigated the mechanism of connection/separation. They could socialise or be alone. The trampolines were placed near their homes, enabling them to balance a sense of independence with connectedness to their family relationships. The children also liked to show off how good they were. They craved recognition/(mis)recognition, particularly in comparison to adults who they felt did not necessarily belong on them. Additionally, the trampolines were given to them by their carers, who saw them as an essential part of both childhood and UK culture. The kinship carers demonstrated they provided mature care and a sense of contained freedom by providing a sizeable, semi-permanent display that occupied significant space.

Once again, this serves as an example. Just as pets should not be seen as a universal solution for ensuring the development and wellbeing of children in kinship care, it is equally absurd to suggest that trampolines are essential for all children to flourish safely. The focus should be on values rather than specific items or strategies. It is proposed that children be supported with objects, activities, and connections that help them manage and navigate the values, tensions, and things that matter to them. These should be negotiated based on what is practical and how particular children navigate the connection/separation, care and protection/independence and risk, and recognition/(mis) recognition mechanisms that allow them to manage relational spaces.

Listen to children

The most important finding from the project and subsequent discussions and publications is that children in kinship care arrangements are competent in giving considered, nuanced, and sophisticated understandings of their fractured family life experiences. They live and manage their everyday lives with tensions, ambivalences, and nuances. These findings are consistent with the growing body of evidence that attests to young people's competence to participate in research as leaders and agents of change (Heinsch et al, 2020).

The children were adamant that their wishes and feelings should be recognised more, especially regarding maintaining connections. They strongly disagreed that a child's wishes and feelings should be valued differently based on age or understanding (Family Rights Group, 2017). The children in the study, who were 5–16 years old, demonstrated an ability to grasp the complex nature of their experiences, regardless of age. They also wished to be given opportunities to participate from the outset. The participation process must be dialogically driven from the start. It is about cultivating suitable space and relationships for a dialogical process. Families and professionals must also consider the tools and strategies children use or prefer to use, acknowledging that these preferences may evolve over time. Everyday child participation is an ongoing process of mature care, where empowerment becomes a collective reciprocal responsibility. However, the children emphasised that final decisions should rest with adults responsible for prioritising their safety and wellbeing.

There are many ways of knowing – everything is fallible

Theory must inform child welfare practice, especially social work practice. It is only with a meaningful understanding of the issues at hand that appropriate child welfare assessments and interventions can be provided (Frost and Dolan, 2021; Muurinen and Kääriäinen, 2022). This book and the children's accounts demonstrate that relying on a single school of thought regarding family, kinship, childhood, and permanence cannot adequately explain their lives or serve as the sole basis for policy and practice. As hypothesised in the early chapters, it is insufficient to depend solely on psychological, sociological, or even psychosocial theorising to understand the complexity of a child's world, relationships, or sense of permanence. Instead, a critical multidisciplinary approach is necessary, because everything is fallible. This approach may provide a more complex and messier picture, but it mirrors reality by acknowledging the tensions inherent in children's lives. It also reflects social work's political requirement to address change on both individual and societal levels (IFSW, 2014).

Many theories this book that are used to illuminate and understand how children navigate family life have sociological foundations. Sociology customarily addresses the dialogical, dualisms, and the dialectical, helping recognise not only the lives of children in kinship care arrangements but also the tensions and contradictions inherent in social work (Simpson and Price, 2007). For example, sociology helps explain why children feel that the ethics of care and justice are essential and intertwined. Yet, overall, the ethics of care must take precedence. What we do is important, but how we do it – with sensitivity, empathy, compassion, competence, responsiveness, and trust – is the most vital for engagement. Working in the dialectical helps explain how understanding autonomous interdependence is crucial when considering children's lives, as well as the public versus private and the service versus upbringing by family debate. A modernised sociology of childhood and theories of recognition have been crucial in understanding the children's views and their experiences of family life and permanence in kinship care. When combined with theories grounded in human development, sociological explanations can give researchers, policy makers, practitioners, and students a clearer picture. Sociological theories ensure that social work research, policy, and practice do not privilege simplistic notions of empowerment, participation, and individual capacity. They ensure that contexts such as culture, gender, politics, neoliberalisation, and consumer capitalism are considered within debates.

Using time and space to mobilise family and permanence

The children demonstrated that a sense of permanence, affinity, belonging, and interdependence within the family network is more important than legal permanence or stability from remaining with one or two primary carers throughout their childhoods. It is not about substitute care. Instead, it is about having a growing sense of family to care for them. Permanence happens across the family network. The children viewed blood ties as an indicator of family networks but do not necessarily consider them a requirement. Family life and care can take various forms and include members who are not genealogically related, or species related in the case of pets.

This disrupts the over-reliance on physical and legal permanence and questions the traditional static views of family and home often assumed in policy, research, and practice. Typically, family forms are hierarchical, gendered, institutionalised, and dependent on individual carers, frequently based on genetic relations (Morris et al, 2017). Stability is usually associated with a permanent residence with the same carers, secured until adulthood. However, the children demonstrated that homes, like the roles of family members, are not static concepts and change according to needs and experiences.

Legal permanence may help to achieve the trusting, caring relationships they desired. Nevertheless, the primary goal is having an emotional sense of permanence in terms of 'a sense of security, continuity, commitment and identity' (DfE, 2010, p 12). It is more important than having legal certainty of care or seemingly arbitrary timescales often enforced by social work and courts. Children's timescales should not be based just on judicial and developmental life trajectories that govern child welfare practice, but also on how individual children use their agency to mobilise time itself.

For kinship care, time has been explored regarding how court orders and assessments may not allow for appropriate time for thorough assessments or how certain orders do not necessitate stability (Harwin, Alrouh et al, 2019). Limited critical attention has also been given to spatiality and temporality in other areas of child welfare and social work (Jeyasingham, 2014). Davies was one of the first to highlight the incompatibility of bureaucratic 'clocktime' and 'process time' associated with the 'rationality of care' (1994, p 278). More recent research by Ferguson (2004; 2008; 2009a; 2009b; 2010a; 2010b; 2010c; 2018) and Yuill and Mueller-Hirth (2019) examines social work practitioners' use of space and time. Staples et al (2023) explored the negotiation of temporality in life story conversations with care-experienced children. The journal *Qualitative Social Work* dedicated a whole issue to place and space in social work (Bryant and Williams, 2020). However, there was no specific article about social work with children not in their birth parents' care. The children's insights have provided a new direction for further research to explore how they use space and time to navigate their sense of belonging and permanence.

The children also proposed that providing adequate time and space for separation/connection is not just an individual responsibility; the necessity of time and space must also be recognised by the community, professionals, and the state. Such opportunities depend on having sufficient financial means and resources as well as safe real/virtual spaces. For example, Harmony as a teenager, wished for more 'freedom' outside the family home. She also felt unsafe in her neighbourhood, and often felt that her nan was preoccupied with work and trying to obtain contact with Harmony's adopted younger brother. Additionally, her home had poor internet access. These circumstances impacted her choices and sense of wellbeing, ultimately influencing her decision to move from her nan's care to her father's.

The children's insights also propose that religion, hobbies, school, friends, gender roles, heritage, politics, consumer capitalism, and children's popular culture impact their sense of worth, wellbeing, and belonging. This is often forgotten or minimised in policy, literature, and research about children (Spyrou et al, 2018). Therefore, support children's wellbeing and sense of permanence is not just reliant on the individualised, neoliberalised ideologies and interventions on which European social work is often based (Webb, 2016).

Maintaining safe connections

It would be remiss to discuss negotiating relational spaces without addressing the often messy and febrile subject of contact. While it should be considered alongside life story work and embedded as part of permanence work, contact warrants its own focus. In English legislation (Children's Act 1989), contact typically refers to the arrangements for children in state care to maintain relationships between the child and their family, usually their birth parents. Contact was a significant issue for the children and remains a complex challenge for child welfare when planning for children in kinship and 'out-of-home' care (Sen and Broadhurst, 2011).

The children had a variety of contact with their birth parents and diverse ways of managing the mechanism of connection/separation. Zack preferred his birth mum to turn up on an ad hoc basis. Megan preferred to learn about her mum only through the storytelling of other family members:

> And it's nice because they all, like, remember, like, my mum and stuff, and they can talk about her. It's like when our mum was young or when our nan was young, and she was bringing up my mum. Obviously, it was, like, very different. And memories would have been brought out in photos and everything like that. So, it's like she's still there but not there.

Louise expressed that she was content with the possibility of never seeing her birth mother again, finding comfort in just having a photograph of her. However, she acknowledged that her birth mother was the key to seeing her younger sister. This situation caused Louise anxiety due to the strained relationships within her family.

The children in this study only used the term 'contact' when referring to specific provisions established by social services. Also, when mentioned, it was often in a negative context. For instance, Erica and Kimberley described feeling forced to attend contact sessions. They perceived these sessions as commodified and used as bargaining tools to appease the professionals involved in their care. Additionally, they felt that granting contact was a way to compensate for the parents' loss of daily parenting of the children. Kimberley said:

> Yes, we both have to see our parents because, erm, we've been told by a couple of people that it's, erm, important, important to see our mum and dad, and by law we have to see them. Because they say that, erm, they are our mum and dad and they care about us, and they, like, love us, and it will be hard for them, if, erm, we didn't see them. If they don't see us. Well, we already know that they are our mum and dad. We know that. Like they've told us that they love us, and they miss us. And we know that. And we don't have to go and see them for them to tell us that.

Rainbow and Lucy understood that they might reconnect with their parents when they got older, hoping the situation would become more manageable over time. The children believed this would be possible either because their birth parents would have changed or because they themselves would be stronger, both physically and emotionally. Although the methods of maintaining connections with their parents varied, it was clear that any form of contact was complex and emotive, even when generally positive. Contact is never a benign experience (Neil and Howe, 2004).

While the term 'contact' is commonly used in social work, it may be time to find a different word that is less detached and better describes daily interactions. Even the newer phrase 'family time' (UK Fostering, 2024) can suggest specific events for specific types of children. However, as the children's insights demonstrate, navigating the relational space of family time is an ongoing daily process. Contact and family time also do not necessarily require physical presence and can be maintained through 'everyday interactions [through which] kinship relations are maintained' (Cossar and Neil, 2013, p 74). A more fitting phrase may be 'maintaining safe connections'.

The children described maintaining safe connections throughout their lives and over an intergenerational life course rather than during specific events. Their experiences highlight that connections across families can be complicated and challenging, representing an ongoing and ever-changing phenomenon. It is an active process – much like the concept of family itself – where the children have agency. This perspective acknowledges the multiple families to which children belong, which are inherently in flux (Rustin, 1994).

The children expressed that relationships with their families are so enmeshed that they are unlikely to be untangled by prescriptive contact arrangements, contact orders, contact plans, or contact centre regulations. For them, contact quality mattered more than quantity. Additionally, relationships need to be reciprocal and built on trust and respect. They questioned the point of attending a contact centre if a family member was misusing substances, prioritising their own needs, posing a risk, or if birth parents had previously failed to show up. The ethics of rights must be upheld. For example, keeping connections must happen. However, the ethics of rights cannot supersede or be seen as separate from the ethics of care and mature care. Eliza said:

> If you're going to have contact with that person, it needs to be regular, and you need to know what's going on all the time, and it just makes things easier to keep healthy relationships. There needs to be a mutual ... everyone needs to know what's going on and what's going to happen. Like every time.

Working with the entire family is crucial to maintaining positive and safe connections. For contact to be beneficial, there must be some semblance of positive, functional family relationships. This means addressing all spheres of recognition and involving other family and community members, not just birth parents, carers and children. Furthermore, because the children view permanence, identity, and knowing that others are OK as a responsibility of the family as a whole, these issues do not have to be addressed by direct connections with the birth parents. For example, a child's needs regarding connection/separation can be addressed through face-to-face meetings with an aunt who is more able to focus on the children's needs. Family connections should be approached holistically rather than strictly following Bowlby's views on substitute care and primary attachments. It is about the whole family, in whatever form is meaningful and safe for the child (Kiraly and Humphreys, 2016).

Recognition of relational spaces

As highlighted in the previous chapter, recognition ties all the book's themes and the children's insights together. Recognition is essential for everyone, and (mis)recognition was identified by these children as the primary source of their unhappiness. The children sought recognition for their achievements and struggles, and they wanted to feel a sense of belonging, attachment, and affiliation within their family – their whole family – as well as within their communities and society. Moreover, they wanted their lives to be acknowledged for the realities in which they lived. The children struggled for recognition in the following ways:

- They wanted their family to be seen as another way of being a normal family. They did not wish to be seen as 'dramatically different' from other families.

- They did not see themselves within the typical adoption and fostering narratives. Instead, they wished for their lives to be seen as part of the diversity of normal family living, which includes a broader sense of family, home, and care.
- They used phrases like contact, placements, permanence, and life story work rarely, and only when describing social work processes. They felt these terms did not adequately represent their lives or how they wanted themselves or their families to be perceived.
- They wished for services, especially schools, to better understand kinship care as a family arrangement. They hoped for more attuned support in line with their specific needs.
- They knew the impact of insufficient recognition and lack of help from services and the state, including practical, financial, and housing support. This lack limited their options, such as attending clubs and family holidays, and made some neighbourhoods feel unsafe, preventing them from displaying their family life as normal.
- They often felt excluded from discussions about their lives and were frequently seen as vulnerable, inadequate, and unable. They felt they were not listened to by child welfare judiciary services, practitioners, researchers, and policy makers.

This leads to a fundamental principle reiterated throughout this book: child welfare must recognise kinship care and these children's family lives for what they are, not for what they are not. We know the children are not living with their birth parents, nor are they in stranger foster care or adoptive placements. The professionalisation of kinship care as a placement or placement-adjacent service only partly describes and addresses their care. The children felt this approach diminished their family experiences and needs. Inappropriate processes and specific phrases can reduce real-life experiences to arbitrary, impersonal, sanitised procedures to be measured. Policy, practice, and explanations will fall short if based on such premeditations. The complete de-professionalisation and an over-reliance on the families' often fractured social capital and limited economic capital will also fall short.

Kinship care is a complex family arrangement that lies between private and public care. It is a complicated permanency option that lies between substitute psychological parenting, parenting by birth families, and theories of multiple family affiliations. Child welfare policy and practice must be based on real accounts of the children's lives. One of the most effective ways to achieve this is for researchers, policy makers, and practitioners to ask the children living within such arrangements. Meaningful participation can be achieved by including them in research and policy development from the start, and by practitioners incorporating their views at all assessment levels and in interventions and support.

Engaging in reflexivity

Child welfare and social work are political endeavours, as are kinship care, research with children, participatory practice, and critical realism. They focus on the primary mission of 'empowering' the 'weak' and ensuring wellbeing (Bordonaro and Payne, 2012). Therefore, identifying power dynamics and working with reflexivity was crucial to the initial project and the book, and it remains vital to me as a social worker, educator, and researcher. This is a challenging task. The more I investigate, the more certain ideologies persuade me, while others dissuade and even anger me. I get particularly angry about the exploitation of kinship care and children's views for political gain. I do not see this as a weakness of my work, and I feel that everybody should feel anger about injustice.

However, I must be reflexive and aware of my positionality. As someone with a unique background and identities, my liberal, Left-leaning Minority World politics can produce biases that close down and dismiss other perspectives. For instance, when approaching concepts such as autonomous interdependence, I realise this is a particularly socialist view of the world. David Graeber (2014) even argues that collectivism, interconnectivity, and the wish to help others are communist principles. The political view of human sociability and the idealised view of society are further compounded by this book's recommendation that the ethics of care and other specific liberal political values are necessary to guide child welfare practice, kinship care, and child participation.

I also constantly return to the deep anxiety that research and child welfare can constitute an act of symbolic violence, even with ongoing consent. For example, while we intend to promote children's wellbeing and safety, inviting them to reflect on pressing and potentially distressing issues may cause further emotional harm, both now and in the future. This raises the question of whether this is all for our own gain, vanity, and need to be needed and helpful. As previously mentioned, exploitation angers me. Therefore, I am always mindful of intent and the power of emotions, and I encourage others, including children and carers, to be aware of them too.

Most importantly, the alternative to discussing issues with children and including them in research and plans about their own lives would be to further subjugate and silence this marginalised group. The children have shown that they think about their lives and its challenges and contradictions whether we engage with them or not, and they do so in nuanced and sophisticated ways. The children central to this book have demonstrated not only the value of having space to talk about such thoughts for child welfare policy making and practice, but also how children value such recognition and participation.

This level of reflexivity is not a limitation. Instead, it is necessary to enrich and drive our work. For example, Longhofer and Floersch (2014) propose that social work research must be value-informed and that social work practice and values must be research-informed. Such arguments return to the ought/is and the fact/value debates. Child welfare policy, practice, and research must engage in both normativity (what matters most to people and what allows for flourishing rather than suffering) and judgmental rationality (which accounts are better or worse explanations).

This book also does not, and must not, imply that those who do not share the identified values and approaches should be excluded from practising child welfare or informing policy on kinship care or permanence. This book contributes to a body of knowledge and is not intended to replace it. It offers a valuable alternative perspective, with children's views central to the analysis. Like the children's views, the book's social scientific truth claim must be open to scrutiny, criticism, and corroboration. Everything is fallible, including the interpretations of an early-career social work researcher. This is the essence of critical realist paradigms, dialogical participation, and child welfare research. It is to advance knowledge through collective learning and to continuously and reflexively engage in the dialectical, sharing our inner conversations, the values that motivate us, our current strategies for making life work, our fears, and, most importantly, our hopes.

Final reflections

This book and the original research wished to explore whether listening to children can enhance our understanding of kinship care, permanence, and child participation. Can children's voices cut through the ongoing cyclical debates and dilemmas centred on what adults feel matters? Can they guide child welfare researchers, policy makers, and practitioners towards more effective ways of supporting them?

I continue to be profoundly influenced by the children's insights. Their wisdom and honesty offer fresh perspectives each time I read and reflect on them. I am consistently struck by how they inspire me to promote a more compassionate and realistic approach to kinship care, family life, permanence, child participation, child welfare, and social work. Together, we have developed theories and nuanced, intelligent, reflexive understandings that illuminate the essence of family life – the values that truly matter to them. We have highlighted the importance of relationships, trust, belonging, and our collective responsibility in navigating relational spaces. Some aspects do remain sobering and tricky to hear. The children have also stated they still do not feel genuinely heard in research, policy, practice, and family life. We also frequently fail to fully consider what it means for them to feel safe.

Nevertheless, I want to thank you, the reader, along with those who have helped promote the children's voices through seminars, workshops, conferences, book chapters, journals, podcasts, and everyday discussions.

Including these children's perspectives in conversations about how they are making do and getting by in their family life matters. At the risk of ending on an 'upbeat note' (Lesko and Talburt, 2012, p 280), the children have shown that they can guide us toward better recognising the realities of their lives so that we can support them more effectively. Children want to be heard. We just have to provide space to listen, understand, reflect, and respond. As Louise said: 'When people just don't listen to you, and they like go on to try and change the subject, I'm like "Oh no you don't. I'm still talking about this."'

References

Abbott, P. and Sapsford, R. (1998) *Research Methods for Nurses and the Caring Professions* (2nd edn), Open University Press.

Abebe, T. (2019) 'Reconceptualising children's agency as continuum and interdependence', *Social Sciences*, 8(3): 81–97.

Aebi, V., Sabato, G., and Schmid, M. (2012) 'Risk management, corporate governance, and bank performance in the financial crisis', *Journal of Banking and Finance*, 36(12): 3213–26.

Akhtar, F. (2013) *Mastering Social Work Values and Ethics*, Jessica Kingsley.

Albertini, M., Kohli, M., and Vogel, C. (2016) 'Intergenerational transfers of time and money in European families: common patterns – different regimes?', *Journal of European Social Policy*, 17(4): 319–34.

Alderson, P. (2013) *Childhoods Real and Imagined: Volume 1: An Introduction to Critical Realism and Childhood Studies*, Routledge.

Alderson, P. (2016) 'The philosophy of critical realism and childhood studies', *Global Studies of Childhood*, 6(2): 199–210.

Alderson, P. and Morrow, V. (2020) *The Ethics of Research with Children and Young People: A Practical Handbook*, SAGE.

Aldgate, J. (2009) 'Living in kinship care: a child-centred view', *Adoption and Fostering*, 33(3): 51–63.

Aldgate, J. and McIntosh, M. (2006) *Looking After the Family: A Study of Children Looked After in Kinship Care in Scotland*, Social Work Inspection Agency.

Altshuler, S.J. (1999) 'Children in kinship foster care speak out: "we think we're doing fine"', *Child and Adolescent Social Work Journal*, 16(3): 215–35.

Andersen, S.H. and Fallesen, P. (2015) 'Family matters? The effect of kinship care on foster care disruption rates', *Child Abuse and Neglect*, 48: 68–79.

Appleton, C. (2011) '"Critical friends", feminism and integrity: a reflection on the use of critical friends as a research tool to support researcher integrity and reflexivity in qualitative research studies', *Women in Welfare Education*, 1–13.

Arce, M.C. (2018) 'Who is (to be) the subject of children's rights?', in S. Spyrou, R. Rosen, and D.T. Cook (eds) *Reimagining Childhood Studies*, Bloomsbury Academic, pp 169–83.

Archer, M.S. (2003) *Structure, Agency and the Internal Conversation*, Cambridge University Press.

Archer, M.S. (2012) *The Reflexive Imperative in Late Modernity*, Cambridge University Press.

Archer, M., Bhaskar, R., Collier, A., Lawson, T., and Norrie, A. (2013) *Critical Realism: Essential Readings*, Routledge.

References

Argent, H. (2009) 'What's the problem with kinship care?', *Adoption and Fostering*, 33(3): 6–14.

Arnstein, S.R. (1969) 'A ladder of citizen participation', *Journal of the American Institute of Planners*, 35(4): 216–24.

Ba', S. (2021) 'The critique of sociology of childhood: human capital as the concrete "social construction of childhood"', *Power and Education*, 13(2): 73–87.

Bacon, K. (2016) 'Children's use and control of bedroom space', in S. Punch, R. Vanderbeck, and T. Skelton (eds) *Families, Intergenerationality, and Peer Group Relations*, Springer, pp 1–21.

Baginsky, M. (2023) 'Parents' views on improving relationships with their social workers', *Journal of Social Work*, 23(1): 3–18.

Bahn, S. and Barratt-Pugh, L. (2013) 'Getting reticent young male participants to talk: using artefact-mediated interviews to promote discursive interaction', *Qualitative Social Work*, 12(2): 186–99.

Bainbridge, A. (2015) 'Pedagogy of recognition: Winnicott, Honneth and learning in psychosocial spaces', *Journal of Pedagogic Development*, 5(3): 9–20.

Bainham, A. (2007) 'Permanence for children: special guardianship or adoption?', *The Cambridge Law Journal*, 66(3): 520–3.

Barad, K. (2018) 'Troubling time/s and ecologies of nothingness: re-turning, re-membering, and facing the incalculable', *New Formations: A Journal of Culture/Theory/Politics*, 92(1): 56–86.

Baraitser, L. (2013a) 'Collecting time: some reflections on the psychopolitics of belonging', *New Formations*, 79: 8–25.

Baraitser, L. (2013b) 'Mush time: communality and the temporal rhythms of family life', *Families, Relationships and Societies*, 2(1): 147–53.

Barnes, M. (2012) *Care in Everyday Life: An Ethic of Care in Practice*, Bristol University Press.

Barnes, V. (2012) 'Social work and advocacy with young people: rights and care in practice', *The British Journal of Social Work*, 42(7): 1275–92.

Barthes, R. (1973) *Mythologies*, Hill and Wang.

BASW (2021) 'Code of ethics', *BASW*. Available from: https://basw.co.uk/policy-practice/standards/code-ethics (Accessed 29 September 2024).

BASW England (2021) *BASW England's Response to the Care Review Case for Change*. Available from: https://basw.co.uk/sites/default/files/resources/basw_england_response_to_care_review_case_for_change_-_16_aug_21.pdf (Accessed 29 September 2024).

Baumrind, D. (1989) 'Rearing competent children', in W. Damon (ed) *Child Development Today and Tomorrow*, Jossey-Bass/Wiley, pp 349–78.

Baynes, P. (2008) 'Untold stories: a discussion of life story work', *Adoption and Fostering*, 32(2): 43–9.

Beck, U. (1998) *Risk Society* (5th edn), SAGE.

Bekaert, S., Paavilainen, E., Schecke, H., Baldacchino, A., Jouet, E., Zalocka-Żytka, L. et al (2021) 'Family members' perspectives of child protection services, a metasynthesis of the literature', *Children and Youth Services Review*, 128: art 106094. doi: 10.1016/j.childyouth.2021.106094

Bell, D.C. and Bell, L.G. (2018) 'Accuracy of retrospective reports of family environment', *Journal of Child and Family Studies*, 27(4): 1029–40.

Benton, P.T. and Craib, P.I. (2010) *Philosophy of Social Science: The Philosophical Foundations of Social Thought* (2nd edn), Palgrave Macmillan.

Beresford, J. (1997) 'Ask the children', *Reading*, 31(1): 17–18.

Berrick, J.D. and Hernandez, J. (2016) 'Developing consistent and transparent kinship care policy and practice: state mandated, mediated, and independent care', *Children and Youth Services Review*, 68: 24–33.

Bhaskar, R. (1986) *Scientific Realism and Human Emancipation*, Verso.

Bhaskar, R. (1989) *Reclaiming Reality: A Critical Introduction to Contemporary Philosophy*, Verso.

Bhaskar, R. (1993) *Dialectic: The Pulse of Freedom*, Verso.

Bhaskar, R. (1998) *The Possibility of Naturalism: A Philosophical Critique of the Contemporary Human Sciences*, Routledge.

Bhaskar, R. (2008) *A Realist Theory of Science*, Routledge.

Biehal, N. (2014) 'A sense of belonging: meanings of family and home in long-term foster care', *The British Journal of Social Work*, 44(4): 955–71.

Biehal, N., Ellison, S., Baker, C., and Sinclair, I. (2010) *Belonging and Permanence: Outcomes in Long-Term Foster Care and Adoption*, British Association for Adoption and Fostering.

Boddy, J. (2017) *Understanding Permanence for Looked After Children*, Care Inquiry.

Boddy, J. (2019) 'Troubling meanings of "family" for young people who have been in care: from policy to lived experience', *Journal of Family Issues*, 40(16): 2239–63.

Boddy, J. (2023) *Thinking Through Family: Narratives of Care Experienced Lives*, Bristol University Press.

Bolshaw, P. and Josephidou, J. (2022) *Understanding the Media in Young Children's Lives: An Introduction to the Key Debates*, Routledge.

Boone, K., Roets, G., and Roose, R. (2019) 'Social work, participation, and poverty', *Journal of Social Work*, 19(3): 309–26.

Bordonaro, L.I. and Payne, R. (2012) 'Ambiguous agency: critical perspectives on social interventions with children and youth in Africa', *Children's Geographies*, 10(4): 365–72.

Boss, P. (2000) *Ambiguous Loss: Learning to Live with Unresolved Grief*, Harvard University Press.

Bottrell, D. (2009) 'Understanding "marginal" perspectives: towards a social theory of resilience', *Qualitative Social Work*, 8(3): 321–39.

Bourdieu, P. (1977) *Outline of a Theory of Practice*, edited by J. Goody, Cambridge University Press.

Bourdieu, P. (1999) 'Understanding', in G Balazs and P. Bourdieu (eds) *The Weight of the World: Social Suffering in Contemporary Society*, Stanford University Press, pp 607–26.

Bowen, B. (2021) 'The matrix of needs: reframing Maslow's hierarchy', *Health*, 13(5): 538–63.

Bowlby, J. (1980) *Attachment and Loss, Vol 3: Loss, Sadness and Depression*, Basic Books.

Bowyer, S., Wilkinson, J., and Gadsby-Waters, J. (2015) *Impact of the Family Justice Reforms on Front-Line Practice Phase Two: Special Guardianship Orders*, Research in Practice.

Brenner, N. and Theodore, N. (2002) *Spaces of Neoliberalism: Urban Restructuring in North America and Western Europe*, Wiley-Blackwell.

Broad, B. (2004) 'Kinship care for children in the UK: messages from research, lessons for policy and practice', *European Journal of Social Work*, 7(2): 211–27.

Broad, B. (2006) 'Some advantages and disadvantages of kinship care: a view from research', in C. Talbot and M.C. Calder (eds) *Assessment in Kinship Care*, Russell House, pp 145–61.

Broad, B., Hayes, R., and Rushforth, C. (2001) *Kith and Kin: Kinship Care for Vulnerable Young People*, National Children's Bureau.

Bronfenbrenner U. (1979) *The Ecology of Human Development: Experiments by Nature and Design*, Harvard University Press.

Brown, R. and Ward, H. (2012) *Decision-Making within a Child's Timeframe: An Overview of Current Research Evidence for Family Justice Professionals Concerning Child Development and the Impact of Maltreatment*, Childhood Wellbeing Research Centre.

Brown, R., Broadhurst, K., Harwin, J., and Simmonds, J. (2019) *Special Guardianship: International Research on Kinship Care*, Nuffield Family Justice Observatory.

Brown, S., Cohon, D., and Wheeler, R. (2002) 'African American extended families and kinship care: how relevant is the foster care model for kinship care?', *Children and Youth Services Review*, 24(1): 53–77.

Bryant, L. and Williams, C. (2020) 'Place and space in social work', *Qualitative Social Work*, 19(3): 321–36.

Burgess, A.L. and Borowsky, I.W. (2010) 'Health and home environments of caregivers of children investigated by child protective services', *Pediatrics*, 125(2): 273–81.

Burgess, C., Rossvoll, F., Wallace, B., and Daniel, B. (2010) '"It's just like another home, just another family, so it's nae different": Children's voices in kinship care: a research study about the experience of children in kinship care in Scotland', *Child and Family Social Work*, 15(3): 297–306.

Burr, V. (2015) *Social Constructionism* (3rd edn), Routledge.

Butler, J. (1993) 'Critically queer', *GLQ: A Journal of Lesbian and Gay Studies*, 1(1): 17–32.

Butler, I. (2002) 'A code of ethics for social work and social care research', *British Journal of Social Work*, 32(2): 239–48.

Butler, J. (2006) *Gender Trouble: Feminism and the Subversion of Identity*, Routledge.

Butler, J., Gambetti, Z., and Sabsay, L. (2016) *Vulnerability in Resistance*, Duke University Press.

Bywaters, P., Bunting, L., Davidson, G., Hanratty, J., Mason, W., McCartan, C., and Steils, N. (2016) *The Relationship between Poverty, Child Abuse and Neglect: An Evidence Review*, Joseph Rowntre Foundation.

Cain, A.O. (1985) 'Pets as family members', *Marriage and Family Review*, 8(3–4): 5–10.

Canosa, A. and Graham, A. (2020) 'Tracing the contribution of childhood studies: maintaining momentum while navigating tensions', *Childhood*, 27(1): 25–47.

Capella, C. and Boddy, J. (2021) 'Listening to the opinista? Relational understandings of voice and silence in a multiperspective narrative study of child psychotherapy', *Children and Society*, 35(6): 835–49.

Care Crisis Review (2018) *Care Crisis Review: Options for Change*, Family Rights Group.

Carr, S. and Rockett, B. (2017) 'Fostering secure attachment: experiences of animal companions in the foster home', *Attachment and Human Development*, 19(3): 259–77.

Carter, E.A. and McGoldrick, M. (eds) (1989) *The Changing Family Life Cycle: Framework for Family Therapy* (3rd edn), Allyn and Bacon.

Casas, F. (2011) 'Subjective social indicators and child and adolescent well-being', *Child Indicators Research*, 4(4): 555–75.

Casey, L. (2012) *Listening to Troubled Families*, Department for Communities and Local Government.

Cassidy, J., Jones, J.D., and Shaver, P.R. (2013) 'Contributions of attachment theory and research: a framework for future research, translation, and policy', *Development and Psychopathology*, 25(402): 1415–34.

Chambers, D. (2021) 'Family as place: family photograph albums and the domestication of public and private space', in J.M. Schwartz and J.R. Ryan (eds) *Picturing Place*, Routledge, pp 96–114.

Chang, J.S. (2017) 'The docent method: a grounded theory approach for researching place and health', *Qualitative Health Research*, 27(4): 609–19.

Chapman, C. (2023) 'Affinity through vulnerability: the politics of positionality in child welfare', *Medicine Anthropology Theory*, 10(1): 1–9.

Cheney, K. (2018) 'Decolonizing childhood studies: overcoming patriarchy and prejudice in child-related research and practice', in S. Spyrou, R. Rosen, and D.T. Cook (eds) *Reimagining Childhood Studies*, Bloomsbury Academic, pp 91–104.

Children's Commissioner (2021) 'The Big Ask – Big Answers', 20 September. Available from: www.childrenscommissioner.gov.uk/resource/the-big-ask-big-answers/ (Accessed 14 March 2025).

Chipman, R., Wells, S., and Johnson, M. (2002) 'The meaning of quality in kinship foster care: caregiver, child, and worker perspectives', *Families in Society: The Journal of Contemporary Social Services*, 83(5): 508–20.

Cho, J., Ha, J.H., and Jue, J. (2020) 'Influences of the differences between mothers' and children's perceptions of parenting styles', *Frontiers in Psychology*, 11: art 552585. doi: 10.3389/fpsyg.2020.552585

Chudacoff, H.P. (2007) *Children at Play: An American History*, NYU Press.

Clapton, W. (2021) 'The exceptionalism of risk: Trump's wall and travel ban', *European Journal of International Security*, 6(2): 129–47.

Clark, A. and Morriss, L. (2017) 'The use of visual methodologies in social work research over the last decade: a narrative review and some questions for the future', *Qualitative Social Work: Research and Practice*, 16(1): 29–43.

Clark, C.D. (2003) *In Sickness and in Play: Children Coping with Chronic Illness*, Rutgers University Press.

Clark, T. (2011) 'Gaining and maintaining access: exploring the mechanisms that support and challenge the relationship between gatekeepers and researchers', *Qualitative Social Work: Research and Practice*, 10(4): 485–502.

Clarke, A., Healy, K., Lynch, D., and Featherstone, G. (2024) 'Stability in statutory kinship care: a grounded theory study of placement stability in Australia', *Children and Youth Services Review*, 156: art 107289. doi: 10.1016/j.childyouth.2023.107289

Clements, J. and Birch, S. (2023) 'Exploring risk and protective factors in kinship family environments: a systematic literature review of the views of children in kinship care', *Educational Psychology in Practice*, 39(4): 475–99.

Clinton, H.R. (2007) *It Takes a Village: And Other Lessons Children Teach Us*, Simon & Schuster.

Collingridge, M. and Curry, S. (2020) *Ethical Practice in Social Work: An Applied Approach*, Routledge.

Collins, S. (2018) 'Ethics of care and statutory social work in the UK: critical perspectives and strengths', *Practice*, 30(1): 3–18.

Coman, W., Dickson, S., McGill, L., and Rainey, M. (2016) 'Why am I in care? A model for communicating with children about entry to care that promotes psychological safety and adjustment', *Adoption and Fostering*, 40(1): 49–59.

Compeau, L.D., Monroe, K.B., Grewal, D., and Reynolds, K. (2016) 'Expressing and defining self and relationships through everyday shopping experiences', *Journal of Business Research*, 69(3): 1035–42.

Cong, Z. and Silverstein, M. (2012) 'Caring for grandchildren and intergenerational support in rural China: a gendered extended family perspective', *Ageing and Society*, 32(3): 425–50.

Connolly, M. and Morris, K. (2011) *Understanding Child and Family Welfare: Statutory Responses to Children at Risk*, Palgrave Macmillan.

Connolly, M., Kiraly, M., McCrae, L., and Mitchell, G. (2016) 'A kinship care practice framework: using a life course approach', *British Journal of Social Work*, 47(1): 87–105.

Conway, T. and Hutson, R. (2007) *Is Kinship Care Good for Kids*, Centre for Law and Social Policy.

Cook, D.T. (2018) 'Panaceas of play: stepping past the creative child', in S. Spyrou, R. Rosen, and D.T. Cook (eds) *Reimagining Childhood Studies*, Bloomsbury Academic, pp 123–36.

Cook, L.L. (2020) 'The home visit in child protection social work: emotion as resource and risk for professional judgement and practice', *Child and Family Social Work*, 25(1): 18–26.

Cornwall, A. and Jewkes, R. (1995) 'What is participatory research?', *Social Science and Medicine*, 41(12): 1667–76.

Cossar, J. (2004) *Kinship Care: Retracing the Relationship Between Family and State* (new edn), Social Work Monographs.

Cossar, J. and Neil, E. (2013) 'Making sense of siblings: connections and severances in post-adoption contact', *Child and Family Social Work*, 18(1): 67–76.

Cossar, J., Brandon, M., and Jordan, P. (2016) '"You've got to trust her and she's got to trust you": Children's views on participation in the child protection system', *Child & Family Social Work*, 21(1): 103–12.

Costa Santos, S., Parnell, R., Abo Kanon, H., Pattinson, E., Pitsikali, A., and Sarhan, H. (2024) '"… nice to get some alone time": children's spatial negotiation of alone time needs in the family home', *Children's Geographies*, 22(4): 513–29.

Craib, I. (2000) *Classical Social Theory: An Introduction to the Thought of Marx, Weber, Durkheim and Simmel* (reprint), Oxford University Press.

Crawford, B. and Bradley, M.S. (2016) 'Parent gender and child removal in physical abuse and neglect cases', *Children and Youth Services Review*, 65: 224–30.

Cree, V.E. (2000) *Sociology for Social Workers and Probation Officers*, Psychology Press.

Cree, V.E., Kay, H., and Tisdall, K. (2002) 'Research with children: sharing the dilemmas', *Child and Family Social Work*, 7(1): 47–56.

References

Crisp, B.R. (2024) 'How do we decolonise the social work curriculum?', *Australian Social Work*: 1–13. doi: 10.1080/0312407X.2024.2329233

Crosby, C., Duggan, L., Ferguson, R., Floyd, K., Joseph, M., Love, H. et al (2012) 'Queer studies, materialism, and crisis: a roundtable discussion', *GLQ: A Journal of Lesbian and Gay Studies*, 18(1): 127–47.

Cruickshank, J. (2007) *Critical Realism: The Difference it Makes*, Routledge.

Crumbley, J. and Little, R.L. (1997) *Relatives Raising Children: An Overview of Kinship Care*, Child Welfare League of America.

Cudjoe, E., Abdullah, A., and Chiu, M.Y.L. (2019) 'What makes kinship caregivers unprepared for children in their care? Perspectives and experiences from kinship care alumni in Ghana', *Children and Youth Services Review*, 101: 270–6.

Danermark, B., Ekström, M., and Karlsson, J.C. (2019) *Explaining Society: Critical Realism in the Social Sciences* (2nd edn), Routledge.

Davey, J. (2016) *The Care of Kin: A Case Study Approach to Kinship Care in the South of England and Zululand, South Africa*, Bournemouth University.

Davidson, G., Bunting, L., Bywaters, P., Featherstone, B., and McCartan, C. (2017) 'Child welfare as justice: why are we not effectively addressing inequalities?', *The British Journal of Social Work*, 47(6): 1641–51.

Davies, H., Boaz, A., Fraser, A., and Nutley, S. (eds) (2019) *What Works Now? Evidence-Informed Policy and Practice*, Policy Press.

Davies, K. (1994) 'The tensions between process time and clock time in care-work: the example of day nurseries', *Time and Society*, 3(3): 277–303.

Davies, K. (2015) 'Siblings, stories and the self: the sociological significance of young people's sibling relationships', *Sociology*, 49(4): 679–95.

Delap, E. and Mann, G. (2019) *The Paradox of Kinship Care: The Most Valued but Least Resourced Care Option – A Global Study*, Family for Every Child. Available from: https://familyforeverychild.org/wp-content/uploads/2022/01/The-Paradox-of-Kinship-Care-text-full-English-report-04-03-12.pdf (Accessed 14 March 2025).

Delap, E., Gilham, G., Clulow, S., and Mutama, B. (2024) *How to Support Kinship Care: Lessons Learnt Across the World*, Family for Every Child. Available from: https://familyforeverychild.org/resources/how-to-support-kinship-care-lessons-learnt-from-around-the-world/ (Accessed 14 March 2025).

Delfabbro, P. (2020) *Developmental Outcomes of Children and Young People in Relative/Kinship Care and Foster Care*, NSW Department of Communities and Justice.

del Valle, J.F., Lázaro-Visa, S., López, M., and Bravo, A. (2011) 'Leaving family care: transitions to adulthood from kinship care', *Children and Youth Services Review*, 33(12): 2475–81.

DfE (Department for Education) (2010) *The Children Act 1989 Guidance and Regulations. Volume 2: Care Planning, Placement and Case Review*. Available from: https://assets.publishing.service.gov.uk/media/60e6fb43d3bf7f56896127e5/The_Children_Act_1989_guidance_and_regulations_Volume_2_care_planning__placement_and_case_review.pdf (Accessed 13 March 2025).

DfE (Department for Education) (2012) *An Action Plan for Adoption: Tackling Delay*. Available from: https://assets.publishing.service.gov.uk/media/5a7a3eab40f0b66a2fc00f13/action_plan_for_adoption.pdf (Accessed 13 March 2025).

DfE (Department for Education) (2021) *Adoption Strategy: Achieving Excellence Everywhere*. Available from: https://www.gov.uk/government/publications/adoption-strategy-achieving-excellence-everywhere (Accessed 15 May 2025).

DfE (Department for Education) (2023) *Championing Kinship Care: National Kinship Care Strategy*. Available from: www.gov.uk/government/publications/championing-kinship-care-national-kinship-care-strategy (Accessed 27 September 2024).

DfE (Department for Education) (2024) *Family and Friends Care: Statutory Guidance for Local Authorities*. Available from: https://assets.publishing.service.gov.uk/media/670d3ed5e84ae1fd8592f2fa/Kinship_Care_-_statutory_guidance_for_local_authorities__October_2024.pdf#:~:text=This%20guidance%20sets%20out%20a%20framework%20for%20the,who%20are%20unable%20to%20live%20with%20their%20parents (Accessed 13 March 2025).

Dermott, E. and Seymour, J. (eds) (2011) *Displaying Families: A New Concept for the Sociology of Family Life*, Palgrave Macmillan.

de St Croix, T. (2012) '"If someone is not a success in life it's their own fault": What Coalition youth policy says about young people and youth workers', *In Defence of Youth Work*. Available from: https://indefenceofyouthwork.com/2012/08/15/if-someone-is-not-a-success-in-life-its-their-own-fault-coalition-youth-policy-revisited/ (Accessed 14 March 2025).

Dianiska, R.E., Quas, J.A., and Lyon, T.D. (2024) 'Using rapport building to improve information yield when interviewing adolescents: a systematic review and call for research', *Child Abuse and Neglect*, 154: art 106898. doi: 10.1016/j.chiabu.2024.106898

Diaz, C. and Hill, L. (2019) 'A critical evaluation of the extent to which the reform and modernisation agenda has impacted on the professionalisation of social work in England', *Child Care in Practice*, 26(3): 272–84.

Dickson, K., Sutcliffe, K., and Gough, D. (2010) *What Outcomes Matter to Looked After Children and Young People and Their Families and Carers? A Systematic Review of Their Experiences, Views and Preferences*, EPPI Centre, Institute of Education.

Dill, K.A. (2010) *'Fitting a Square Peg into a Round Hole': Understanding Kinship Care Outside of the Foster Care Paradigm*, University of Toronto.

Dockett, S., Einarsdottir, J., and Perry, B. (2017) 'Photo elicitation: reflecting on multiple sites of meaning', *International Journal of Early Years Education*, 25(3): 225–40.

Dolbin-MacNab, M.L. and Keiley, M.K. (2009) 'Navigating interdependence: how adolescents raised solely by grandparents experience their family relationships', *Family Relations*, 58(2): 162–75.

Dominelli, L. and Campling, J. (2002) *Feminist Social Work Theory and Practice*, Palgrave.

Domingues, J.M. (2022) 'From global risk to global threat: state capabilities and modernity in times of coronavirus', *Current Sociology*, 70(1): 6–23.

Dorval, A., Lamothe, J., Hélie, S., and Poirier, M.-A. (2020) 'Different profiles, different needs: an exploration and analysis of characteristics of children in kinship care and their parents', *Children and Youth Services Review*, 108(C): 1–8.

Downie, J.M., Hay, D.A., Horner, B.J., Wichmann, H., and Hislop, A.L. (2010) 'Children living with their grandparents: resilience and wellbeing', *International Journal of Social Welfare*, 19(1): 8–22.

Drew, I., Pierre, R., and Sen, R. (2023) 'Exploring and re-imagining children's services in England through a decolonial frame', in R. Sen and C. Kerr (eds) *The Future of Children's Care*, Policy Press, pp 101–21.

Easton, G. (2010) 'Critical realism in case study research', *Industrial Marketing Management*, 39(1): 118–28.

Edwards, D. and Parkinson, K. (2018) *Family Group Conferences in Social Work: Involving Families in Social Care Decision Making*, Policy Press.

Edwards, E. (1994) *Anthropology and Photography, 1860–1920* (new edn), Yale University Press.

Edwards, R., McCarthy, J.R., and Gillies, V. (2012) 'The politics of concepts: family and its (putative) replacements', *The British Journal of Sociology*, 63(4): 730–46.

Emlen, A. (1981) 'Development of the permanency planning concept', in S. Downs, L. Bayles, A. Dreyer, and L. Emlen (eds) *Foster Care in the 70's: Final Report of the Permanency Planning Dissemination Project*, Regional Research Institute for Human Services.

Emmel, N. and Clark, A. (2009) 'The methods used in Connected Lives: investigating networks, neighbourhoods and communities', ESRC National Centre for Research Methods Working Paper 06/09, ESRC.

Enke, B. (2019) 'Kinship, cooperation, and the evolution of moral systems', *The Quarterly Journal of Economics*, 134(2): 953–1019.

Epstein, L. and Heymann, I. (1967) 'Some decisive processes in adoption planning for older children', *Child Welfare*, 46(1): 5–46.

Esacove, A. (2024) 'Common patterns of cisgender use in public health articles and their implications for gender inclusivity efforts, 2013-2020', *American Journal of Public Health*, 114(2): 202–8.

Esping-Andersen, G. (1990) *The Three Worlds of Welfare Capitalism*, Princeton University Press.

Evans, J. and Jones, P. (2011) 'The walking interview: methodology, mobility and place', *Applied Geography*, 31(2): 849–58.

Fabian, J. (1990) *Power and Performance: Ethnographic Explorations through Proverbial Wisdom and Theater in Shaba, Zaire*, University of Wisconsin Press.

Facca, D., Gladstone, B., and Teachman, G. (2020) 'Working the limits of "giving voice" to children: a critical conceptual review', *International Journal of Qualitative Methods*, 19: 1–10.

Fahlberg, V. (2008) *A Child's Journey Through Placement*, British Association for Adoption and Fostering.

Fairhall, N. and Woods, K. (2021) 'Children's views on children's rights: a systematic literature review', *The International Journal of Children's Rights*, 29(4): 835–71.

Family Justice Council (2019) *Interim Guidance on Special Guardianship*. Available from: www.judiciary.uk/wp-content/uploads/2019/05/fjc-sg-interim-guidance-pfd-approved-draft-21-may-2019-1-1.pdf (Accessed 24 March 2021).

Family Rights Group (2017) *Initial Family and Friends Care Assessment: A Good Practice Guide*, Family Rights Group.

Farmer, E. (2010) 'What factors relate to good placement outcomes in kinship care?', *British Journal of Social Work*, 40(2): 426–44.

Farmer, E. and Moyers, S. (2008) *Kinship Care: Fostering Effective Family and Friends Placements*, Jessica Kingsley.

Farmer, E., Selwyn, J., and Meakings, S. (2013) '"Other children say you're not normal because you don't live with your parents". Children's views of living with informal kinship carers: social networks, stigma and attachment to carers', *Child and Family Social Work*, 18(1): 25–34.

Fawcett, B., Featherstone, B., Fook, J., and Rossiter, A. (2005) *Practice and Research in Social Work: Postmodern Feminist Perspectives*, Routledge.

Featherstone, B., White, S., and Morris, K. (2014) *Re-Imagining Child Protection: Towards Humane Social Work with Families*, Policy Press.

Featherstone, B., Gupta, A., and Mills, S. (2018) *The Role of the Social Worker in Adoption – Ethics and Human Rights: An Enquiry*, British Association of Social Workers.

Featherstone, B., Gupta, A., Morris, K., and Warner, J. (2018) 'Let's stop feeding the risk monster: towards a social model of "child protection"', *Families, Relationships and Societies*, 7(1): 7–22.

Ferguson, H. (2004) *Protecting Children in Time: Child Abuse, Child Protection and the Consequences of Modernity*, Palgrave Macmillan.

Ferguson, H. (2008) 'Liquid social work: welfare interventions as mobile practices', *The British Journal of Social Work*, 38(3): 561–79.

Ferguson, H. (2009a) 'Driven to care: the car, automobility and social work', *Mobilities*, 4(2): 275–93.

Ferguson, H. (2009b) 'Performing child protection: home visiting, movement and the struggle to reach the abused child', *Child and Family Social Work*, 14(4): 471–80.

Ferguson, H. (2010a) 'Mobilities of welfare: the case of social work', in M. Buscher, J. Urry, and K. Witchger (eds) *Mobile Methods*, Routledge, pp 72–87.

Ferguson, H. (2010b) 'Therapeutic journeys: the car as a vehicle for working with children and families and theorising practice', *Journal of Social Work Practice*, 24(2): 121–38.

Ferguson, H. (2010c) 'Walks, home visits and atmospheres: risk and the everyday practices and mobilities of social work and child protection', *The British Journal of Social Work*, 40(4): 1100–17.

Ferguson, H. (2018) 'Making home visits: creativity and the embodied practices of home visiting in social work and child protection', *Qualitative Social Work*, 17(1): 65–80.

Ferguson, I. (2012) 'Personalisation, social justice and social work: a reply to Simon Duffy', *Journal of Social Work Practice*, 26(1): 55–73.

Ferguson, I., Ioakimidis, V., and Lavalette, M. (2018) *Global Social Work in a Political Context: Radical Perspectives*, Policy Press.

Ferguson, J. (1994) 'The anti-politics machine: "development" and bureaucratic power in Lesotho', *The Ecologist*, 24(5): 176–81.

Ferraro, A.C., Maher, E.J., and Grinnell-Davis, C. (2022) 'Family ties: a quasi-experimental approach to estimate the impact of kinship care on child well-being', *Children and Youth Services Review*, 137: art 106472. doi: 10.1016/j.childyouth.2022.106472

Fenton-Glynn, C. (2016) 'Adoption without consent: update 2016', European Parliament, Directorate-General for Internal Policies. Available from: https://www.europarl.europa.eu/RegData/etudes/STUD/2016/556940/IPOL_STU(2016)556940_EN.pdf (Accessed 15 May 2025).

Fielding, M. (2008) 'Personalisation, education and the market', *Soundings*, 38: 56–69.

Finch, J. (2007) 'Displaying families', *Sociology*, 41(1): 65–81.

Fitzgerald, R.M., Graham, A.P., Smith, A.B., and Taylor, N. (2009) 'Children's participation as a struggle over recognition', in B. Percy-Smith and N. Thomas (eds) *A Handbook of Children and Young People's Participation: Perspectives from Theory and Practice*, Routledge, pp 293–305.

Fives, A., Russell, D.W., Canavan, J., Lyons, R., Eaton, P., Devaney, C. et al (2015) 'The ethics of randomized controlled trials in social settings: can social trials be scientifically promising and must there be equipoise?', *International Journal of Research and Method in Education*, 38(1): 56–71.

Fletcher, A.J. (2017) 'Applying critical realism in qualitative research: methodology meets method', *International Journal of Social Research Methodology*, 20(2): 181–94.

Font, S.A. (2015) 'Is higher placement stability in kinship foster care by virtue or design?', *Child Abuse and Neglect*, 42: 99–111.

Fook, J. (2016) *Social Work: A Critical Approach to Practice*, SAGE Publications.

Forman, H. (2015) 'Events and children's sense of time: a perspective on the origins of everyday time-keeping', *Frontiers in Psychology*, 6(259): 1–5.

Fraser, N. (2003) 'Social justice in an age of identity politics: redistribution, recognition and participation', in N. Fraser and A. Honneth (eds) *Redistribution or Recognition?* Verso, pp 7–109.

Freeman, J.D. and Stoldt, R.G. (2019) 'Grandma or mommy: familial labels as constructs of identity in grandfamilies', *Journal of Intergenerational Relationships*, 17(4): 411–29.

Freistadt, J. and Strohschein, L. (2013) 'Family structure differences in family functioning: interactive effects of social capital and family structure', *Journal of Family Issues*, 34(7): 952–74.

Frost, N. and Dolan, P. (2021) 'Theory, research and practice in child welfare: the current state of the art in social work', *Child and Family Social Work*, 26(3): 498–506.

Furstenberg, F.F. (2020) 'Kinship reconsidered: research on a neglected topic', *Journal of Marriage and Family*, 82(1): 364–82.

Gage, F.H. (2002) 'Neurogenesis in the adult brain', *Journal of Neuroscience*, 22(3): 612–13.

Gallagher, M. (2008) 'Foucault, power and participation', *The International Journal of Children's Rights*, 16(3): 395–406.

Garrett, P.M. (2010) 'Recognizing the limitations of the political theory of recognition: Axel Honneth, Nancy Fraser and social work', *The British Journal of Social Work*, 40(5): 1517–33.

Garrett, P.M. (2013) *Social Work and Social Theory: Making Connections*, Policy Press.

Garrett, P.M. (2017) 'Keywords, care and neoliberalism', *Critical and Radical Social Work*, 5(3): 269–85.

Geen, R. (2004) 'The evolution of kinship care policy and practice', *The Future of Children*, 14(1): 130–49.

Geldard, K., Geldard, D., and Foo, R.Y. (2017) *Counselling Children: A Practical Introduction*, SAGE.

Giddens, A. (1991) *Modernity and Self-Identity* (new edn), Polity Press.

Gilgun, J.F. (2015) 'Beyond description to interpretation and theory in qualitative social work research', *Qualitative Social Work*, 14(6): 741–52.

Gillies, V., Edwards, R., and Horsley, N. (2017) *Challenging the Politics of Early Intervention: Who's 'Saving' Children and Why*, Policy Press.

Gilligan, C. (1982) *In a Different Voice: Psychological Theory and Women's Development*, Harvard University Press.

Godden, N.J. (2017) 'The participation imperative in co-operative inquiry: personal reflections of an initiating researcher', *Systemic Practice and Action Research*, 30(1): 1–18.

Goldacre, A. and Hood, R. (2022) 'Factors affecting the social gradient in children's social care', *The British Journal of Social Work*, 52(6): 3599–617.

Goldberg, A.E. (2019) *Open Adoption and Diverse Families: Complex Relationships in the Digital Age*, Oxford University Press.

Goldman-Segall, R. and Goldman, R. (2014) *Points of Viewing Children's Thinking*, Psychology Press.

Goldstein, J., Freud, A., and Solnit, A.J. (1979) *Beyond the Best Interests of the Child*, Free Press.

Goldstein, J., Freund, A., and Solnit, A.J. (1986) *Before the Best Interests of the Child* (reprint), Free Press.

Goldstein, J., Freud, A., Solnit, A.J., and Goldstein, S. (1986) *In the Best Interests of the Child: Professional Boundaries*, Macmillan.

Goredema-Braid, B. (2010) 'Ethical research with young people', *Research Ethics*, 6(2): 48–52.

Gorla, L., Fusco, C., and Santona, A. (2023) 'A retrospective study on adoptive parenthood in the first year after the adoption: the role of parents' attachment and empathy on communicative openness', *Healthcare*, 11(24): art 3128. doi: 10.3390/healthcare11243128

Graeber, D. (2014) 'On the moral grounds of economic relations: a Maussian approach', *Journal of Classical Sociology*, 14(1): 65–77.

Graham, A.P. and Fitzgerald, R.M. (2010) 'Progressing children's participation: exploring the potential of a dialogical turn', *Childhood*, 17(3): 343–59.

Graham, M. (2011) 'Changing paradigms and conditions of childhood: implications for the social professions and social work', *The British Journal of Social Work*, 41(8): 1532–47.

Greenhow, S., Hackett, S., Jones, C., and Meins, E. (2017) 'Adoptive family experiences of post-adoption contact in an internet era', *Child and Family Social Work*, 22(S1): 44–52.

Greig, A., Taylor, J., and MacKay, T. (2007) *Doing Research with Children*, SAGE.

Griffiths, M., Rogers, A. and Anderson, B. (2013) 'Migration, time and temporalities: review and prospect', COMPAS Research Resources Paper, University of Oxford. Available from: https://www.compas.ox.ac.uk/publication/migration-time-and-temporalities-review-and-prospect (Accessed 16 May 2025).

Grimwood, T. (2015) *Key Debates in Social Work and Philosophy*, Routledge.

Gross, H.E. (1993) 'Open adoption: a research-based literature review and new data', *Child Welfare*, 72(3): 269–84.

Groundwater-Smith, S., Dockett, S., and Bottrell, D. (2015) *Participatory Research with Children and Young People*, SAGE Publications.

Guterman, J.T. (2006) *Mastering the Art of Solution-Focused Counseling*, American Counseling Association.

Habermas, J. (1985) *The Theory of Communicative Action: Volume 1: Reason and the Rationalization of Society*, Beacon Press.

Hagen, A.L. (2021) 'Egalitarian ideals, conflicting realities: introducing a model for thick youth participation', in A.L. Hagen and B. Andersen (eds) *Ung medvirkning: Kreativitet og konflikt i planlegging*, Cappelen Damm Akademisk/NOASP, pp 277–306.

Halberstam, J. (2005) *In a Queer Time and Place: Transgender Bodies, Subcultural Lives: 3 (Sexual Cultures)*, New York University Press.

Hallett, N., Garstang, J., and Taylor, J. (2021) 'Kinship care and child protection in high-income countries: a scoping review', *Trauma, Violence, and Abuse*, advance online publication. doi: 10.1177/15248380211036073

Hammersley, M. (2017) 'Childhood studies: a sustainable paradigm?', *Childhood*, 24(1): 113–27.

Hammond, S.P., Young, J., and Duddy, C. (2020) 'Life story work for children and young people with care experience: a scoping review', *Developmental Child Welfare*, 2(4): 293–315.

Hanley, J. (2021) 'Networks of power and counterpower in social work with children and families in England', *Critical Social Policy*: advance online publication. doi: 10.1177/02610183211034727

Hannah, M. (2008) *An Introduction to Kitbag: Building Psychological Capacity in Powerful Times*, International Futures Forum.

Hantrais, L. (2004) *Family Policy Matters*, Bristol University Press.

Hardecker, S., Schmidt, M.F.H., and Tomasello, M. (2017) 'Children's developing understanding of the conventionality of rules', *Journal of Cognition and Development*, 18(2): 163–88.

Harden, B.J., Clyman, R.B., Kriebel, D.K., and Lyons, M.E. (2004) 'Kith and kin care: parental attitudes and resources of foster and relative caregivers', *Children and Youth Services Review*, 26(7): 657–71.

Harden, J., Scott, S., Backett-Milburn, K., and Jackson, S. (2000) 'Can't talk, won't talk? Methodological issues in researching children', *Sociological Research Online*, 5(2): 1–12.

References

Hardy, M. (2020) 'Claim, blame, shame: how risk undermines authenticity in social work', in L. Frost, V. Magyar-Haas, H. Schoneville, and A. Siccora (eds) *Shame and Social Work: Theory, Reflexivity and Practice*, Policy Press, pp 163–86.

Harper, P.C. (2020) 'ASMR: bodily pleasure, online performance, digital modality', *Sound Studies*, 6(1): 95–8.

Harris, J. (2003) *The Social Work Business*, Routledge.

Hart, R.A. (1997) *Children's Participation*, Routledge.

Hartman, A. (1995) 'Diagrammatic assessment of family relationships', *Families in Society: The Journal of Contemporary Social Services*, 76(2): 111–22.

Hartwig, M. (ed) (2007) *Dictionary of Critical Realism*, Routledge.

Harwin, J., Alrouh, B., Golding, L., McQuarrie, T., Karen, P., and Cusworth, L. (2019) *The Contribution of Supervision Orders and Special Guardianship to Children's Lives and Family Justice*, Centre for Family Justice Research, Lancaster University.

Hassall, A., Janse van Rensburg, E., Trew, S., Hawes, D.J., and Pasalich, D.S. (2021) 'Does kinship vs. foster care better promote connectedness? A systematic review and meta-analysis', *Clinical Child and Family Psychology Review*, 24(4): 813–32.

Hedin, L. (2012) *Foster Youth's Sense of Belonging in Kinship, Network and Traditional Foster Families: An Interactive Perspective on Foster Youth's Everyday Life*, Örebro University.

Hedin, L. (2014) 'A sense of belonging in a changeable everyday life – a follow-up study of young people in kinship, network, and traditional foster families: a sense of belonging in a changeable daily life', *Child and Family Social Work*, 19(2): 165–73.

Hegar, R.L. (1999) 'The cultural roots of kinship care', in R.L. Hegar and M. Scannapieco (eds) *Kinship Foster Care: Policy, Practice, and Research*, Oxford University Press, pp 17–28.

Hegel, G.W.F. (2018) *Georg Wilhelm Friedrich Hegel: The Phenomenology of Spirit* (edited and translated by T. Pinkard and M. Baur), Cambridge University Press.

Heinsch, M., Agllias, K., Tickner, C., Wells, H., Cootes, H., Sampson, D., and Kay-Lambkin, F. (2020) '"Speaking with them, not about them": engaging undergraduate social work students in research with young people', *Social Work Education*, 39(1): 111–25.

Held, V. (2006) *The Ethics of Care: Personal, Political, and Global*, Oxford University Press.

Hennink, M.M., Kaiser, B.N., and Marconi, V.C. (2017) 'Code saturation versus meaning saturation: how many interviews are enough?', *Qualitative Health Research*, 27(4): 591–608.

Herlofson, K. and Hagestad, G.O. (2012) 'Transformations in the role of grandparents across welfare states', in S. Arber and V. Timonen (eds) *Contemporary Grandparenting: Changing Family Relationships in Global Contexts*, Policy Press, pp 27–49.

Heslop, P. (2019) 'Foster fathers performing gender: the negotiation and reproduction of parenting roles in families who foster', *Journal of Family Social Work*, 22(4–5): 352–68.

Hickle, K. (2020) 'Introducing a trauma-informed capability approach in youth services', *Children & Society*, 34(6): 537–51.

Hicks, S. (2005) 'Lesbian and gay foster care and adoption: a brief UK history', *Adoption and Fostering*, 29(3): 42–56.

Hicks, S. (2016) 'Theory and social work: a conceptual review of the literature', *International Journal of Social Welfare*, 25(4): 399–414.

Hiles, M., Essex, S., Fox, A., and Luger, C. (2008) 'The words and pictures storyboard: making sense for children and families', *Context*, 97: 10–16.

Hiller, R.M., Halligan, S.L., Meiser-Stedman, R., Elliott, E., and Rutter-Eley, E. (2020) 'Supporting the emotional needs of young people in care: a qualitative study of foster carer perspectives', *BMJ Open*, 10(3): art e033317. doi: 10.1136/bmjopen-2019-033317

Hingley-Jones, H., Allain, L., Gleeson, H., and Twumasi, B. (2020) '"Roll back the years": a study of grandparent special guardians' experiences and implications for social work policy and practice in England', *Child and Family Social Work*, 25(3): 526–35.

Hislop, M.A., Horner, M.B., and Hay, D. (2004) *The Perceived Experiences of Children and Adolescents Living with their Grandparents*, Curtin University of Technology, Wanslea Family Services.

HM Government (2018) *Working Together to Safeguard Children*. Available from: https://assets.publishing.service.gov.uk/media/669e7501ab418ab05 5592a7b/Working_together_to_safeguard_children_2023.pdf (Accessed 28 March 2025).

Hodes, M. (1992) 'Commissioned review, the clinical relevance of the social anthropology of childhood', *Association of Child Psychology and Psychiatry Newsletter*, 14(6): 257–61.

Hodgetts, D., Chamberlain, K., and Radley, A. (2007) 'Considering photographs never taken during photo-production projects', *Qualitative Research in Psychology*, 4(4): 263–80.

Holland, S., Renold, E., Ross, N.J., and Hillman, A. (2010) 'Power, agency and participatory agendas: a critical exploration of young people's engagement in participative qualitative research', *Childhood*, 17(3): 360–75.

Holmes, H. and Burgess, G. (2022) 'Digital exclusion and poverty in the UK: how structural inequality shapes experiences of getting online', *Digital Geography and Society*, 3: art 100041. doi: 10.1016/j.diggeo.2022.100041

References

Holmes, L., Neagu, M., Sanders-Ellis, D., and Harrison, N. (2020) *Lifelong Links Evaluation Report*, Department for Education.

Holtan, A. (2008) 'Family types and social integration in kinship foster care', *Children and Youth Services Review*, 30(9): 1022–36.

Holtan, A., Rønning, J.A., Handegård, B.H., and Sourander, A. (2005) 'A comparison of mental health problems in kinship and nonkinship foster care', *European Child and Adolescent Psychiatry*, 14(4): 200–7.

Honneth, A. (1996) *Struggle for Recognition: The Moral Grammar of Social Conflicts*, Polity.

Hood, R. (2023) *Inequality and Social Work*, SAGE Publications.

Hook, M.P.V. (2019) *Social Work Practice with Families: A Resiliency-Based Approach*, Oxford University Press.

Horgan, D. (2017) 'Child participatory research methods: attempts to go "deeper"', *Childhood*, 24(2): 245–59.

Horgan, D., Fernández, E., and Kitching, K. (2023) 'Walking and talking with girls in their urban environments: a methodological meandering', *Irish Journal of Sociology*, 31(1): 101–24.

Horgan, D., Forde, C., Martin, S., and Parkes, A. (2017) 'Children's participation: moving from the performative to the social', *Children's Geographies*, 15(3): 274–88.

Horton, J. (2010) '"The best thing ever": how children's popular culture matters', *Social and Cultural Geography*, 11(4): 377–98.

Houston, S. (2001) 'Beyond social constructionism: critical realism and social work', *The British Journal of Social Work*, 31(6): 845–61.

Houston, S. (2010) 'Prising open the black box: critical realism, action research and social work', *Qualitative Social Work*, 9(1): 73–91.

Houston, S. (2016a) 'Beyond individualism: social work and social identity', *The British Journal of Social Work*, 46(2): 532–48.

Houston, S. (2016b) 'Empowering the "shamed" self: recognition and critical social work', *Journal of Social Work*, 16(1): 3–21.

Houston, S. (2022) 'The "powers of horror": abjection, critical realism and social work', *The British Journal of Social Work*, 53(2): 2314–30.

Houston, S. and Swords, C. (2022) 'Critical realism, mimetic theory and social work', *Journal of Social Work*, 22(2): 345–63.

Howe, D. (2011) *Attachment across the Lifecourse: A Brief Introduction*, Red Globe Press.

Hugman, R. (2009) 'Social work research and ethics', in I. Shaw, K. Briar-Lawson, J. Orme, and R. Ruckdeschel (eds) *The SAGE Handbook of Social Work Research*, SAGE Publications, pp 149–163.

Humphries, D.B. (2008) *Social Work Research for Social Justice*, Palgrave Macmillan.

Hunt, J. (2001) *Friends and Family Care: A Scoping Paper for the Department of Health*, Department of Health.

Hunt, J. (2020) *Two Decades of UK Research on Kinship Care: An Overview*, Family Rights Group.

Hunt, J. and Waterhouse, S. (2013) *It's Just Not Fair! Support, Need and Legal Status in Family and Friends Care*, Family Rights Group.

Hunt, J., Macleod, A., and Thomas, C. (1999) *The Last Resort: Child Protection, the Courts and the 1989 Children Act*, Stationery Office.

Hunt, J., Waterhouse, S., and Lutman, E. (2008) *Keeping Them in the Family*, British Association for Adoption and Fostering.

Hunt, J., Waterhouse, S., and Lutman, E. (2010) 'Parental contact for children placed in kinship care through care proceedings research', *Child and Family Law Quarterly*, 22(1): 71–92.

Ide, Y. and Beddoe, L. (2024) 'Challenging perspectives: reflexivity as a critical approach to qualitative social work research', *Qualitative Social Work*, 23(4): 725–40.

IFSW (International Federation of Social Workers) (2014) 'Global definition of social work'. Available from: www.ifsw.org/what-is-social-work/global-definition-of-social-work/ (Accessed 14 March 2025).

Ingham, D. and Mikardo, J. (2022) 'Kinship care: uncannily close for comfort?', *Journal of Child Psychotherapy*, 48(3): 334–50.

International Futures Forum (nd) 'Kitbag'. Available from: www.iffkitbag.com/ (Accessed 15 March 2025).

Irvine, L. and Cilia, L. (2017) 'More-than-human families: pets, people, and practices in multispecies households', *Sociology Compass*, 11: art e12455. doi: 10.1111/soc4.12455

Iversen, C., Flinkfeldt, M., Tuncer, S., and Laurier, E. (2022) 'The uses of small talk in social work: weather as a resource for informally pursuing institutional tasks', *Qualitative Social Work*, 21(6): 1043–62.

Iyer, P., Boddy, J., and Lynch, C. (2020) 'Contact following placement in care, adoption, or special guardianship: implications for children and young people's well-being', Evidence review. Nuffield Family Justice Observatory. Available from: https://www.nuffieldfjo.org.uk/resource/contact-well-being (Accessed 15 May 2025).

Jackson, S. and Ho, P.S.Y. (2020) 'What makes a family? Meanings and practices', in S. Jackson and P.S. Ying Ho (eds) *Women Doing Intimacy: Gender, Family and Modernity in Britain and Hong Kong*, Palgrave Macmillan, pp 87–118.

James, A. and Prout, A. (1997) *Constructing and Reconstructing Childhood: Contemporary Issues in the Sociological Study of Childhood* (2nd edn), Falmer Press.

James, A., Jenks, C., and Prout, A. (1998) *Theorizing Childhood*, Polity Press.

James-Brown, C. (2022) 'Introduction: transforming child welfare through anti-racist approaches', *Child Welfare*, 100(1): ix–xiv.

Jessiman, P., Kidger, J., Spencer, L., Geijer-Simpson, E., Kaluzeviciute, G., Burn, A. et al (2022) 'School culture and student mental health: a qualitative study in UK secondary schools', *BMC Public Health*, 22(1): art 619. doi: 10.1186/s12889-022-13034-x

Jessop, B. (2005) 'Critical realism and the strategic-relational approach', *New Formations*, 54(2): 40–53.

Jeyasingham, D. (2014) 'The production of space in children's social work: insights from Henri Lefebvre's spatial dialectics', *British Journal of Social Work*, 44(7): 1879–94.

Jones, R. (2018) *In Whose Interest? The Privatisation of Child Protection and Social Work*, Policy Press.

Jonsson, G. (1975) 'Negative social inheritance', in L. Levi (ed) *Society, Stress and Disease: Childhood and Adolescence Vol 2*, Oxford University Press, pp 181–6.

Jordan, B. (2011) 'Individualism and social work: the case of the third way in the UK', *Revista de Asistenta Social*, X(1): 15–24.

Kachel, U., Moore, R., and Tomasello, M. (2018) 'Effects of "we" – framing on young children's commitment, sharing, and helping', *Child Development*, 89(4): 1130–8.

Kaiser, D.H., McAdams, C.R., and Foster, V.A. (2012) 'Disequilibrium and development: the family counseling internship experience', *The Family Journal*, 20(3): 225–32.

Kallinen, K.P. (2021) 'Family relationships of children in kinship foster care', *Nordic Social Work Research*, 11(4): 319–32.

Kelch-Oliver, K. (2011) 'African American grandchildren raised in grandparent-headed families: an exploratory study', *The Family Journal*, 19(4): 396–406.

Kemmis, S. and McTaggart, R. (2005) 'Communicative action and the public sphere', in N.K. Denzin and Y.S. Lincoln (eds) *The SAGE Handbook of Qualitative Research* (3rd edn), Sage, pp 559–603.

Kennan, D., Brady, B., and Forkan, C. (2018) 'Supporting children's participation in decision making: a systematic literature review exploring the effectiveness of participatory processes', *The British Journal of Social Work*, 48(7): 1985–2002.

Kettle, M. and Jackson, S. (2017) 'Revisiting the rule of optimism', *The British Journal of Social Work*, 47(6): 1624–40.

Kinship (2024) *Out of Order: The Case for Boosting Financial Support for Kinship Arrangements Outside the Care System*. Available from: https://kinship.org.uk/wp-content/uploads/out-of-order-2024.pdf (Accessed 14 March 2025).

Kinship Care Parliamentary Taskforce (2020) *First Thought Not Afterthought: Report of the Parliamentary Taskforce on Kinship Care*. Available from: https://frg.org.uk/publications/ (Accessed 14 March 2025).

Kiraly, M. (2015) 'A review of kinship carer surveys: the "Cinderella" of the care system?', *Child, Family, Community, Australia (CFCA) Information Exchange*, 31: 1–28.

Kiraly, M. (2019) 'Nonfamilial kinship carers: who are they and what support do they need to nurture children?', *Child & Family Social Work*, 24: 449–57.

Kiraly, M. and Humphreys, C. (2013a) 'Family contact for children in kinship care: a literature review', *Australian Social Work*, 66(3): 358–74.

Kiraly, M. and Humphreys, C. (2013b) 'Perspectives from young people about family contact in kinship care: "don't push us – listen more"', *Australian Social Work*, 66(3): 314–27.

Kiraly, M. and Humphreys, C. (2016) '"It's about the whole family": family contact for children in kinship care', *Child and Family Social Work*, 21(2): 228–39.

Kiraly, M. and Kertesz, M. (2021) '"It's good because my sister is young, and she knows what's going on": children's views about their young kinship carers', *Child and Family Social Work*, 26(4): 592–600.

Kirk, S. (2007) 'Methodological and ethical issues in conducting qualitative research with children and young people: A literature review', *International Journal of Nursing Studies*, 44(7): 1250–60.

Kirton, D. (2020) 'Adoption wars: inequality, child welfare and (social) justice', *Families, Relationships and Societies*, 9(2): 253–68.

Kjørstad, M. and Solem, M.-B. (eds) (2017) *Critical Realism for Welfare Professions*, Routledge.

Koh, E. (2010) 'Permanency outcomes of children in kinship and non-kinship foster care: testing the external validity of kinship effects', *Children and Youth Services Review*, 32(3): 389–98.

Koh, E. and Testa, M.F. (2008) 'Propensity score matching of children in kinship and nonkinship foster care: do permanency outcomes differ?', *Social Work Research*, 32(2): 105–16.

Koh, E. and Testa, M.F. (2011) 'Children discharged from kin and non-kin foster homes: do the risks of foster care re-entry differ?', *Children and Youth Services Review*, 33(9): 1497–505.

Kolb, B. (2008) 'Involving, sharing, analysing – potential of the participatory photo interview', *Forum: Qualitative Sozialforschung/Forum: Qualitative Social Research*, 9(3): art 12. doi: 10.17169/fqs-9.3.1155

Konijn, C., Admiraal, S., Baart, J., van Rooij, F., Stams, G.-J., Colonnesi, C. et al (2019) 'Foster care placement instability: a meta-analytic review', *Children and Youth Services Review*, 96: 483–99.

Kosher, H. and Ben-Arieh, A. (2020) 'Social workers' perceptions of children's right to participation', *Child and Family Social Work*, 25(2): 294–303.

Kraftl, P. and Horton, J. (2018) 'Children's geographies and the "new wave" of childhood studies', in S. Spyrou, R. Rosen, and D. Cook (eds) *Reimagining Childhood Studies*, Bloomsbury, pp 105–21.

References

Križ, K. and Skivenes, M. (2017) 'Child welfare workers' perceptions of children's participation: a comparative study of England, Norway and the US (California)', *Child and Family Social Work*, 22(S2): 11–22.

Kuyini, A.B., Alhassan, A.R., Tollerud, I., Weld, H., and Haruna, I. (2009) 'Traditional kinship foster care in northern Ghana: the experiences and views of children, carers and adults in Tamale', *Child and Family Social Work*, 14(4): 440–9.

Lambert, M. (2019) 'Between "families in trouble" and "children at risk": historicising "troubled family" policy in England since 1945', *Children and Society*, 33(1): 82–91.

Lansdown, G. (2010) 'The realisation of children's participation rights', in B. Percy-Smith and N. Thomas (eds) *A Handbook of Children and Young People's Participation: Perspectives from Theory and Practice*, Routledge, pp 11–23.

Lara, M.S. (2011) *Kinship Care Policy: Women's Oppression and Neoliberal Familialization: Exacerbating Women's Multiple Oppressions through Developing Neoliberal Policy in Child Welfare*, master's thesis, McMaster University. Available from: https://macsphere.mcmaster.ca/handle/11375/11407 (Accessed 14 March 2025).

Lefevre, M. (2018) *Communicating and Engaging with Children and Young People: Making a Difference* (2nd edn), Policy Press.

Lefevre, M., Hickle, K., and Luckock, B. (2019) '"Both/and" not "either/or": reconciling rights to protection and participation in working with child sexual exploitation', *The British Journal of Social Work*, 49(7): 1837–55.

Lehto, X.Y., Choi, S., Lin, Y.-C., and MacDermid, S.M. (2009) 'Vacation and family functioning', *Annals of Tourism Research*, 36(3): 459–79.

Leigh, J., Beddoe, L., and Keddell, E. (2020) 'Disguised compliance or undisguised nonsense? A critical discourse analysis of compliance and resistance in social work practice', *Families, Relationships and Societies*, 9(2): 269–85.

Leitch, J. (2022) '"Learning to hold a paradox": a narrative review of how ambiguous loss and disenfranchised grief affects children in care', *Practice*, 34(5): 355–69.

Leitner, S. (2003) 'Varieties of familialism: the caring function of the family in comparative perspective', *European Societies*, 5(4): 353–75.

Lenette, C., Stavropoulou, N., Nunn, C., Kong, S.T., Cook, T., Coddington, K., and Banks, S. (2019) 'Brushed under the carpet: examining the complexities of participatory research', *Research for All*, 3(2): 161–79.

Lesko, N. and Talburt, S. (2012) 'Enchantment', in S Talburt and N Lesko (eds) *Keywords in Youth Studies: Tracing Affects, Movements, Knowledges*, Routledge, pp 279–89.

LeVine, R.A. (2014) 'Attachment theory as cultural ideology', in H. Otto and H. Keller (eds) *Different Faces of Attachment: Cultural Variations on a Universal Human Need*, Cambridge University Press, pp 50–65.

Levingston, J., Adebiyi, M., Hadley, B., Al-Hassan, Y., Back, D., Cook, M., and Edginton, C. (2019) 'Slime bash social: a tactile manipulative for child and youth play', *Journal of STEM Arts, Crafts, and Constructions*, 4(1): 52–62.

Lindsay, J., Tanner, C., Leahy, D., Supski, S., Wright, J., and Maher, J. (2021) 'The family meals imperative and everyday family life: an analysis of children's photos and videos', *Critical Public Health*, 31(1): 77–89.

Linn, S. (2009) *Case for Make Believe: Saving Play in a Commercialized World* (reprint), The New Press.

Litrownik, A.J., Newton, R., Mitchell, B.E., and Richardson, K.K. (2003) 'Long-term follow-up of young children placed in foster care: subsequent placements and exposure to family violence', *Journal of Family Violence*, 18(1): 19–28.

Loeffler, T.A. (2005) 'Looking deeply in: using photo-elicitation to explore the meanings of outdoor education experiences', *Journal of Experiential Education*, 27(3): 343–6.

Longhofer, J. and Floersch, J. (2014) 'Values in a science of social work: values-informed research and research-informed values', *Research on Social Work Practice*, 24(5): 527–34.

Lorenz, W. (2016) 'Reaching the person—social work research as professional responsibility', *European Journal of Social Work*, 19(3–4): 455–67.

Lundy, L. (2007) '"Voice" is not enough: conceptualising Article 12 of the United Nations Convention on the Rights of the Child', *British Educational Research Journal*, 33(6): 927–42.

Lyotard, J.-F. (1984) *The Postmodern Condition: A Report on Knowledge* (translated by G. Bennington and B. Massumi), University of Minnesota Press

MacAlister, J. (2022) *Independent Review of Children's Social Care: Final Report*, Department for Education. Available from: www.gov.uk/government/publications/independent-review-of-childrens-social-care-final-report (Accessed 14 March 2025).

MacDonald, M., Hayes, D., and Houston, S. (2018) 'Understanding informal kinship care: a critical narrative review of theory and research', *Families, Relationships and Societies*, 7(1): 71–87.

Mackenzie, C. and Stoljar, N. (2000) *Relational Autonomy: Feminist Perspectives on Autonomy, Agency, and the Social Self*, Oxford University Press.

Maconochie, H. (2013) *Young Children's Participation in a Sure Start Children's Centre*, PhD thesis, Sheffield Hallam University.

Madigan, S., Quayle, E., Cossar, J., and Paton, K. (2013) 'Feeling the same or feeling different? An analysis of the experiences of young people in foster care', *Adoption and Fostering*, 37(4): 389–403.

Maechler, S. and Graz, J.-C. (2022) 'Is the sky or the earth the limit? Risk, uncertainty and nature', *Review of International Political Economy*, 29(2): 624–45.

Maluccio, A.N., Fine, E., and Olmstead, K.A. (1986) *Permanency Planning for Children: Concepts and Methods*, Tavistock Publications.

Mannay, D. (2015) *Visual, Narrative and Creative Research Methods: Application, Reflection and Ethics*, Routledge.

Mannion, G. (2009) 'After participation: the socio-spatial performance of intergenerational becoming', in B. Percy-Smith and N. Thomas (eds) *A Handbook of Children's Participation: Perspectives from Theory and Practice*, Routledge, pp 330–42.

Manzano, A. (2016) 'The craft of interviewing in realist evaluation', *Evaluation*, 22(3): 342–60.

Maree, J.G. (2022) 'The psychosocial development theory of Erik Erikson: critical overview', in R. Evans and O.N. Saracho (eds) *The Influence of Theorists and Pioneers on Early Childhood Education*, Routledge, pp 119–33.

Martens, L. (2018) 'Researching children, childhood, and consumer culture', in L. Martens (ed) *Childhood and Markets: Infants, Parents and the Business of Child Caring*, Palgrave Macmillan, pp 23–55.

Marthinsen, E., Skjefstad, N., Juberg, A., and Garrett, P.M. (eds) (2021) *Social Work and Neoliberalism*, Routledge.

Maslow, A.H. (1954). *Motivation and Personality*, Harper.

Mason, J. (2008) 'Tangible affinities and the real life fascination of kinship', *Sociology*, 42(1): 29–45.

Mason, J. and Hood, S. (2011) 'Exploring issues of children as actors in social research', *Children and Youth Services Review*, 33(4): 490–5.

Massoud, M.F. (2022) 'The price of positionality: assessing the benefits and burdens of self-identification in research methods', *Journal of Law and Society*, 49(S1): S64–S86.

Mattsson, T. (2014) 'Intersectionality as a useful tool: anti-oppressive social work and critical reflection', *Affilia*, 29(1): 8–17.

Mayall, B. (2002) *Towards a Sociology For Childhood: Thinking from Children's Lives*, Open University Press.

McCafferty, P. (2017) 'Implementing Article 12 of the United Nations Convention on the Rights of the Child in child protection decision-making: a critical analysis of the challenges and opportunities for social work', *Child Care in Practice*, 23(4): 327–41.

McCafferty, P. (2020) '"Do I read it? No". Knowledge utilisation in child welfare decisions', *Child Care in Practice*, 26(3): 276–92.

McCartan, C., Bunting, L., Bywaters, P., Davidson, G., Elliott, M., and Hooper, J. (2018) 'A four-nation comparison of kinship care in the UK: the relationship between formal kinship care and deprivation', *Social Policy and Society*, 17(4): 619–35.

McCarthy, J.R. (2013) 'What is at stake in family troubles? Existential issues and value frameworks', in J. Ribbens McCarthy, C.-A. Hooper, and V. Gillies (eds) *Family Troubles?* Policy Press, pp 326–53.

McFadden, A., Varcoe, C., and Brown, H. (2023) 'Examining child-led tours and child standpoint theory as a methodological approach to mitigate asymmetrical adult-child power dynamics in ethnographic research: a child-led tour of elfish antics and sensorial knowledge', *International Journal of Qualitative Methods*, 22. doi: 16094069231182878

McFarland, L. and Laird, S.G. (2020) '"She's only two": parents and educators as gatekeepers of children's opportunities for nature-based risky play', in A. Cutter-Mackenzie-Knowles, K. Malone, and E. Barratt Hacking (eds) *Research Handbook on Childhoodnature: Assemblages of Childhood and Nature Research*, Springer International Publishing, pp 1075–98.

McGhee, J., Bunting, L., McCartan, C., Elliott, M., Bywaters, P., and Featherstone, B. (2018) 'Looking after children in the UK – convergence or divergence?', *The British Journal of Social Work*, 48(5): 1176–98.

McGrath, P. (2021) *Becoming and Being a Grandparent Special Guardian: An Interpretative Phenomenological Analysis*, PhD thesis, University of East Anglia.

McGrath-Brookes, M., Hanley, J., and Higgins, M. (2021) 'A Fisher-eye lens on social work reform', *Journal of Social Work*, 21(5): 1261–77.

McKie, L. and Callan, S. (2011) *Understanding Families: A Global Introduction*, SAGE Publications.

McMullin, C., Maguire, T., and McFadden, P. (2023) 'A scoping review on applied drama methods used in social work education', *Journal of Practice Teaching and Learning*, 21(2). doi: 10.1921/jpts.v21i2.2078

McSherry, D. and Fargas Malet, M. (2018) 'The extent of stability and relational permanence achieved for young children in care in Northern Ireland', *Children Australia*, 43(2): 124–34.

Meehan, C. (2016) 'Every child mattered in England: but what matters to children?', *Early Child Development and Care*, 186(3): 382–402.

Meloni, F., Vanthuyne, K., and Rousseau, C. (2015) 'Towards a relational ethics: rethinking ethics, agency and dependency in research with children and youth', *Anthropological Theory*, 15(1): 106–23.

Meng, K., Yuan, Y., Wang, Y., Liang, J., Wang, L., Shen, J., and Wang, Y. (2020) 'Effects of parental empathy and emotion regulation on social competence and emotional/behavioral problems of school-age children', *Pediatric Investigation*, 4(2): 91–8.

Mercer, A., Lindley, B., Hopkins, A., and Ashley, C. (2015) *Could Do Better… Must Do Better: A Study of Family and Friends Care Local Authority Policies*, Family Rights Group.

Messing, J.T. (2006) 'From the child's perspective: a qualitative analysis of kinship care placements', *Children and Youth Services Review*, 28(12): 1415–34.

Michelan, C.S. and Correia, L.S.B. (2014) 'Children taking over their own space in the house: consumption and negotiation of meanings', *Strenæ. Recherches sur les livres et objets culturels de l'enfance*, 7. doi: 10.4000/strenae.1221

Mitchell, M. (2022) '"Because I'm a kid ...": the struggle for recognition of children and young people involved in child and family social work', *Child and Family Social Work*, 27(3): 526–34.

Montserrat, C. (2007) 'Kinship foster care: a study from the perspective of the caregivers, the children and the child welfare workers', *Psychology in Spain*, 11: 42–52.

Montserrat, C. and Casas, F. (2006) 'Kinship foster care from the perspective of quality of life: research on the satisfaction of the stakeholders', *Applied Research in Quality of Life*, 1(3): 227–37.

Moran, L., McGregor, C., and Devaney, C. (2020) 'Exploring the multi-dimensionality of permanence and stability: emotions, experiences and temporality in young people's discourses about long-term foster care in Ireland', *Qualitative Social Work*, 19(5–6): 1111–29.

Moran-Ellis, J. (2010) 'Reflections on the sociology of childhood in the UK', *Current Sociology*, 58(2): 185–205.

Moran-Ellis, J., Bandt, A., and Sünker, H. (2014) 'Children's well-being and politics', in A. Ben-Arieh, F. Casas, I. Frønes, and J.E. Korbin (eds) *Handbook of Child Well-Being: Theories, Methods and Policies in Global Perspective*, Springer Netherlands, pp 415–35.

Morgan, D. (1996) *Family Connections: An Introduction to Family Studies: His Life and Work*, Polity.

Morgan, D.H.G. (2011) 'Locating "family practices"', *Sociological Research Online*, 16(4): 174–82.

Morgan, D.H.J. (2020) 'Family practices in time and space', *Gender, Place and Culture*, 27(5): 733–43.

Morris, K. (ed) (2008) *Social Work and Multi-Agency Working: Making a Difference*, Policy Press.

Morris, K., White, S., Doherty, P., and Warwick, L. (2017) 'Out of time: theorizing family in social work practice', *Child and Family Social Work*, 22: 51–60.

Morton, P. (2006) 'Using critical realism to explain strategic information systems planning', *Journal of Information Technology Theory and Application*, 8(1): 3–20.

Munby, J. (2019) 'Keynote speech (Coram permanence event, Nov 2019)', Coram. Available from: www.coram.org.uk/resource/keynote-speech-sir-james-munby-coram-permanence-event-nov-2019 (Accessed 18 November 2020).

Munro, E. (2011) *The Munro Review of Child Protection. Final Report: A Child-Centred System*, Department for Education.

Munro, E. (2019) 'Decision-making under uncertainty in child protection: creating a just and learning culture', *Child & Family Social Work*, 24(1): 123–30.

Munro, E.R. and Gilligan, R. (2013) 'The "dance" of kinship care in England and Ireland: navigating a course between regulation and relationships', *Psychosocial Intervention*, 22(3): 185–92.

Murphy, C. (2023) 'How learning from the lived experiences of child protection social workers, can help us understand the factors underpinning workforce instability within the English child protection system', *Journal of Social Work Practice*, 37(2): 263–76.

Murris, K. (2020) 'Posthuman child: de(con)structing Western notions of child agency', in W.O. Kohan and W. Barbara (eds) *Thinking, Childhood, and Time: Contemporary Perspectives on the Politics of Education*, Lexington Books, pp 161–78.

Murris, K. and Kohan, W. (2020) 'Troubling troubled school time: posthuman multiple temporalities', *International Journal of Qualitative Studies in Education*, 34(7): 581–97.

Muurinen, H. and Kääriäinen, A. (2022) 'Using theory in practice – an intervention supporting research dissemination in social work', *Human Service Organizations: Management, Leadership and Governance*, 46(1): 1–10.

Myers, J. (2017) *Serious Case Review ADS14: Polly*. Derbyshire Safeguarding Children Board. Available from: https://basw.co.uk/policy-and-practice/resources/derbyshire-safeguarding-children-board-serious-case-review-ads14 (Accessed 14 March 2025).

Nandy, S. and Selwyn, J. (2013) 'Kinship care and poverty: using census data to examine the extent and nature of kinship care in the UK', *British Journal of Social Work*, 43(8): 1649–66.

Nandy, S., Selwyn, J., Farmer, E., and Vaisey, P. (2011) *Spotlight on Kinship Care*, Policy Press.

Narey, M. (2011) 'The Narey report: a blueprint for the nation's lost children', *The Times*, 6 July.

Neil, E. and Howe, D. (eds) (2004) *Contact in Adoption and Permanent Foster Care: Research, Theory and Practice*, British Association for Adoption and Fostering.

Neil, E., Gitsels, L., and Thoburn, J. (2019) 'Children in care: where do children entering care at different ages end up? An analysis of local authority administrative data', *Children and Youth Services Review*, 106: art 104472. doi: 10.1016/j.childyouth.2019.104472

Nellhaus, T. (2017) 'Embodied collective reflexivity: Peircean performatives', *Journal of Critical Realism*, 16(1): 43–69.

Noble, C., Rasool, S., Harms-Smith, L., Muñoz-Arce, G., and Baines, D. (eds) (2024) *The Routledge International Handbook of Feminisms in Social Work*, Routledge.

Nolas, S.-M., Varvantakis, C., and Aruldoss, V. (2017) 'Talking politics in everyday family lives', *Contemporary Social Science*, 12(1–2): 68–83.

References

Norrie, A. (2009) *Dialectic and Difference: Dialectical Critical Realism and the Grounds of Justice*, Routledge.

Norton, D.F. and Norton, M.J. (2006) *David Hume, a Treatise of Human Nature* (Clarendon Hume edn), Clarendon.

Nuuffield Family Justice Observatory, Harwin, J., Simmonds, J., Broadhurst, K., and Brown, R. (2019) *Special Guardianship: A Review of English Research Studies*, Nuffield Family Justice Research.

Nybell, L.M. (2013) 'Locating "youth voice:" considering the contexts of speaking in foster care', *Children and Youth Services Review*, 35(8): 1227–35.

Oakley, M. (2021) *Fostering the Future: Recruiting and Retaining More Foster Carers*, Social Market Foundation.

O'Brien, V. (2012) 'The benefits and challenges of kinship care', *Child Care in Practice*, 18(2): 127–46.

Ochs, E. and Izquierdo, C. (2009) 'Responsibility in childhood: three developmental trajectories', *Ethos*, 37(4): 391–413.

Okpokiri, C. (2021) 'Parenting in fear: child welfare micro strategies of Nigerian parents in Britain', *The British Journal of Social Work*, 51(2): 427–44.

Oliver, C. (2012) 'Critical realist grounded theory: a new approach for social work research', *British Journal of Social Work*, 42(2): 371–87.

O'Reilly, L. and Dolan, P. (2016) 'The voice of the child in social work assessments: age-appropriate communication with children', *British Journal of Social Work*, 46(5): 1191–207.

Oswell, D. (2012) *The Agency of Children: From Family to Global Human Rights*, Cambridge University Press.

Owusu-Bempah, K. (2010) *The Wellbeing of Children in Care: A New Approach for Improving Developmental Outcomes*, Routledge.

Pampaka, M., Williams, J., and Homer, M. (2016) 'Is the educational "what works" agenda working? Critical methodological developments', *International Journal of Research and Method in Education*, 39(3): 231–6.

Pawson, R. (1996) 'Theorizing the interview', *British Journal of Sociology*, 47(2): 295–314.

Pawson, R. (2006) *Evidence-Based Policy: A Realist Perspective*, SAGE Publications.

Pawson, R. (2013) *The Science of Evaluation: A Realist Manifesto*, SAGE Publications.

Pawson, R. and Tilley, N. (1997) *Realistic Evaluation*, SAGE Publications.

Percy-Smith, B. (2015) 'Negotiating active citizenship: young people's participation in everyday spaces', in K.P. Kallio, S. Mills, and T. Skelton (eds) *Politics, Citizenship and Rights*, Springer, pp 401–22.

Percy-Smith, B. and Thomas, N. (2009) *A Handbook of Children and Young People's Participation: Perspectives from Theory and Practice*, Routledge.

Perry, G., Daly, M., and Kotler, J. (2012) 'Placement stability in kinship and non-kin foster care: a Canadian study', *Children and Youth Services Review*, 34(2): 460–5.

Pettersen, T. (2012) 'Conceptions of care: altruism, feminism, and mature care', *Hypatia*, 27(2): 366–89.

Pilgrim, D. (2023) 'Race, ethnicity and the limitations of identity politics', *Journal of Critical Realism*, 22(2): 240–55.

Pink, S., Ferguson, H., and Kelly, L. (2022) 'Digital social work: conceptualising a hybrid anticipatory practice', *Qualitative Social Work*, 21(2): 413–30.

Pinney, C. (2004) *Photos of the Gods: The Printed Image and Political Struggle in India*, Reaktion Books.

Pitcher, D. (ed) (2013) *Inside Kinship Care: Understanding Family Dynamics and Providing Effective Support*, Jessica Kingsley.

Ponnert, L. (2017) 'Emotional kinship care and neutral non-kinship care – the struggle between discourses', *Child and Family Social Work*, 22(2): 1084–93.

Pösö, T., Skivenes, M., and Thoburn, J. (eds) (2021) *Adoption from Care: International Perspectives on Children's Rights, Family Preservation and State Intervention*, Policy Press.

Pratt, J., Brown, D., Brown, M., Hallsworth, S. and Morrison, W. (eds) (2005) *The New Punitiveness: Trends, Theories, Perspectives*, Willan Publishing.

Pratchett, R. and Rees, P. (2017) 'Theories underpinning kinship care', in J. Horton and M. Pyer (eds) *Children, Young People and Care*, Routledge, pp 44–57.

Prout, A. (2011) 'Taking a step away from modernity: reconsidering the new sociology of childhood', *Global Studies of Childhood*, 1(1): 4–14.

Punch, S. (2002) 'Research with children: the same or different from research with adults?', *Childhood*, 9(3): 321–41.

Punch, S. (2005) 'The generationing of power: a comparison of child–parent and sibling relations in Scotland', *Sociological Studies of Children and Youth*, 10: 169–88.

Qvortrup, J. (1994) *Childhood Matters: An Introduction*, Avebury.

Rees, A., Holland, S., and Pithouse, A. (2012) 'Food in foster families: care, communication and conflict', *Children and Society*, 26(2): 100–11.

Rees, J. (2017) *Life Story Books for Adopted and Fostered Children: A Family Friendly Approach* (2nd edn), Jessica Kingsley.

Reisch, M. and Jani, J.S. (2012) 'The new politics of social work practice: understanding context to promote change', *The British Journal of Social Work*, 42(6): 1132–50.

Ricketts, D. (2023) 'An autoethnographic perspective of life story work', *The British Journal of Social Work*, 53(3): 1325–40.

Robson, C. and McCartan, K. (2015) *Real World Research* (4th edn), John Wiley and Sons.

Rock, S., Michelson, D., Thomson, S., and Day, C. (2015) 'Understanding foster placement instability for looked after children: a systematic review and narrative synthesis of quantitative and qualitative evidence', *The British Journal of Social Work*, 45(1): 177–203.

Rogers, C. (1995) *On Becoming a Person: A Therapist's View of Psychotherapy* (2nd edn), Mariner Books.

Rogers, J. (2017) 'Eco-maps and photo-elicitation: reflections on the use of visual methods in social work research with children and young people', *Journal of Applied Youth Studies*, 1(4): 59–74.

Rogowski, S. (2020) *Social Work: The Rise and Fall of a Profession*, Policy Press.

Rose, N. (1996) 'The death of the social? Re-figuring the territory of government', *Economy and Society*, 25(3): 327–56.

Rowe, J. and Lambert, L. (1973) *Children Who Wait: A Study of Children Needing Substitute Families*, British Association for Adoption and Fostering.

Rowlson, E. and Shabbar, F. (2024) 'Exploring stability within kinship care from the perspective of kinship carer advocates', *Child and Family Social Work*, advance online publication. doi: 10.1111/cfs.13216

Rubin, D., Springer, S.H., Zlotnik, S., Kang-Yi, C.D., and Council on Foster Care (2017) 'Needs of kinship care families and pediatric practice', *Pediatrics*, 139(4): art e20170099. doi: 10.1542/peds.2017-0099

Rubin, D.I. (2019) 'Navigating the "space between" the Black/White binary: a call for Jewish multicultural inclusion', *Culture and Religion*, 20(2): 192–206.

Ruch, G., Winter, K., Morrison, F., Hadfield, M., Hallett, S., and Cree, V. (2020) 'From communication to co-operation: reconceptualizing social workers' engagement with children', *Child & Family Social Work*, 25(2): 430–8.

Ruch, G., Turney, D., and Ward, A. (eds) (2010) *Relationship-Based Social Work: Getting to the Heart of Practice*, Jessica Kingsley.

Rustin, M. (1994) 'Multiple families in mind', *Clinical Child Psychology and Psychiatry*, 4(1): 51–62.

Ryan, S.D., Hinterlong, J., Hegar, R.L., and Johnson, L.B. (2010) 'Kin adopting kin: in the best interest of the children?', *Children and Youth Services Review*, 32(12): 1631–9.

Saar-Heiman, Y. and Gupta, A. (2020) 'The poverty-aware paradigm for child protection: a critical framework for policy and practice', *The British Journal of Social Work*, 50(4): 1167–84.

Sacker, A., Murray, E.T., Lacey, R., and Maughan, B. (2021) *The Lifelong Health and Wellbeing Trajectories of People Who Have Been in Care*, Nuffield Foundation.

Samuel, M. (2023) 'Are regional care co-operatives the answer to care placement challenge?', *Community Care*, 20 February. Available from: www.communitycare.co.uk/2023/02/20/are-regional-care-co-operatives-the-answer-to-care-placement-challenge/ (Accessed 14 March 2025).

Samuels, G.M. (2009) 'Ambiguous loss of home: the experience of familial (im)permanence among young adults with foster care backgrounds', *Children and Youth Services Review*, 31(12): 1229–39.

Saraceno, C. and Keck, W. (2010) 'Can we identify intergenerational policy regimes in Europe?', *European Societies*, 12(5): 675–96.

Sayer, A. (1992) *Method in Social Science: A Realistic Approach*, Routledge.

Sayer, A. (2011) *Why Things Matter to People: Social Science, Values and Ethical Life*, Cambridge University Press.

Sayer, A. (2017) 'Normativity in the social sciences and professions', in M. Kjørstad and M.-B. Solem (eds) *Critical Realism for Welfare Professions*, Routledge, pp 23–37.

Sayer, A. (2019) 'Normativity and naturalism as if nature mattered', *Journal of Critical Realism*, 18(3): 258–73.

Sayer, R.A. (2000) *Realism and Social Science*, SAGE.

Schoenwold, E., Smyth, E., Gwyther, J., O'Higgins, A., Briggs, E., Gurau, O., and Alam, A. (2022) *Understanding Formal Kinship Care Arrangements in England: Analysis of Administrative Data*, What Works for Children's Social Care.

Schöffl, I., Ehrlich, B., Rottermann, K., Weigelt, A., Dittrich, S., and Schöffl, V. (2021) 'Jumping into a healthier future: trampolining for increasing physical activity in children', *Sports Medicine – Open*, 7(1): art 53. doi: 10.1186/s40798-021-00335-5

Schofield, G., Beek, M., and Ward, E. (2012) 'Part of the family: planning for permanence in long-term family foster care', *Children and Youth Services Review*, 34(1): 244–53.

Seedat, S. and Rondon, M. (2021) 'Women's wellbeing and the burden of unpaid work', *BMJ*, 374: art n1972. doi: 10.1136/bmj.n1972

Segal, M. (2023) 'The conflict between maintaining confidentiality in social work and protecting a minor from harm', *Journal of Family Social Work*, 26(1): 31–44.

Sellick, C. (1999) 'Independent fostering agencies: providing high quality services to children and carers?', *Adoption and Fostering*, 23(4): 7–14.

Selman, S.B. and Dilworth-Bart, J.E. (2024) 'Routines and child development: a systematic review', *Journal of Family Theory and Review*, 16(2): 272–328.

Selwyn, J. and Briheim-Crookall, L. (2023) 'The views of children and young people in kinship foster care on their well-being', 10,000 Voices insight paper. Rees Centre, University of Oxford & Coram Voice. Available from: https://coramvoice.org.uk/resource-library/the-views-of-children-and-young-people-in-kinship-foster-care-on-their-well-being/ (Accessed 21 May 2025).

Selwyn, J. and Nandy, S. (2014) 'Kinship care in the UK: using census data to estimate the extent of formal and informal care by relatives', *Child and Family Social Work*, 19(1): 44–54.

Selwyn, J., Magnus, L., and Stuijfzand, B. (2018) *Our Lives Our Care: Looked After Children's Views on their Well-Being in 2017*, School for Policy Studies, University of Bristol.

Selwyn, J., Wijedasa, D., and Meakings, S. (2014) *Beyond the Adoption Order: Challenges, Interventions and Adoption Disruption*, Department for Education.

Selwyn, J., Wood, M., and Newman, T. (2017) 'Looked after children and young people in England: developing measures of subjective well-being', *Child Indicators Research*, 10(2): 363–80.

Selwyn, J., Farmer, E., Meakings, S., and Vaisey, P. (2013) *The Poor Relations? Children and Informal Kinship Carers Speak Out*, School for Policy Studies, University of Bristol.

Sen, R. and Broadhurst, K. (2011) 'Contact between children in "out-of-home" placements and their family and friends networks: a research review', *Child and Family Social Work*, 16(3): 298–309.

Sen, R. and Kerr, C. (2023) *The Future of Children's Care: Critical Perspectives on Children's Services Reform*, Policy Press.

Sevenhuijsen, S. (2000) 'Caring in the third way: the relation between obligation, responsibility and care in Third Way discourse', *Critical Social Policy*, 20(1): 5–37.

Sharma, S. (2011) 'The biopolitical economy of time', *Journal of Communication Inquiry*, 35(4): 439–44.

Shaw, C., Brady, L.-M., and Davey, C. (2011) *Guidelines for Research with Children and Young People*, National Children's Bureau Research Centre.

Shaw, I. and Holland, S. (2014) *Doing Qualitative Research in Social Work*, SAGE.

Shaw, I. and Lorenz, W. (2016) 'Special issue: private troubles or public issues? Challenges for social work research', *European Journal of Social Work*, 19(3–4): 305–9.

Shaw, P.A. (2020) 'Photo-elicitation and photo-voice: using visual methodological tools to engage with younger children's voices about inclusion in education', *International Journal of Research and Method in Education*, advance online publication. doi: 10.1080/1743727X.2020.1755248

Shuttleworth, P.D. (2021) *What Matters to Children Living in Kinship Care: 'Another Way of Being a Normal Family'*, PhD thesis, University of Sussex. Available from: https://sussex.figshare.com/articles/thesis/What_matters_to_children_living_in_kinship_care_another_way_of_being_a_normal_family_/23482181 (Accessed 14 March 2025).

Shuttleworth, P.D. (2023a) 'Kinship care for England and Wales in the 2020s: assumptions, challenges and opportunities', in R. Sen and C. Kerr (eds) *The Future of Children's Care*, Policy Press, pp 122–44.

Shuttleworth, P.D. (2023b) 'What matters for child participation: the role of valuation-based dialogical participation for children living in kinship care in England', *Children and Youth Services Review*, 149: art 106959. doi: 10.1016/j.childyouth.2023.106959

Siippainen, A., Närvi, J., and Alasuutari, M. (2023) 'The puzzles of daily life: the temporal orders of families when parents have non-standard work schedules', *International Journal of Social Welfare*, 32(3): 291–305.

Simmonds, J. (2014) 'Permanence planning for children in family and friends care', in D. Pitcher (ed) *Inside Kinship Care: Understanding Family Dynamics and Providing Effective Support*, Jessica Kingsley, pp 135–51.

Simpson, G. and Price, V. (2007) *Transforming Society? Social Work and Sociology*, Policy Press.

Sinclair, R. (2004) 'Participation in practice: making it meaningful, effective and sustainable', *Children & Society*, 18(2): 106–18.

Sinclair, I. (2005) *Fostering Now: Messages from Research*, Jessica Kingsley.

Sinclair, I., Baker, C., Lee, J., and Gibbs, I. (2007) *The Pursuit of Permanence: A Study of the English Child Care System*, Jessica Kingsley.

Singh, S. (2021) 'Punishing mothers for men's violence: failure to protect legislation and the criminalisation of abused women', *Feminist Legal Studies*, 29(2): 181–204.

Skauge, B., Storhaug, A.S., and Marthinsen, E. (2021) 'The what, why and how of child participation – a review of the conceptualization of "child participation" in child welfare', *Social Sciences*, 10(2): art 54. doi: 10.3390/socsci10020054

Skeggs, B. (2004) 'Exchange, value and affect: Bourdieu and "the self"', *The Sociological Review*, 52(s2): 75–95.

Skivenes, M. and Thoburn, J. (2016) 'Pathways to permanence in England and Norway: a critical analysis of documents and data', *Children and Youth Services Review*, 67: 152–60.

Skivenes, M. and Benbenishty, R. (2022) 'Securing permanence for children in care: a cross-country analysis of citizen's view on adoption versus foster care', *Child and Family Social Work*, 29(2): 432–42.

Skoglund, J. and Thørnblad, R. (2019) 'Kinship care or upbringing by relatives? The need for "new" understandings in research', *European Journal of Social Work*, 22(3): 435–45.

Skoglund, J., Thørnblad, R., and Holtan, A. (2022) *Childhood in Kinship Care: A Longitudinal Investigation*, Routledge.

Smart, C. (2011) 'Families, secrets and memories', *Sociology*, 45(4): 539–53.

Smith, A.B. (2015) *Enhancing Children's Rights: Connecting Research, Policy and Practice*, Palgrave Macmillan.

References

Smith, M., Cameron, C., and Reimer, D. (2017) 'From attachment to recognition for children in care', *The British Journal of Social Work*, 47(6): 1606–23.

Smith, R. (2010) 'Social work, risk, power', *Sociological Research Online*, 15(1): 37–46.

Social Work England (2019) 'Professional standards'. Available from: www.socialworkengland.org.uk/standards/professional-standards/ (Accessed 29 September 2024).

Spagnola, M. and Fiese, B.H. (2007) 'Family routines and rituals: a context for development in the lives of young children', *Infants and Young Children*, 20(4): 284–99.

Spyrou, S. (2011) 'The limits of children's voices: from authenticity to critical, reflexive representation', *Childhood*, 18(2): 151–65.

Spyrou, S. (2019) 'An ontological turn for childhood studies?', *Children and Society*, 33(4): 316–23.

Spyrou, S., Rosen, R., and Cook, D.T. (2018) *Reimagining Childhood Studies*, Bloomsbury.

Staines, J. and Selwyn, J. (2020) '"I wish someone would explain why I am in care": the impact of children and young people's lack of understanding of why they are in "out-of-home" care on their well-being and felt security', *Child and Family Social Work*, 25(S1): 97–106.

Staples, E.M., Watson, D., and Riches, K. (2023) 'Being, becoming, belonging: negotiating temporality, memory and identity in life story conversations with care-experienced children and young people', *Qualitative Social Work*, 23(1): 41–57.

Strijker, J., Zandberg, T., and van der Meulen, B.F. (2003) 'Kinship foster care and foster care in the Netherlands', *Children and Youth Services Review*, 25(11): 843–62.

Subramani, S. (2019) 'Practising reflexivity: ethics, methodology and theory construction', *Methodological Innovations*, 12(2): 1–11.

Sussman, M.B. (2016) *Pets and the Family*, Routledge.

Sutton, C. (2006) *Helping Families with Troubled Children: A Preventive Approach* (2nd edn), Wiley.

Swadener, B.B., Kabiru, M., and Njenga, A. (2000) *Does the Village Still Raise the Child? A Collaborative Study of Changing Child-Rearing and Early Education in Kenya*, SUNY Press.

Syed, J., Mingers, J., and Murray, P.A. (2010) 'Beyond rigour and relevance: a critical realist approach to business education', *Management Learning*, 41(1): 71–85.

Sykes, J., Sinclair, I., Gibbs, I., and Wilson, K. (2002) 'Kinship and stranger foster carers: how do they compare?', *Adoption and Fostering*, 26(2): 38–48.

Tay-Lim, J. and Lim, S. (2013) 'Privileging younger children's voices in research: use of drawings and a co-construction process', *International Journal of Qualitative Methods*, 12(1): 65–83.

Taylor, C. (1994) 'The politics of recognition', in A. Gutmann (ed) *Multiculturalism: Examining the Politics of Recognition* (revised edn), Princeton University Press, pp 25–73.

Taylor, C. and White, S. (2016) 'Knowledge, truth and reflexivity: the problem of judgement in social work', *Journal of Social Work*, 1(1): 37–59.

Taylor, D. (2018) 'Ellie Butler's grandfather says authorities have "blood on their hands"', *The Telegraph*, 10 April.

Taylor, E.P., Di Folco, S., Dupin, M., Mithen, H., Wen, L., Rose, L., and Nisbet, K. (2020) 'Socioeconomic deprivation and social capital in kinship carers using a helpline service', *Child and Family Social Work*, 25(4): 845–55.

The Care Inquiry (2013) *Making Not Breaking: Building Relationships for Our Most Vulnerable Children*, Nuffield Foundation.

The Fostering Network (2024) 'More children to end up in unsuitable homes if more foster carers aren't urgently recruited', 13 May. Available from: www.thefosteringnetwork.org.uk/news/more-children-to-end-up-in-unsuitable-homes-if-more-carers-aren-t-urgently-recruited/ (Accessed 28 September 2024).

Thoburn, J. (1994) *Child Placement: Principles and Practice* (2nd edn), Ashgate.

Thomas, N. and O'Kane, C. (2000) 'Discovering what children think: connections between research and practice', *The British Journal of Social Work*, 30(6): 819–35.

Thornock, C.M., Nelson, L.J., Porter, C.L., and Evans-Stout, C.A. (2019) 'There's no place like home: the associations between residential attributes and family functioning', *Journal of Environmental Psychology*, 64: 39–47.

Thunberg, S. and Arnell, L. (2022) 'Pioneering the use of technologies in qualitative research: A research review of the use of digital interviews', *International Journal of Social Research Methodology*, 25(6): 757–68.

Tinkler, P. (2013) *Using Photographs in Social and Historical Research*, SAGE.

Tisdall, E.K.M. (2012) 'The challenge and challenging of childhood studies? Learning from disability studies and research with disabled children', *Children and Society*, 26(3): 181–91.

Tisdall, E.K.M. (2016) 'Subjects with agency? Children's participation in family law proceedings', *Journal of Social Welfare and Family Law*, 34(4): 362–79.

Tomkins, L. and Bristow, A. (2021) 'Evidence-based practice and the ethics of care: "what works" or "what matters"?', *Human Relations*, 76(1): 118–43.

Tompkins, C.J. and Vander Linden, K. (2020) 'Compounding complexity: examining multiple factors leading to challenges within grandfamilies', *The Gerontologist*, 60(6): 1094–102.

Trell, E.-M. and van Hoven, B. (2010) 'Making sense of place: exploring creative and (inter)active research methods with young people', *Fennia – International Journal of Geography*, 188(1): 91–104.

Tronto, J. (1994) *Moral Boundaries: Political Argument for an Ethic of Care*, Routledge.

Trowler, I. (2018) *Care Proceedings in England: The Case for Clear Blue Water*, University of Sheffield.

Tunstill, J. (2018) 'Pruned, policed and privatised: the knowledge base for children and families social work in England and Wales in 2019', *Social Work and Social Sciences Review*, 20(2): 57–76.

Turley, R., Roberts, S., Foster, C., Warner, N., El-Banna, A., Evans, R. et al (2022) 'Staff wellbeing and retention in children's social work: systematic review of interventions', *Research on Social Work Practice*, 32(3): 281–309.

Turnell, A. and Essex, S. (2014) '"It takes a village" – placing grandparents and extended family at the center of safeguarding vulnerable children', in D. Pitcher (ed) *Inside Kinship Care: Understanding Family Dynamics and Providing Effective Support*, Jessica Kingsley, pp 96–121.

UK Fostering (2024) 'Family time/contact', UK Fostering.

United Nations General Assembly (1989) Convention on the Rights of the Child, General Assembly resolution 44/25, adopted 20 November. Available from: www.ohchr.org/en/instruments-mechanisms/instruments/convention-rights-child (Accessed 14 March 2025).

Uprichard, E. (2008) 'Children as "being and becomings": children, childhood and temporality', *Children and Society*, 22(4): 303–13.

van Bijleveld, G.G., Bunders-Aelen, J.F.G., and Dedding, C.W.M. (2020) 'Exploring the essence of enabling child participation within child protection services', *Child and Family Social Work*, 25(2): 286–93.

van Bijleveld, G.G., de Vetten, M., and Dedding, C.W. (2021) 'Co-creating participation tools with children within child protection services: what lessons we can learn from the children', *Action Research*, 19(4): 693–709.

Vandenbroeck, M. (2006) 'Children's agency and educational norms: a tensed negotiation', *Childhood*, 13(1): 127–43.

van der Kolk, M.D.B. (2015) *The Body Keeps the Score: Brain, Mind, and Body in the Healing of Trauma* (reprint), Penguin Books.

van Deth, J.W., Abendschön, S., and Vollmar, M. (2011) 'Children and politics: an empirical reassessment of early political socialization', *Political Psychology*, 32(1): 147–73.

van Petegem, S., Beyers, W., Vansteenkiste, M., and Soenens, B. (2012) 'On the association between adolescent autonomy and psychosocial functioning: examining decisional independence from a self-determination theory perspective', *Developmental Psychology*, 48(1): 76–88.

Veitch, J., Flowers, E., Ball, K., Deforche, B., and Timperio, A. (2020) 'Exploring children's views on important park features: a qualitative study using walk-along interviews', *International Journal of Environmental Research and Public Health*, 17(13): art 4625. doi: 10.3390/ijerph1713462

Vis, S.A., Strandbu, A., Holtan, A., and Thomas, N. (2011) 'Participation and health: a research review of child participation in planning and decision-making', *Child and Family Social Work*, 16(3): 325–35.

Wade, J., Sinclair, I.A.C., Stuttard, L., and Simmonds, J. (2014) *Investigating Special Guardianship: Experiences, Challenges and Outcomes*, Department for Education.

Walsh, D. and Evans, K. (2014) 'Critical realism: an important theoretical perspective for midwifery research', *Midwifery*, 30(1): e1–e6.

Wang, C. and Burris, M.A. (1997) 'Photovoice: concept, methodology, and use for participatory needs assessment', *Health Education and Behavior: The Official Publication of the Society for Public Health Education*, 24(3): 369–87.

Ward, H., Brown, R., and Hyde-Dryden, G. (2014) *Assessing Parental Capacity to Change When Children Are on the Edge of Care: An Overview of Current Research Evidence*, Department for Education.

Watson, D., Hahn, R., and Staines, J. (2020) 'Storying special objects: material culture, narrative identity and life story work for children in care', *Qualitative Social Work*, 19(4): 701–18.

Watson, D.L., Latter, S., and Bellew, R. (2015) 'Adopted children and young people's views on their life storybooks: the role of narrative in the formation of identities', *Children and Youth Services Review*, 58: 90–8.

Watts, L. (2019) 'Reflective practice, reflexivity, and critical reflection in social work education in Australia', *Australian Social Work*, 72(1): 8–20.

Webb, C., Bywaters, P., Scourfield, J., Davidson, G., and Bunting, L. (2020) 'Cuts both ways: ethnicity, poverty, and the social gradient in child welfare interventions', *Children and Youth Services Review*, 117: art 105299. doi: 10.1016/j.childyouth.2020.105299

Webb, S.A. (2010) '(Re)assembling the left: the politics of redistribution and recognition in social work', *The British Journal of Social Work*, 40(8): 2364–79.

Webb, S.A. (2016) 'European individualism and social work', in K. Fabian, L. Walter, O. Hans-Uwe, and S. White (eds) *European Social Work: A Compendium*, Barbara Budrich, pp 114–38.

Wellard, S., Meakings, S., Farmer, E., and Hunt, J. (2017) *Growing Up in Kinship Care*, Grandparents Plus.

Wendt, S. and Moulding, N. (eds) (2016) *Contemporary Feminisms in Social Work Practice*, Routledge.

Weston, K. (1991) *Families We Choose: Lesbians, Gays, Kinship*, Columbia University Press.

White, A., Bushin, N., Carpena-Méndez, F., and Ní Laoire, C. (2010) 'Using visual methodologies to explore contemporary Irish childhoods', *Qualitative Research*, 10(2): 143–58.

White, S. and Gibson, M. (2019) *Reassessing Attachment Theory in Child Welfare: A Critical Appraisal*, Policy Press.

White, N. and Hughes, C. (2017) *Why Siblings Matter: The Role of Brother and Sister Relationships in Development and Well-Being*, Routledge.

Wiegmann, W.L. (2017) 'Habitus, symbolic violence, and reflexivity: applying Bourdieu's theories to social work', *The Journal of Sociology and Social Welfare*, 44(4): art 6. doi: 10.15453/0191-5096.3815

Wijedasa, D. (2015) *The Prevalence and Characteristics of Children Growing Up with Relatives in the UK: Part I*, University of Bristol.

Wiles, R., Crow, G., Heath, S., and Charles, V. (2008) 'The management of confidentiality and anonymity in social research', *International Journal of Social Research Methodology*, 11(5): 417–28.

Williams, F. (2004) *Rethinking Families*, Calouste Gulbenkian Foundation.

Willow, C. (2023) 'Where now? Children's rights in England into the 2020s', in R. Sen and C. Kerr (eds) *The Future of Children's Care*, Policy Press, pp 14–37.

Winnicott, D.W. (1953) 'Transitional objects and transitional phenomena: a study of the first not-me possession', *The International Journal of Psychoanalysis*, 34: 89–97.

Winnicott, D.W. (1960) 'Ego distortion in terms of true and false self', in *The Maturational Processes and the Facilitating Environment: Studies in the Theory of Emotional Development*, Karnac Books, pp 140–52.

Winnicott, D.W. (2002) *Winnicott On the Child*, Perseus.

Winokur, M.A., Holtan, A., and Batchelder, K.E. (2018) 'Systematic review of kinship care effects on safety, permanency, and well-being outcomes', *Research on Social Work Practice*, 28(1): 19–32.

Winter, K. (2010) 'The perspectives of young children in care about their circumstances and implications for social work practice', *Child and Family Social Work*, 15(2): 186–95.

Winter, K. and Cree, V.E. (2016) 'Social work home visits to children and families in the UK: a Foucauldian perspective', *British Journal of Social Work*, 46(5): 1175–90.

Winter, K., Morrison, F., Cree, V., Ruch, G., Hadfield, M., and Hallett, S. (2019) 'Emotional labour in social workers' encounters with children and their families', *The British Journal of Social Work*, 49(1): 217–33.

Wissö, T., Johansson, H., and Höjer, I. (2019) 'What is a family? Constructions of family and parenting after a custody transfer from birth parents to foster parents', *Child and Family Social Work*, 24(1): 9–16.

Wood, M. and Selwyn, J. (2017) 'Looked after children and young people's views on what matters to their subjective well-being', *Adoption and Fostering*, 41(1): 20–34.

Wright, P., Turner, C., Clay, D., and Mills, H. (2006) *The Participation of Children and Young People in Developing Social Care, Participation Practice Guide*, Social Care Institute of Excellence.

Wulff, D., St George, S., Faul, A.C., Frey, A., and Frey, S. (2010) 'Drama in the academy: bringing racism to light', *Qualitative Social Work*, 9(1): 111–27.

Wyness, M. (2018) 'Children's participation: definitions, narratives and disputes', in C. Baraldi and T. Cockburn (eds) *Theorising Childhood*, Springer, pp 53–72.

Xu, Y. and Bright, C.L. (2018) 'Children's mental health and its predictors in kinship and non-kinship foster care: a systematic review', *Children and Youth Services Review*, 89: 243–62.

Xu, Y., Bright, C.L., Ahn, H., Huang, H., and Shaw, T. (2020) 'A new kinship typology and factors associated with receiving financial assistance in kinship care', *Children and Youth Services Review*, 110: art 104822. doi: 10.1016/j.childyouth.2020.104822

Yip, C., Han, N.-L.R., and Sng, B.L. (2016) 'Legal and ethical issues in research', *Indian Journal of Anaesthesia*, 60(9): 684–8.

Yuill, C. and Mueller-Hirth, N. (2019) 'Paperwork, compassion and temporal conflicts in British social work', *Time and Society*, 28(4): 1532–51.

Zinn, J.O. (2020) 'Responsibilisation: blaming or empowering risk-taking', in J.O. Zinn (ed) *Understanding Risk-Taking*, Springer International Publishing, pp 225–52.

Zutlevics, T. (2016) 'Could providing financial incentives to research participants be ultimately self-defeating?', *Research Ethics*, 12(3): 137–48.

Index

References to figures appear in *italic* type; those in **bold** type refer to tables.

A

abduction 100–1
abuse
 blame for 20, 27
 care for children who
  experienced 40, 43
 intergenerational 22–3, 45, 53
 participation and 63, 75, 113
 right to protection from 26, 192
 risks of 53–4
 value judgements on 91–2
 views of children, and 61
acts
 Adoption and Children Act 2002 45
 Adoption of Children Act 1926 43
 Children Act 1975 45
 Children Act 1989 2, 26, 28, 30, 37, 39, 40, 53, 61, 75
 Children and Families Act 2014 40, 46, 48
 Children and Young Persons Act 2008 40
 Housing Act 1985 136
Adoption and Children Act 2002 45
Adoption of Children Act 1926 43, 44
adoption orders 43–4
adoptions
 benefits of 49
 as gold standard 43, 48, 51
 open adoptions 44, 48
 severance, post-adoption 43–4, 49–50
Alderson, P. 97
Aldgate, J. 70
ambiguous loss 127
animals *see* pets
anonymity 110–11
anti-racist practices 25, 35
Appleton, C. 107
Archer, M.S. 88, 93, 99, 106
Armenia 26
assent 109–10
attachment theories 38, 66
austerity 10, 33, 49, 191
Australia 7, 8, 26, 69
author of book *see* research by author
autonomous interdependence 154–6, 159, 161, 169–70, 199, 203, 209
autonomy 160, 165, 178

B

Bacon, K. 136
Barthes, R. 66
Beck, U. 23
Beddoe, L. 106
best interests of the child 2, 44, 49, 54, 176
Bhaskar, Roy 87, 89, 95, 99, 127, 156, 198–9
Biehal, N. 38–9, 49, 72
Big Ask survey 62
binary thinking *see* monological thinking
birth families 6, 38, 41, 43–4, 45, 48–50, 53, 131–2, 208 *see also* contact; research participants
Black people 6, 24–5, 183
Boddy, J. 49, 68
Boss, P. 127
Bourdieu, P. 107
Bowlby, J. 47, 49, 207
Bowyer, S. 40
British Association of Social Workers (BASW) 49
Bronfenbrenner, U. 175
brothers *see* siblings
Butler, Ellie 22
Butler, J. 107, 176–7

C

Cameron, David 24
Canada 7, *18*, 48
Capella, C. 68
capitalism 21, 177–8
care *see* adoptions; ethics; formal kinship care; foster care; informal kinship care; kinship care; mature care; non-kinship care; state care, rise of children in
care and protection/independence and risk mechanism
 author's summary of 169–71
 autonomous interdependence 154–6
 care 150–2, 152–3
 ethics of care 159–60
 mature care 150, 160–2, 167, 169–70, 202, 207
 permanence and 162–9
 rules 156–7
 safety 153–4, 200
 social workers 157–9
care arrangement orders 6–7, 45–6, 165

Care Crisis Review: Options for Change 30
Care Inquiry 50
care planning guidance (Department for Education) 40, 49
carers *see* contact; foster carers; kinship carers; support for kinship care
Case Proceedings in England: The Case for Clear Blue Water (Trowler) 30–1
Casey, L. 22
causations *see* correlations/causations
Census data 2, 7–8, 9
Chang, J.S. 117
child participation *see* participation; participatory research
child welfare systems
　author's recommendations for 144–5, 192–3
　challenges, systemic 21–2
　contact with family 124–5
　critical realism and 95–7
　cultural models of kinship care 16–17, *18*, 19
　kinship care within 28–9, 33–6, *34*, 54–6
　values of 19
　'what works' approach 10
　see also permanence; social work
child-led walking tours 111, 114, 117
children *see* kinship care; participation; research participants; rights of children; values; views of children; voices of children
Children Act 1975 45
Children Act 1989 2, 26, 28, 30, 37, 39, 40, 53, 61, 75
Children and Families Act 2014 40, 46, 48
Children and Young Persons Act 2008 40
Children England 43
children with disabilities 8, 25, 42, 54, 75
children's views *see* views of children
children's voices *see* voices of children
China 6, 26
chosen families 20, 168–9
Clark, A. 117
Clear Blue Water 30–1
Clinton, Hillary 5
confidentiality 110, 111, 120
connection/separation mechanism
　absence/presence 124–7, 140
　activities 143–4
　birth parents 131–2
　'doing' family 144–5, 145–6
　families 128–31, 134–5, 200
　memories 140–3
　pets 133–4
　sharing (time, space, stories) 135–40, 145–6
　siblings 132–3, 146, 200

consent 104, 107, 108, 109–10, 112, 120, 139–40, 209
Conservative government 10
constructionism *see* social constructionism
constructivism *see* social constructivism
consumer capitalism 177–8
contact
　adoptions and 44, 48
　child welfare focus on 124–5
　children on 165–6, 179, 188, 205–7
　critical realism and 96
　kinship care and 52–3, 70, 158
　past carers, with 56
　severance of 43–4, 45, 47, 49–50
contexts 88–9, 89–90
correlations/causations 10, 11, 23, 25, 71, 83
Cossar, J. 49
cost-effectiveness 25–6, 29, 30, 31, 32, 33, 36, 42, 191, 193
courts
　children on decisions by 178–9
　court proceedings 30–1
　role of 47
　time-limits for family court 40, 46
COVID-19 pandemic 23, 25, 62, 118
critical friends 107
critical realism
　author's overview of 81, 86, 90, 94–5, 105
　author's use of 11–12, 13–14
　benefits of using 95–9, 180–1, 198
　challenges with 12
　child welfare, and 95–7
　embodiment 94
　evaluation process/cycle 89–90
　family, and 130–1
　'is/ought problem' 90–2
　kinship care, and 97–8, 192
　normality and 19
　positivism, and 82–3
　reality, levels of 87, *87*
　theory building 89–90, 98–9, 113–14, 114–22
　see also contexts; dialogical approaches; mechanisms; research by author
Crumbley, J. 23
cultural norms 2, 16–17, *18*, 19, 177, 188–9

D

Davies, K. 204
de St Croix, T. 66–7
deaths
　children, of 20, 21–2
　focus on by children 126, 161, 167, 178
Delap, E. 9
Department for Education (DfE) 37, 39, 40, 49

Index

dialectical thinking 77, 198–200, 203
dialogical approaches
  author's overview of 76–9, **77**
  challenges with 83–4, 90
  consent and 109–10
  critical realism and 98–9
  ethics, and 107–8
  space and 78
  voices of children and 77–8, 170–1, 187–8
disabilities, children with 8, 25, 42, 54, 75
displaying of family 191–2, 208
drama/role-play 120–1
drift 39, 40
dualisms 199

E

eco-maps 118
economic crisis *see* global financial crisis
either/or thinking *see* monological thinking
embodiment 94, 95, 97, 117, 121
Emmel, N. 117
emotional permanence 41–2, 46–7, 51–2, 166–7, 170–1
enacted permanence 41, 46, 72
enslaved people 6
Epstein, L. 39
Erikson, E. 155
Esping-Andersen's framework 17
essentialist determinism 10–11, 83, 93, 95, 191
ethics
  of care 150, 159–61, 166, 170, 171, 194, 195, 203, 207, 209
  of justice 159–60, 166, 171, 203
  research practices 107–8, 111–13
  of rights 160, 165, 170, 171, 180, 194, 207
Ethiopia 26

F

Fabian, J. 121
fallibility 88, 89, 90, 97, 98, 103, 202–3, 210
familialism 15, 16–17, 162, 192
families
  displaying family 191–2, 208
  'doing' family 144–5, 145–6
  meaning of 130–1
  power relations in 133
  risky, as 16, 23–4, 45, 53
  siblings 132–3, 146, 167–8
  troubled families 23, 24
  see also birth families; research participants
families, chosen 20, 168–9
family displaying 191–2, 208
Family Justice Council 40
family mottos 163, 167, 173
family norms 19–20, 24, 34, 50, 157
Family Rights Group 7

Farmer, E. 54
Featherstone, B. 49
Ferguson, H. 204
Ferraro, A.C. 55
financial crisis *see* global financial crisis
Finch, J. 191
Finland *18*, 69
Floersch, J. 209–10
food 101–2
formal kinship care 6–7, 24, 26–27, 28–29, 44, 193
foster care
  debates on 49
  drift, and 39, 40
  short-term care, as 39
  voices of children 62
foster carers 27, 42, 45
Fraser, Nancy 174, 180, 191
Freud, A. 47

G

Garrett, P.M. 180
gatekeepers 109, 113
gender norms 17, 35, 177
gender roles 20, 50, 176–7
genograms 118
Ghana 26, 68
Giddens, A. 23
Gillick ruling 109
Gilligan, C. 161
global financial crisis 10, 23, 25
Goldstein, J. 38, 47
Graeber, David 209
Guterman, J.T. 84

H

Habermas, J. 78
Hammersley, M. 74, 90
Hantrais, L. 17
Harris, J. 22
Hassall, A. 2
Hegel, G.W.F. 155, 175
Heymann, I. 39
hierarchy of needs *see* Maslow's hierarchy of needs
Hodes, M. 65
Honneth, Axel 174, 175, 178, 180, 187, 189, 190, 191
Housing Act 1985 136
Hume, David 90
Hunt, J. 7, 16
hyperrealism 83

I

Ide, Y. 106
Independent Review of Children's Social Care *see* MacAlister review
India 26

individualism 20–2, 24, 65, 66, 67, 79, 205
informal kinship care 6–7, 24–5, 28–29, 193
intergenerational abuse/risk 22–3, 45, 53
Interim Guidance on Special Guardianship (Family Justice Council) 40
International Federation of Social Workers 65
interpretivism 13, 86, 88, 199
'is/ought problem' 90–2

J

jargon 12
Jonsson, G. 22
justice, ethics of 159–60, 166, 171, 203

K

Keck, W. 17
Kinship (charity) 15
kinship care
  author's overview of 2–3, 28–9
  author's recommendations for 34–6
  challenges with 33–6, *34*, 72–3
  concerns with 31–3, 51, 52, 53–4
  court proceedings and 30–1
  critical realism and 97–8, 192
  cultural models of 16–17, *18*, 19
  demographics 8
  familialism 15, 16–17, 162, 192
  groups for 186–7
  history of 5–6
  legal definitions of 6–7
  non-familial 20
  scholarship on 2, 6, 8–9, 16, 68–73
  statistics 2, 6, 32, 193
  support, factors that impact 19–26
  the term *kinship care* 6
  see also contact; cost-effectiveness; formal kinship care; informal kinship care; permanence; support for kinship care
Kinship Care: Statutory Guidance for Local Authorities 27, 39
Kinship Care Strategy 31, 32
kinship carers
  adoption with 51
  assessments of 40
  challenges faced by 52, 53, 54, 56
  demographics 7–8
  motivations of 27
  regulation of 26–27
  special guardianship orders 45
  see also support for kinship care
Kitbag 115–16, *116*
Kolb, B. 119
Križ, K. 76

L

Lambert, L. 49
legal permanence 41, 43–6, 50–1, 165–6, 199, 203, 204

LGBTQIA+ people 20
life story work 141–2, 143, 146–7, 208
Lifelong Links 50
Little, R.L. 23
Longhofer, J. 209–10
loss 66, 70, 126, 127, 135, 146, 186, 205–6
love 175–8
Lundy, L. 77, **77**

M

MacAlister, J. 7, 31
MacAlister review 10, 31, 33, 43, 61, 62, 158
MacDonald, M. 6
Maluccio, A.N. 48–9
managerialism 21, 22, 35, 88, 160
Mannion, G. 78
Manzano, A. 104, 114, 121
Manzano's interview sequence 114–22
Maslow's hierarchy of needs 150–1, *151*, 152, 153–4
mature care 150, 160–2, 167, 169–70, 202, 207
McCartan, C. 17
McIntosh, M. 70
mechanisms
  author's overview of 87–8
  author's summary of 200–1, 201–10
  children in kinship care, for 99–100, *100*, 101–2, *102*, 103
  contexts and 88–9
  critical realisms evaluation cycles 89–90
  trampolines 201–2
  see also care and protection/independence and risk mechanism; connection/separation mechanism; recognition/(mis)recognition mechanism
(mis)recognition 173 *see also* recognition/(mis)recognition mechanism
Mitchell, M. 174
modernisation 22, 160
monological thinking 59, 73–6, 80, 83, 93, 97, 99, 105, 109, 124, 127
Moran, L. 38
mottos, family 163, 167, 173
Mueller-Hirth, N. 204
Munro, Eileen 61
murders 21–2

N

Narey, M. 45, 48
National Adoption Strategy 2021 48
National Kinship Care Strategy 31, 32
needs *see* Maslow's hierarchy of needs
Neil, E. 49

neoliberalism 20–1, 24, 35, 65, 67–8, 79, 205
neologisms 12
new sociology of childhood 67–8, 74, 194–5
Nolas, S.-M. 118
non-familial kinship care 20
non-kinship care 26–27, 32, 51, 54 *see also* adoptions; foster care
normal
  being seen as 185–6, 190, 192, 200, 207–8
  the term *normal* 17, 19
normality 19, 185–6
norms
  cultural norms 2, 16–17, *18*, 19, 177, 188–9
  family norms 19–20, 24, 34, 50, 157
  gender norms 17, 35, 177
  societal norms 84, 85, 157
Norrie, A. 99
Norway 16–17, *18*, 69
Nuffield Looked-after Children Grown Up Project 55

O

objective permanence 41
open adoptions 44, 48
orders *see* adoption orders; care arrangement orders; residence orders; special guardianship orders; supervision orders
Oregon Project 40
Our Lives, Our Care survey 72

P

pandemic *see* COVID-19 pandemic
participation
  author's overview of 63–5
  ethics, conversations about 107–8
  monological thinking 59, 73–6
  new sociology of childhood, and 67–8
  recognition and 193–5, 208
participatory research
  author's overview of 59–61
  author's recommendations for 59
  benefits of 62–3
  challenges with 58, 60–1, 62, 85
  child-led walking tours 111, 114, 117
  Manzano's interview sequence 114–22
  monological thinking 59, 73–6
  views, children's right to express 61–2
  see also dialogical approaches
Pawson, R. 79, 89, 99, 115
permanence
  author's overview of 2, 37–8, 41, 199
  author's recommendations for 170–1
  author's summary of 54–6, 203–5
  enacted permanence 41, 46, 72
  factors that influence 38
  history of 39–40
  kinship care and 38–9
  mature care 160–2, 162–9
  objective permanence 41
  scholarship on 38–9, 42, 49–50, 50–2, 54–6, 71
  subjective permanence 41, 42, 46
  uncontested permanence 41, 46
  see also emotional permanence; legal permanence; mechanisms; physical permanence/stability
pets 72, 82, 86, 99, 133–4, 146, 168
Pettersen, T. 161
philosophical thinking 81, 82, 83, 90, 99, 155, 182
photo-elicitation 119
photovoice 119–20
physical permanence/stability 41–3, 46–7, 50, 51, 71, 72, 160, 163–5, 199, 203–4
play 143–4, 201–2
Poland 16, *18*
positionality 104, 105–6, 112, 120, 122, 209
positivism 13, 58, 82–3, 86, 88, 102
power relations
  author's exploration of 11
  ethics, and 107–8
  in families 133
  participatory research and 59–60, 63–4
  play and 143–4, 201–2
  positionality and 104
  recognition and 175
  time and 138, 145–6
professionals *see* social workers
psychological parenting 47–8
Punch, S. 133

Q

qualitative research 58, 59, 83, 95, 105, 109, 114 *see also* participatory research
quantitative research 10, 58, 83, 98
Qvortrup, J. 74

R

racism *see* anti-racist practices; systemic racism
recognition/(mis)recognition mechanism
  author's overview of 173
  author's recommendations for 192–3
  author's summary of 207–8
  community recognition 190, 200
  displaying of family 191–2
  participation of children 193–5, 208
  recognition theories 173–5
  slime 189
  spheres of recognition 175–8, 178–84, 184–9
Rees, J. 146

reflexivity 88, 93, 98, 104, 106–7, 120, 209–10
research
  critical realist approach to 96–9
  qualitative research 58, 59, 83, 95, 105, 109, 114
  quantitative research 10, 58, 83, 98
  see also critical realism; participatory research; scholarship
research by author
  about the author 3–5, 11, 107
  author's overview of 11–12, 197–8
  challenges faced during 112–13
  children in 11, 197, 202
  confidentiality/anonymity 110–11
  consent 104, 107, 108, 109–10, 112, 120, 139–40, 209
  drama/role-play 120–1
  ethical practices 107–8, 111–13
  findings 100, *100*, 200–8
  language in, importance of 12
  photovoice 119–20
  positionality of author 105–6, 112, 122, 209
  power relations 11, 108
  theory building 113–14, 114–22
  visual methods 118–19, 121–2, *122*
  see also critical realism; participatory research; research participants; 'what matters' approach; 'What matters to children living in kinship care' study
research participants
  about 11, 197, 202
  on activities 143–4, 169
  on anonymity 110–11
  on birth parents 129, 131–2, 139, 141, 153, 164, 165–6
  on care 37, 150–1, 152, 153, 160–2
  on childhood 181–2
  on contact 205–7
  on court decisions 178–9
  on cultural backgrounds 188
  on death 126, 161, 167, 178
  on families 124, 125–7, 128–30, 131, 134–5, 167, 170
  on family mottos 163, 167, 173
  on feeling safe 149, 153–4, 168–9, 178
  on gender differences 176–7
  on home 162, 163
  on independence 155–6
  on kinship care 134–5, 182–3
  on learning/education 181, 184
  on legal statuses 165–6
  on listening to children 58, 179–80, 183, 187–8, 210
  on memories/stories/traditions 140–2
  on needs 152
  on normality 186–7
  on pets 133–4, 168
  on relationships 175–6, 184–5
  on rules 156–7
  on shopping 177–8
  on siblings 132–3
  on slime 189
  on social workers 157–9, 160, 165–6, 180, 188, 194
  on space, private/shared 135–8
  on support for kinship carers 8, 15, 182–3, 191
  on time 138–40
  on what matters 81
residence orders 45–6
resilience 66, 83
Rethinking Families (Williams) 130
retroductive reasoning 86, 87–8, 96, 100–1, 103, 200
rights of children
  abuse, protection from 26, 192
  contact with family, to 52–3
  ethics of 160, 165, 170, 171, 180, 194, 207
  family life, to 2
  risks, to take 149
  sphere of recognition, as 175, 178–84
  state, and role of 32
  UN Convention on the Rights of the Child, under 26
  view of children 61–2, 195
  voices of children 179–80
risks
  kinship care, in 22–4, 53–4
  rights of children, and 149
  see also care and protection/independence and risk mechanism
risky
  children as 73, 108
  families as 16, 23–4, 45, 53
  kinship care as 20, 23, 192
Rogers, C. 155
role-play/drama 120–1
Rose, N. 64, 146
Rowe, J. 49
Ryan, S.D. 51

S

safety 153–4, 156–7, 160, 164, 165–6, 168–9, 192, 205–7
Saraceno, C. 17
Sayer, Andrew 12, 13, 81, 92–3, 94, 155
scholarship
  on adoption 49–50, 51
  on concerns with kinship care 31–2
  on contact 52–3
  on dialogical approaches 76–9
  on ethics of care 159–60
  on familialism 16–17

on family and care 34
gaps in 56–7
on kinship care 2, 6, 8–9, 16, 68–73
on monological thinking 73–6
on neoliberalism 21
on participation 63–5
on participatory research 63
on permanence 38–9, 42, 49–50, 50–2, 54–6, 71
on recognition 174–5, 180
on risks 22–4, 53–4
on social workers 76
on support for kinship care 6–7, 29
on systemic racism 24–5
on time 204
on wellbeing 54
section 20 arrangements 30, 32
Sellick, C. 42
Sevenhuijsen, S 160
severance 43–4, 45, 47, 49–50
sharing
  activities 143–4
  memories 140–3
  narratives 140
  space 135–8
  time 138–40
siblings 132–3, 146, 167–8
Sinclair, I. 41
sisters *see* siblings
Skivenes, M. 76
Skoglund, J. 9
slime 189
social constructionism 84–5, 86, 88, 89
social constructivism 84, 85–6, 88, 89, 120
social work
  critical realism and 95–7
  cultural/religious backgrounds 188–9
  definitions of 65
  ethics of care 159–60
  individualism in 21
  language use in 12
  modernisation/managerialism in 22
  participation of children, and 75, 76
  research 34–5, 60–1, 62, 68–73, 107–8, 121
  theories of children/childhood, and 65–7, 203
  transitional objects 143
  values of 5, 19, 96, 107, 174, 210
  visual tools 118
  see also child welfare systems
social workers
  author's experience as 3–5, 112
  author's recommendations for 147–8, 193–4, 194–5
  care by 157–9
  children on 157–9, 160, 165–6, 180, 188, 194

negative portrayals of 6, 22, 158, 170
  scholarship on 76, 204
societal norms 84, 85, 157
solidarity 175, 184–9
Solnit, A.J. 47
spaces 78, 135–40, 145–6
special guardianship orders 6–7, 40, 43, 44–5, 46, 50, 177
Special Guardianship Regulations 2005 45
Special Guardianship (Amendment) Regulations 2016 46
spheres of recognition 175–8, 178–84, 184–9
Spyrou, S. 64, 68
stability *see* physical permanence/stability
Staples, E.M. 204
state care, rise of children in 30–1
subjective permanence 41, 42, 46
substitute psychological parenting 47–8, 197, 208
supervision orders 46
support for kinship care
  author's overview of 13, 56
  author's recommendations for 35–6
  children on 8, 15, 182–3, 191
  circular debates on 33–4, *34*
  factors that impact 19–26
  formal kinship care 26–27, 29
  informal kinship care 28
  legislation 31
  models of 16–17, *18*, 19
  recognition and 191–2
  types of 8
Sweden *18*, 69
systemic racism 16, 24–5, 88, 183

T

Taylor, Charles 174
theories of children/childhood 65–7, 203
theory building 89–90, 98–9, 113–14, 114–22
Thoburn, J. 49
Thørnblad, R. 9
Tilley, N. 79, 89, 99, 115
time
  limits for family court 40, 46
  power relations and 138, 145–6
  scholarship on 204
  sharing of 138–40
#TimeToDefine campaign 7
trampolines 201–2
transitional objects 142–3
trauma 66, 75, 94
trauma-informed approaches 66, 195
Tronto, J. 160
troubled families 23, 24
Trowler, Isabelle 30, 31, 32
trust 154

U

UK Census data 2, 7–8, 9
uncontested permanence 41, 46
United Nations Convention on the Rights of the Child 2, 26, 32, 38, 53, 61, 75, 149
United States 6, 7, 8, *18*, 26, 39, 41, 43, 48, 52, 69

V

values
  child welfare systems, of 19, 55
  children, that matter to 99–100, *100*, 101–3, *102*, 159–60, 201–2, 209
  family mottos 163, 167, 173
  importance of 81
  'is/ought problem' 90–2
  positionality and 105–6
  rights discourses of children 61
  social work, of 5, 19, 96, 107, 174, 210
Varvantakis, C. 118
views of children
  kinship care research, in 68–73
  political views 183–4
  rights, and 61–2, 195
visual research methods 118–19, 121–2, *122*
voices of children
  absence of 3, 9
  challenges with 75–6
  foster care, in 62
  listening to 194, 202
  political views 183–4
  rights, and 179–80
  see also dialogical approaches

W

walking tours, child-led 111, 114, 117
wellbeing 53–4, 54–6, 56–7, 205
  see also permanence
'what matters' approach
  author's overview of 81, 102–3, 197–8, 200
  family mottos 163, 167, 173
  importance of 11, 13–14, 92–4
  participatory research 65, 78
  theory building 89–90, 98–9, 113–14, 114–22
  values that matter to children 99–100, *100*, 101–3, *102*
  see also critical realism; research by author; research participants
'What matters to children living in kinship care' study
  ethical practices 107–8
  participants 82
  permanence and 37, 43
  use of in this book 1
  value that matter 99–100, *100*, 103
  see also research by author; research participants
'what works' approach
  author's overview of 9–10
  challenges with 10–11, 60–1, 67, 73, 193, 198
  permanence and 50–1, 55
Why Things Matter to People (Sayer) 13, 81, 92
Williams, F. 130
Winnicott, D.W. 175, 185
Wulff, D. 121

Y

Yuill, C. 204

www.ingramcontent.com/pod-product-compliance
Lightning Source LLC
Chambersburg PA
CBHW051533020426
42333CB00016B/1909